Theorizing Practice

Redefining British Theatre History

General Editor: **Professor Peter Holland**

Redefining British Theatre History is a five-volume series under the general editorship of Professor Peter Holland. The series brings together major practitioners in theatre history in order to establish ways in which previous assumptions need fundamental questioning and to initiate new directions for the field. The series aims to establish a new future for theatre history, not least by making theatre historians aware of their own history, current practice and future.

Titles include:

W. B. Worthen and Peter Holland (*editors*)
THEORIZING PRACTICE
Redefining Theatre History

Redefining British Theatre History
Series Standing Order ISBN 0-333-98219-3 (Hardback) 0-333-98220-7 (Paperback)
(*outside North America only*)

You can receive future titles in this series as they are published by placing a standing order. Please contact your bookseller or, in case of difficulty, write to us at the address below with your name and address, the title of the series and the ISBN quoted above.

Customer Services Department, Macmillan Distribution Ltd, Houndmills, Basingstoke, Hampshire RG21 6XS, England

Theorizing Practice

Redefining Theatre History

Edited by
W. B. Worthen

with

Peter Holland

Redefining British Theatre History Series
General Editor: Peter Holland
In Association with the Huntington Library

First published 2003 by
PALGRAVE MACMILLAN
Houndmills, Basingstoke, Hampshire RG21 6XS and
175 Fifth Avenue, New York, N. Y. 10010
Companies and representatives throughout the world

PALGRAVE MACMILLAN is the global academic imprint of the Palgrave Macmillan division of St. Martin's Press, LLC and of Palgrave Macmillan Ltd. Macmillan® is a registered trademark in the United States, United Kingdom and other countries. Palgrave is a registered trademark in the European Union and other countries.

ISBN 1–4039–0793–5 hardback
ISBN 1–4039–0794–3 paperback

This book is printed on paper suitable for recycling and made from fully managed and sustained forest sources.

A catalogue record for this book is available from the British Library.

Library of Congress Cataloging-in-Publication Data

Theorizing practice: redefining theatre history/edited by W.B. Worthen with Peter Holland.
     p. cm. – (Redefining British theatre history)
   Includes bibliographical references and index.
   ISBN 1-4039-0793-5 – ISBN 1-4039-0794-3 (pbk.)
    1. Theater–Great Britain–History–Congresses. 2. English drama–History and criticism–Congresses. I. Worthen, William B., 1955– II. Holland, Peter, 1951– III. Series.

PN2581.T48 2003
792'.0941–dc21

2003053618

10 9 8 7 6 5 4 3 2 1
12 11 10 09 08 07 06 05 04 03

Printed and bound in Great Britain by
Antony Rowe Ltd, Chippenham and Eastbourne

Contents

Dis/Continuities

Absences

List of Illustrations

Notes on Contributors

Susan Bennett is University Professor and Professor of English at the University of Calgary, Canada. She is the author of *Theatre Audiences* (1987) and *Performing Nostalgia* (1996), both published by Routledge, and served as editor of *Theatre Journal* from 1998 to 2001. Her current project is a full-length study of women playwrights and theater history.

Una Chaudhuri is Professor of English and Drama at New York University. She is the author of *No Man's Stage: a Semiotic Study of Jean Genet's Plays* (1986), and *Staging Place: the Geography of Modern Drama* (1995), as well as numerous articles on drama and theater in such journals as *Modern Drama*, *Theater*, and *Theatre Journal*. She is a contributing editor to *Theater*, for which she served as guest editor of a special issue on Theater and Ecology. She is editor of *Rachel's Brain and Other Storms: the Performance Scripts of Rachel Rosenthal*, and co-editor, with Elinor Fuchs, of *Land/Scape/Theater*.

Susan Leigh Foster, choreographer, dancer, and scholar, is Professor in the World Arts and Cultures Program at UCLA. She is author of *Reading Dancing: Bodies and Subjects in Contemporary American Dance* (1986), *Choreography and Narrative: Ballet's Staging of Story and Desire* (1996), and *Dances that Describe Themselves: the Improvised Choreography of Richard Bull* (2002), and editor of *Choreographing History* (1995) and *Corporealities* (1996).

Barbara Hodgdon, Adjunct Professor of English and Theatre at the University of Michigan, is the author of *The End Crowns All: Closure and Contradiction in Shakespeare's History* (Princeton, 1991), *The First Part of King Henry the Fourth: Texts and Contexts* (Bedford-St. Martin's, 1997), and *The Shakespeare Trade: Performances and Appropriations* (University of Pennsylvania Press, 1998); she served as guest editor for a special issue of *Shakespeare Quarterly* (summer 2002) on Shakespeare films and is currently editing *The Taming of the Shrew* for the Arden 3 Shakespeare and co-editing, with W. B. Worthen, the *Blackwell Companion to Shakespeare and Performance*.

Peter Holland is the McMeel Family Professor in Shakespeare Studies in the Department of Film, Television and Theater in the University of Notre Dame. From 1997 to 2002 he was Director of the Shakespeare Institute and Professor of Shakespeare Studies in the University of Birmingham. Among his publications are *The Ornament of Action: Text and Performance in Restoration Comedy* (1979) and *English Shakespeares: Shakespeare on the English Stage in the 1990s* (1997), as well as editions of Wycherley and a number of Shakespeare plays. He is editor of *Shakespeare Survey* and general editor (with Stanley Wells) of *Oxford Shakespeare Topics*.

Dennis Kennedy is Samuel Beckett Professor of Drama and head of the School of Drama in Trinity College Dublin. His books include *Granville Barker and the Dream of Theatre* (1985), *Plays by Harley Granville Barker* (1987), *Looking at Shakespeare: a Visual History of Twentieth-century Performance* (2nd edn., 2001), and as editor, *Foreign Shakespeare* (1993) and *The Oxford Encyclopedia of Theatre and Performance* (2003). He has held distinguished visiting professorships at the National University of Singapore, the Salzburg Seminar, McMaster University, the University of Victoria, and the University of Wisconsin. He was Senior Fulbright Lecturer at the University of Karachi in Pakistan, has twice been a fellow of the National Endowment for the Humanities in the USA and twice won the Freedley Award for theater history. His own plays have been performed in New York, London, and at regional theaters across the US, and he has frequently worked as a dramaturg.

Loren Kruger is the author of *The National Stage* (Chicago, 1992) and *The Drama of South Africa* (Routledge, 1999), and serves on the editorial boards of *Theatre Journal*, *Theatre Survey*, and *scrutiny2*. She teaches at the University of Chicago and is currently completing a book called *Post-imperial Brecht*, to be published by Cambridge University Press.

Thomas Postlewait, Professor of Theatre at Ohio State University, is the series editor of "Studies in Theatre History and Culture" at the University of Iowa Press. He is author of *Introduction to Theatre Historiography* (Cambridge, 2003). With Bruce McConachie he edited *Interpreting the Theatrical Past* (Iowa, 1989) and with Tracy C. Davis he edited *Theatricality* (Cambridge, 2003). He also published *Prophet of the New Drama: William Archer and the Ibsen Campaign* (Greenwood, 1986), and essays in both *The Cambridge History of American Theatre* (1999) and *The Cambridge History of British Theatre* (2003). He is past-President of the American Society for Theatre Research.

Joseph Roach, Charles C. and Dorathea S. Dilley Professor of Theater at Yale, has chaired the Department of Performing Arts at Washington University in St. Louis, the Interdisciplinary PhD in Theatre and Drama at Northwestern University, and the Department of Performance Studies at New York University. He is the author of *The Player's Passion: Studies in the Science of Acting* (1985, rpt

Michigan, 1993) and *Cities of the Dead: Circum-Atlantic Performance* (Columbia, 1996).

Freddie Rokem   is Dean of the Faculty of the Arts and Professor of Theater Studies at Tel Aviv University. He has published articles in scholarly journals and chapters in books on European and Israeli theater. His most recent book, *Performing History: Theatrical Representations of the Past in Contemporary Theatre,* received the ATHE Prize for best book in theater studies for 2001, as well as the *Choice* distinction for outstanding academic work that same year. His next book, *Strindberg's Secret Codes,* will be published by Norvik Press in 2003. He is associate editor of the *Theatre Journal* and of *Assaph: Studies in the Theatre.* He also is a translator, a dramaturg, a member of the executive committee of FIRT/IFTR (The International Federation for Theatre Research) and a docent (permanent visiting professor) at the University of Helsinki in Finland.

W. B. Worthen   is Professor and Chair of the Department of Theater, Dance, and Performance Studies at the University of California, Berkeley. He is the author of a range of articles on modern drama, performance theory, and Shakespeare, and of several books: *The Idea of the Actor: Drama and the Ethics of Performance* (Princeton, 1984), *Modern Drama and the Rhetoric of Theater* (California, 1992), *Shakespeare and the Authority of Performance* (Cambridge, 1997), and *Shakespeare and the Force of Modern Performance* (Cambridge, 2003). He has served as editor of *Theatre Journal,* and as co-editor of *Modern Drama;* he has also edited several widely used teaching anthologies.

Series Introduction: Redefining British Theater History

Peter Holland

On the surface, it doesn't look like much of a problem: conjoining the two words "theater" and "history" to define a particular practice of scholarship has a long and illustrious history. Nor does it appear to over-complicate matters to add the word "British," for all that the word is so furiously questioned at different moments of history (and especially at the moment). Yet what kind of history theater history is and what kind of theater theater history investigates, let alone what the Britishness is of its theater history, is endlessly problematic. For all the availability of shelves full of the outcomes of its practices, theater history is in need of a substantial reassessment. This series is an attempt to place some markers in that vital project.

It is hardly as if theater history is a new area of scholarly enquiry and academic publication. Within a general, varyingly academic mode of publication, one could point, in the UK, to the longevity of *Theatre Notebook*, a journal founded in 1945 by the Society for Theatre Research; its subtitle *A Journal of the History and Technique of the British Theatre* neatly sets out its scope and the assumed scope of theater history. A number of US journals have had similar concerns, including *Theatre Survey* (from the American Society for Theatre Research) and more narrowly defined examples like *Restoration and Eighteenth-Century Theatre Research* or *Nineteenth-Century Theatre Research*. Lying behind such work is the complex institutional history of the formation of university drama and theater departments on both sides of the Atlantic and their vexed and often still unformulated connection both to theater training (the university as feed to a profession) and to departments of English Literature.

For the early modern period theater historians might chart the subject's early twentieth-century history as being encapsulated by the work of E. K. Chambers (especially *The Elizabethan Stage*, 4 vols [Oxford: Clarendon Press, 1923]) or G. E. Bentley in his continuation (*The Jacobean and Caroline Stage*, 7 vols [Oxford: Clarendon Press, 1941–68]), phenomenal individual achievements of documenting theatrical events, theater performers and theatrical contexts. Their work might be matched for a later period by, say, E. L. Avery et al., eds, *The London Stage 1660–1800*, 11 vols (Carbondale, Ill.: Southern Illinois University Press, 1960–8) or Philip Highfill, Kalman Burnim and Edward Langhans, eds, *A Biographical Dictionary of Actors, Actresses, Musicians, Dancers, Managers and Other Stage Personnel in London, 1660–1800*, 16 vols (Carbondale, Ill.: Southern Illinois University Press, 1973–93). Further back still comes the fundamental work of such people as Boaden (*Memoirs of Mrs Siddons*, 2 vols [London, 1827]) and Genest (*Some Account of the English Stage from the Restoration in 1660 to 1830*, 10 vols [Bath, 1832]), who saw themselves neither as scholars nor as academics and yet whose work implicitly defined the accumulative function of data collection as a primary purpose of theater history. Behind them comes the achievement of the greatest of eighteenth-century editors of Shakespeare, Edmond Malone.

Yet, seeing that there is a practice of theater history is not the same as understanding or theorizing such a project. While many academics are engaged in the practice of something they would unhesitatingly term "Theater History" and while they would differentiate it carefully from a variety of other contiguous fields (e.g. performance theory or history of drama), there has been remarkably little investigation of the methodological bases on which the shelves of accumulated scholarship has been based or the theoretical bases on which Theater History has been or might be constructed. Even within organizations as aware of the need for theoretical sophistication as IFTR/FIRT (Fédération Internationale pour la recherche théâtrale) the emphasis has been placed more squarely on performance theory than on the historiographical problems of theater. In part that can undoubtedly be traced to the disciplines or institutional structures out of which the work has evolved: one would need to examine its early and still troubled connection to literary studies, to the analysis of drama and, most visibly, to the study of the history of Shakespeare in performance or, on another tack, to consider the ways in which theater departments have structured their courses in the US and UK.

By comparison with the traditionally positivist accumulation of data that marks, say, *Theatre Notebook*, one could, however, see signs of the emergence of a new concern with the processes of historiography as it affects the specific study of a massive cultural institution like theater in, to take just one significant example, the collection of essays edited by Thomas Postlewait and Bruce McConachie, *Interpreting the Theatrical Past: Essays in the Historiography of Performance* (Iowa City: University of Iowa Press, 1989). But, while individual theater historians are demonstrating an expanding awareness of the specific areas of historiography relevant to their work (e.g. economic history) and while theorizing of performance including its historical traces has grown immensely over the past fifteen years, there is little enough to set out on a large-scale the parameters of something that might hope by now to see itself as a discipline.

The shelves of libraries and bookshops and the reading lists of courses do not show major resources for understanding what theater history is, while an unending stream of books offering to help students understand the history of theater pours from presses. In part this may be connected to the absence of departments of theater history and the further substantial absence, within theater departments, of courses concerned to do more than teach theater history as an assumed and shared methodology based on an acceptance of what constitutes evidence and of how that evidence generates the potential for meaning.

Redefining British Theater History sets out, extremely ambitiously, to make a major statement by bringing together, in the course of its series of five volumes, some fifty major practitioners in theater history in order to establish ways in which previous assumptions need fundamental questioning and in which a future for the field can be enunciated in modes as yet undervalued. It aims to be a significant review of where we are and what we think we are doing.

The project began from an unusual collaboration between research library and publisher. My gratitude goes first and foremost to Dr Roy Ritchie of the Huntington Library and Josie Dixon of Palgrave Macmillan for contacting me to see whether I would develop a proposal that would create a series of conferences and subsequent volumes based on a single theme. Their support, not least financial, has been crucial in bringing the project to a reality both in the pleasures of the conference and the creation of this book. The first conference was held in 2002 and its papers (all bar one) make up this volume. Conference and volume were co-organized with W. B. Worthen, though it would be truer to say (even if embarrassing for me to admit) that far and away the lion's share of the organizational and editorial work was done by Bill, the most scrupulous, efficient and imaginative of collaborators. It has been a privilege to work with him.

The subsequent conferences/volumes travel a chronological path: two, with Stephen Orgel (Stanford University), devoted to the early and early modern periods, one for the long eighteenth century, with Michael Cordner (University of York), and the last, to be held in 2006, for the nineteenth century, with Tracy Davis (Northwestern University). If we succeed, *Redefining British Theater History* should chart the beginnings of a new future for theater history, not least by making theater historians newly and self-consciously aware of their own history, their practice and their future.

Introduction: Theorizing Practice

W. B. Worthen

What is theater history? Is it a distinctive discipline, identified by specific procedures and methods of research, by a defined set of objects of scrutiny, and by clear protocols of research practice? Or is it merely an eccentric aspect of historical studies, blurring off at the margins into literature, art history, architecture, sociology, economics? How has the field been changed by the pressure of adjacent fields – cultural studies, the increasingly materialist bent of literary studies – or by the widely perceived "crisis" in humanities scholarship at large? How has it been affected by shifting paradigms within the field itself, notably the move from dramatic "theater" to "performance" as the sustaining object (and even form) of research?

These questions may suggest something of the energy animating theater history and performance studies today. A field long characterized by an effervescent eclecticism, theater history has nonetheless come to an important moment of definition, as disciplinary frictions remap the borders between and beyond humanities fields. The *Redefining British Theater History* series will engage this friction, as it is played out by an evolving vision of the course of British theater. *Theorizing Practice* opens the series by moving outside the frame of British theater to raise larger questions of the conduct and purpose of scholarship in the field, and to interrogate the boundaries licensed by the notion of a field, a discipline.

"Mapping the field" has become, in recent years, something of a cottage industry in the humanities, and has led to some predictability in the essay collections that do the mapping. The editors typically redefine the critical controversies in the field in terms of general conceptual or methodological categories – in theater studies, such a list might include periodization; economics and theater; the performance of racial, sexual, or class identities; nationalism; and/or a list of critical "approaches," Marxism, psychoanalysis, and so on – and then invite essays that work like "case studies" to exemplify these issues. As important and influential as such collections have been,

Theorizing Practice nonetheless takes a different tack. The work of scholarship is often inspired by the recondite detail, that nagging glimpse of some nugatory bit of the *stuff* of history that seems to challenge received narratives, to obstruct critical practice-as-usual, even to enforce the need to retheorize the basic principles of critical activity itself. Rather than predetermining the questions that shape the field, in *Theorizing Practice* we have invited several of the most energetic scholars in drama, theater, and performance studies to address specific problems in the theory and practice of performance scholarship. Their essays typically take off from a disarmingly local problem – a photographic still, Pepys's masturbatory fantasies, the display of human beings in a New York zoo, the typographic design of Pinter's plays – and use it to generate an inquiry not only into the meaning of the past, but also to prompt renewed interrogation of the narratives, critical practices, and theoretical paradigms that guide our understanding of performance.

The central controversies animating contemporary theater history – questions of the social and political consequences of critical practice, of the meaning of how we construct "history" – are woven throughout the texture of the essays gathered here. Following the impulse of the essays themselves, we have traced a series of organizing themes: the formation of theater history as a research discipline, the nature of historiographical "objectivity" and its construction of performance as the object of research, the continuities and discontinuities enforced by the practice of periodization, and the challenge that performance presents to writing itself, what is and what is not preserved in the space between the words. These categories, though, are only a heuristic: the essays themselves richly document the mobile interdisciplinarity of theater and performance studies today.

Historiographies

Write it up, get it down, get it right – the three essays that open *Theorizing Practice* address the distinctive problems arising in the history of theater history. In "A History of Histories: From Flecknoe to Nicoll," Peter Holland treats the characteristic continuities of writing about the British stage. Concerned to locate the historical trajectory of a discipline, Holland confronts a central issue in the sociology of the contemporary academy: an institutional structure in which "theater history" seems to fall between the battlements of more established disciplines. Yet as he demonstrates here, the history of British theater not only has a distinguished lineage, but one representative of the crises afflicting the practice of historiography more generally – a tension between the antiquarian and the analytical impulses, between the logic of facts and the generalizing power of narrative that represents and inevitably falsifies them.

In many respects, Dennis Kennedy's "Confessions of an Encyclopedist" illustrates the achievement and complexity of the discipline today. The editor of

The Oxford Encyclopedia of Theatre and Performance, Kennedy describes an "adventure" that dwarfs the projects of Malone or Genest or Chambers: two volumes, twelve advisory editors, 100 illustrations, 320 contributors, 1600 pages of print, 4300 main entries, 8000 typed manuscript pages, about 1.3 million words. More to the point, Kennedy takes the *Encyclopedia* as an opportunity not merely to represent the diversity of the field – itself partly signaled by the telling addition "*and Performance*" – but to encourage a rethinking of its traditional boundaries of geography, of genre, and of method. Although he suggests that the *Encyclopedia*'s resistance to individualized biography is its most significant intervention, its topical range and its reorientation away from nationalist narratives represent a complementary image of the discipline in a moment of extraordinary redefinition.

Finally, in "The Criteria for Evidence: Anecdotes in Shakespearean Biography, 1709–2000," Thomas Postlewait engages one of the resident evils of theater history – its penchant for anecdote. While Holland shows the persistence of anecdote as typical of the antiquarian thrust of early histories, Postlewait argues that the anecdote remains constitutive of one of the most central and celebrated areas of historical research: Shakespeare biography. This persistence – amplified by the "new historicism" – dramatizes the tension between a narrative, even myth-making impulse and a documentary impulse that lie at the conflicted heart of writing about the past. What is fascinating about Postlewait's account is how this tension – and how even the most discredited anecdotes – seem necessary to the desire to tell the story.

Objectivities

One of the defining features of modern historiography is the challenge to objectivity. Or, perhaps, the *challenges* to objectivity might be more accurate, capturing a range of dissent from the proprieties of an ideologically overdetermined claim to a "scientific," or disinterested neutrality of representation. Susan Bennett's "Decomposing History (Why Are There So Few Women in Theater History?)" opens a crucial corrective to the traditions of theater history, a history which nods to Aphra Behn and Caryl Churchill, and perhaps to Nell Gwyn and Madame Vestris, and calls its engagement with women quits. Focusing her attention on dramatists, Bennett at once conducts a rich survey of women's near-absence from the standard reference works, supplies the beginnings of a counter-history, and suggests the consequences of the silent regendering of both theater and history as masculine preserves. For as Bennett shows, we have not only failed to read the thousands of plays written and performed by women on British stages, but in so doing we have simply failed to grasp the true complexity of the institutions of theater, a theater whose genres, locations, and even lines of periodization are massively distorted by this critical blindness.

If Bennett decomposes the "objectivity" of a masculinist historiography, Barbara Hodgdon interrogates the reciprocity between an "objective" account of performance and the "objects" that have become an essential part of the evidentiary record: photographs. "Photography, Theater, Mnemonics; or, Thirteen Ways of Looking at a Still" works on two fronts, at once interrogating the accuracy of stills as evidence of what happened onstage (shot at photo call, they often offer contradictory or simply inaccurate evidence about the performance), and rethinking the use of photographs in the public sphere, as advertising, as history, and as cultural memory. Elegantly evoking the power of photographs, Hodgdon's essay illustrates both the framing circumstances inscribed in – and sometimes concealed by – photographic "evidence," and the ways that theatrical memory is shaped by the circulation of images. The limits of photography are illustrated in the most compelling way by what Hodgdon has been forced to leave out of her essay, an essay whose argument depends on what is often absent from the page. As Hodgdon remarks of the photo record generally, the photographs that accompany this essay bear a disproportionate weight, standing in for the many other photographs which could not be acquired and which – given the economics of publishing – cannot be reproduced here.

Objects can be made to function as "evidence," but "objectivity" arises in another sense, too, in the ways that historiography constructs the object of its study, theater and performance. The final two essays in this section situate themselves at the borders of conventional theater history, in ways that reflect the remapping of the field. In "Vicarious: Theater and the Rise of Synthetic Experience," Joseph Roach sees in the Restoration theater a particularly rich nexus: the theater's commodification of vicarious experience renders it both an instance and the epitome of the transformation of the subjective and objective economy in the era of Britain's global expansion. Ranging from Samuel Pepys's erotic fantasies – which connect the church and the stage as sites of vicarious experience – to the eroticization of the "china" trade and the rise of consumer culture in *The Country Wife*, to the transformation of travel to tourism and its exoticized representation in the theater, Roach dispenses with a sense of "theater history" confined to the plane of the aesthetic or to the space of the stage, showing instead *how* the aesthetic at once frames and is framed by the experiential categories of modern social life.

Una Chaudhuri's "Zoo Stories: 'Boundary Work' in Theater History" presses a different limit: the limit of the human. Although theater history has long treated animal acts, bear baiting and circuses as an important if déclassé aspect of the field, Chaudhuri's reading of zoos makes a significantly more searching claim: that modernism, and particularly theatrical modernism, is constituted both paradigmatically and syntagmatically through its imagination of the zoo. Taking her start from the modernists' attraction to the circus, Chaudhuri traces the "boundary work" performed at zoos and by zoos: how zoos constitute the boundary between the human and the non-human, often by theatrical means. Collocating plays from O'Neill's *The Hairy Ape* to Beckett's *Waiting for Godot* to Albee's *Zoo Story* with the controversial modern history of zoo performance (and notably with zoos' displays of *human* subjects), "Zoo Stories" extends and elaborates the sphere of the theatrical, dramatizing the implication of performance in the technologies of the human.

Dis/continuities

Periodization is a crucial enabling instrument of history: the ability to represent historical change, indeed to represent history itself, by marking decisive moments of difference, the "rise" or "emergence" or "crisis" or "waning" of the forms of social life. The two essays in this section interrogate the meaning and utility of periodization from different perspectives. In "History Plays (in) Britain: Dramas, Nations and Inventing the Present," Loren Kruger takes issue with the principle of periodization itself, particularly with the slippery designation of "contemporary" history within the larger sphere of the "modern." Using one of the most dynamic genres of recent dramatic writing in Britain – the history play – as exemplary, Kruger at once challenges the conventional markers of "contemporary British theater" – inaugurated by John Osborne's *Look Back in Anger* and the "angry young [white] men" of the 1950s – and supplies an extraordinarily rich sense of the ways a single "period" may embrace several different trajectories and temporalities of historical change, histories working on different time scales, in a different sync. What emerges here is a history of the present of "contemporary British theater" that is defined by playwrights (Soyinka, Fugard), and issues (a global economy, the devolution of empire and nation, race and diaspora) that fundamentally challenge all three terms: contemporary, British, theater.

Freddie Rokem's "*Deus ex machina* in the Modern Theater: Theater, History and Theater History" opens with a clear discontinuity: when Nietzsche proclaimed the death of God, he also proclaimed the death of a durable theatrical convention, the *deus ex machina*. And yet the signal playwrights of the modernist tradition seem not to have been listening. For as Rokem argues, the course of modern drama can be read as an ongoing effort to reanimate and re-purpose this durable device. Playwrights from Strindberg and Brecht to Beckett and Kushner document a persistent desire to evoke a metaphysical possibility, something "out there," beyond the material horizon of the stage.

Absences

The final two essays in *Theorizing Practice* take up distinctly different projects that turn out to be surprisingly complementary. In "Improvising / History,"

Susan Foster considers a constitutive problem of performance history. Granted, all writing about performance must face its own impossibility: the event is gone, the records are always partial and suspect, and the only thing we know is that nothing we say happened actually took place in precisely that way. Taking dance as paradigmatic of non-textual performance, Foster focuses on a test case: improvisation. For even though a dramatic script hardly provides an account of what happened in performance, the text appears at least to provide something, a record and an instigation connected to the performance. But improvised performance takes place, so to speak, in the white space of the text – both in the script and the historian's description of it – where the event eludes its capture by writing. Choosing to celebrate rather than lament this absence, Foster considers the challenges to history offered by three improvisational performances of the 1960s, how they reshape both our understanding of the past and the writing of history. What is missing from Foster's essay are those performances; what is also missing is her performance – or, rather, *our* performance – of "Improvising/History." Reading the paper at the Huntington, Foster performed two brief "solos" (for example, reading the text printed here in which she discusses Kubota's *Vagina Painting* as it was glued to a large red ribbon that she draped across audience members while walking among the seats); she also developed an improvisational score based on Carolee Schneeman's *Newspaper Event* (1963), giving three of the conference participants each a set of "instructions" to be performed during a section of the paper. The instructions read:

HANDS
roll across the floor until you encounter an obstacle, grasp some part of it
and then let go, all in an exaggerated style
repeat the sequence
say as often as you like: "That is beautiful."

HEAD
concentrate on your head as the source for all movement
sometimes break into a conversation between your hands and facial
expressions
say as frequently as you like: "I need breakfast. I need some breakfast."

FINGERS
do not move about as the others do
sit by yourself
pick at your fingernails, but do not show it
if anyone comes close call them "you little prick" or "you dumb ass" in an
impersonal way

Foster's reading of her essay took place against the background – well, it took place *in the midst* – of these improvisations, as well as through her own performance. Rather than mere "examples" subordinate to an "argument" lodged in the "paper," these improvisations provided the performative context of argument, a palpable dialogue between the three models of historiography described in the paper and the forms of improvisation that resist and reshape them.

"There are things I remember which may never have happened, but as I recall them, so they take place" – Harold Pinter's *Old Times* dramatizes the historian's predicament, the ineffable, inevitable implication of history in improvisation. Foster's essay and the performance it sustained engage what is always absent from writing about performance; in "The Imprint of Performance," W. B. Worthen engages a related problem, how the materiality of writing – its identity, in the modern period, with print – implicates dramatic writing in the contested institutional frontier between "literature" and "theater." Here, white space figures in a different sense, as an aspect of typographic design that becomes legible in the modern period, and so has a specific kind of impact on how we read the marks on the page, what we think dramatic writing tells us, tells anyone, to *do*. For Foster, the white space memorializes the improvisation that print can never recapture; here, white space witnesses a forlorn desire to legislate performance from the page, the desire to preserve the hegemony of print in the theater that is at once doomed to fail and nonetheless constitutive of dramatic theater in the modern era.

Given the conversations that developed about and between the presentations in San Marino, it is important to note a final, crucial absence: Peggy Phelan's superb meditation on Beckett and the visual arts. Illustrating the material constraints on research enforced by property, Phelan's lecture depends on visual materials that cannot – for legal and financial reasons – be reproduced here. In this sense, *Theorizing Practice* enacts the failure engrained in all writing about theater, how the performance disappears from time and space, and sometimes disappears into the space between the words themselves. And yet, ranging across a wide variety of performances, interrogating the narratives of the past in the constructions of the present, *Theorizing Practice* dramatizes the vitality of contemporary performance studies, and the rich contingencies of our reading of the theatrical past.

1

A History of Histories: From Flecknoe to Nicoll

Peter Holland

> "[W]e are almost all of us, now, gone and forgotten."
>
> James Wright, *Historia Histrionica*[1]

On 28 January 1860, a query was printed in that epitome of obsessive antiquarian literary curiosity, *Notes and Queries*, asking for some information about the Reverend John Genest. The enquirer, Mr Hooper, had noted in a recent sale of manuscripts that there was a letter by Genest written "in a large bold hand."[2] The following month C. P. R. replied briefly[3] and his account was the basis for the brief entry on Genest contributed by Joseph Knight to *The Dictionary of National Biography* some years later.[4] Genest was educated at Trinity College, Cambridge, was for many years curate of "a retired Lincolnshire village" and later private chaplain to the Duke of Ancaster. "Compelled by ill-health to retire," as Knight puts it, "he went to Bath for the benefit of the waters. Here he appears to have remained until his death, which took place, after nine years of great suffering" (C. P. R. calls it "most acute suffering"). It is a melancholy little biography of a sad life and is one of the hundreds that made even Leslie Stephen, the first editor of the *DNB*, wonder whether the whole project was worthwhile.[5] Genest's life would have been totally unremarkable but for one extraordinary achievement: as C. P. R. puts it, "during the intervals of leisure there afforded him, he compiled his great work."[6] He had probably started accumulating materials long before his arrival in Bath, but it took Genest only two years of such "intervals" to complete and publish *Some Account of the English Stage from the Restoration in 1660 to 1830*, printed in Bath in ten volumes, each of about 500 pages, in 1832.[7] Knight describes it as "a work of great labour and research, which forms the basis of most exact knowledge concerning the stage" and continues:

> Few books of reference are equally trustworthy, the constant investigation to which it has been subjected having brought to light few errors and none of

grave importance. Genest is not undeservedly hard on his predecessors who followed one another in error. The index to the book is ample, but its arrangement does not greatly facilitate research.

Joseph Knight had good cause to know about the problems of working with Genest. For thirty-eight years drama critic of *The Athenaeum*, one of the central journals of nineteenth-century intellectual life in London, for some of that time he was also, and often simultaneously, drama critic of *The Sunday Times*, *The Globe* and *The Daily Graphic*. In his "intervals of leisure" he was editor of *Notes and Queries* for over twenty years and contributor of no fewer than 351 biographies to the *DNB*. He had used Genest's work often but he might well have agreed with the comments about it offered by R. W. Lowe, an important figure in the sudden growth of interest in British theater history in the late nineteenth century. Lowe, writing in the 1888 preface to his revised edition of Dr Doran's *"Their Majesties' Servants"*, Doran's rhapsodic, stage-struck and magnificently, even campily, excessive *Annals of the Stage*, recognized the dryness of Genest's achievement: "The admirable work of Genest, indispensable as it is to every writer on theatrical history, and to every serious student of the stage, is in no sense a popular work, and is, indeed, rather a collection of facts towards a history than a history itself."[8] Elsewhere the same year Lowe offered the most damning of compliments to Genest ("No words can do adequate justice to the honest and thorough nature of the work"), before going on to note that, published at five guineas, Genest's life-work was remaindered for £1 10s and was "for years a drug on the market" though "now becoming one of the most valued of theatrical books."[9] Lowe's faint praise comes from his *Bibliographical Account of English Theatrical Literature*, itself a crucial "collection of facts towards a history."[10]

Genest, Knight, Doran and Lowe belong to what is usually now seen as a prehistory of theater history, a form of practice of a discipline that had as yet no effective existence. While we may occasionally acknowledge them for their heroic efforts, it is difficult to sense that we are connected to them in our own practice, as theoretically sophisticated as we are able to make it, sensitive to kinds of issues that none of them would have understood. As Lowe worked to correct Doran's text, he noted how Doran's text needed curbing to increase "its authority as a book of reference, by correcting those errors which are scarcely to be avoided by a writer working among the confused, inaccurate, and contradictory documents of theatrical history."[11] Lowe saw that Doran's book had come to hold "a recognized position as the standard popular history of the English stage"[12] but that seemed only to increase his frustration in the activity of correcting errors. When Doran comments of one obscure play, *Elfrid*, that it was "damned in a night," Lowe's footnote moves beyond his normally laconic style: "This is a specimen of one of the greatest difficulties in the revision of

Dr. Doran. He frequently writes of a play as being damned, which really was played for a few nights with no great success. In the present case, 'Elfrid' was played five times."[13] There is no concern here to reexamine Doran's method of historiography, to reconsider the ways in which theater history, even popular theater history, might be written. The model of practice was still acceptable and that, for Lowe, did not warrant further consideration. His own work, editing the playwright and actor Colley Cibber's autobiography, *An Apology for the Life*,[14] or writing a biography of the great Restoration actor Thomas Betterton,[15] may be more accurate than Doran had often been and may be far more restrained in its style but the modes of narrative in Doran and Lowe are directly comparable, positivist and unquestioning accounts of chronology. Facts were the kind of detail that Genest had painstakingly generated and for the limitations of which he apologized on the title-page of each volume in the epigram in Greek and English taken from Evagrius Scholasticus, author of an early ecclesiastical history: "If any thing be overlooked, or not accurately inserted, let no one find fault but take into consideration that this history is compiled from all quarters." Such facts produced apparently natural interpretation, an inevitability of response in which the material could only be read one way as evidence both of event and of cultural context.

My concern in this article, though, is less with the forms of high Victorian writing than with the earliest forms of English theater history: the work of Flecknoe, Wright, and Downes. But I shall also be concerned to trace their subsequent histories, the cultural histories of their histories, tracing the beginnings of an account of the ways in which British theater history has called on and recalled some of what it has regarded as its crucial documents. It matters, as well as perhaps amuses, in this context, that Genest's ten volumes have only once been reprinted, in 1965 by an American publisher, Burt Franklin, as number 93 in their series of "Research and Source Work," sold, presumably, at many times the price at which the volumes were once remaindered, a sign of the economics of facsimile publishing for libraries. Unapologetically, I shall be offering something akin to a bibliographical questing and the risk is that it appears only as another kind of antiquarianism, a rather relentless charting of printings and reprintings. But each act of publication is a new positioning of the texts themselves and it enables me to offer the beginnings of a construction of a kind of narrative history of their histories, in order to find the place these works occupied and now occupy, the disciplinary meanings and resonances, pre-echoes for the most part, that they have been enabled to have in their move from one kind of reading to another, from one location in academic and non-academic history to a very different one.

What lies behind this is a concern to trace the still pervasive anxieties of the discipline, the threats to the particularity of theater history, to its disciplinarity, created conventionally, historically, and most pervasively institutionally by its annexation or service status in relation to other forms of academic work. While theater historians may – to a greater or lesser extent – be clear what they do, it is not always clear that the separateness of the discipline is yet understood, let alone respected, within the structuring of the research and teaching in the forms of the Western university.

The British Academy, the primary organization controlling both funding and prestige for the humanities in the UK, has no theater historians as Fellows and no section to which they might belong, caught between, say, section H6 "Modern Languages, Literatures and other Media" (including, it would seem, Film) and H11 "History of Art and Music." The Arts and Humanities Research Board, another major source of humanities funding in Britain, places "drama, theatre, dance and performance history" within the work of Panel 7, "Music and Performing Arts" in a vast array of types of practice, theory and analysis, thereby associating it with drama but keeping drama hermetically sealed from other literary forms, the preserves of, for instance, Panel 3, "English Language and Literature." There are in the UK no Departments of Theatre History and the status of theater history within the British academy (and Academy) is still bedeviled by conflicts that ought to have been long resolved: the relationship with the study of drama and of other literary forms, the relationship with sociologies of culture, the relationship with the analysis of performance and, most problematically, the relationship with theater practice. The kinds of problems outlined by Ronald Vince in 1989 in his major statement on "Theatre History as an Academic Discipline" continue to stay largely unresolved outside the theory and practice of theater historians themselves/ourselves.[16] The early history of the practice of theater history, then, is a space where the roots of some of these tensions can be charted both at the moment of their appearance and in the histories of their later cultural re-presentations.

I

If the early modern period offered nothing remotely akin to a history of the stage, that was an inevitable consequence of the social positioning of theater. If actors are technically rogues and vagabonds and the theater a space needing strict governmental control, then theater is not a space of activity warranting early modern scholarly attention. While the writing of the history of nation accelerates, the writing of the nation's culture could be ignored. Similarly, the problems Ben Jonson found himself in when he described a volume of his plays as *Workes* in the folio of 1616, mocked for pretentiousness, defines the irrelevance of both drama and theater to any distinct intellectual attention.

But, in another sense, the theater was not a space defined as possessing history, for all its crucial cultural importance as a place for performing history. Theater, as a professional activity based in permanent structures in the capital,

had as yet no significant history, only roots in other kinds of dramatic performance (touring companies, temporary theater spaces, cycle drama and so
on). In many respects early modern drama and theater refused to acknowledge
their origins, refused to construct a sense of their own history, denied their continuity from an antecedent past. Triumphantly working against their own roots
to declare their modernity, the theaters were a space aware of their own cultural
singularity. What history could have been charted?

But it is also the case that there were elements of print that defined theater
as history, denied their immediacy and contemporaneity. Play publication,
both by virtue of its uneasy relationship to the theater companies together
with their rights over the plays and by virtue of the culture of print itself,
located performance as a past event. There is a simple and striking difference
between early modern and Restoration play publication in the form of definition on the title-page of the link to the theater event: where an early modern
play is consistently defined as past, the Restoration play is present; where the
former is identified with the phrase "as it hath been acted," the latter is seen as
belonging in the current repertory, "as it is acted." Each publication of a play
in the early modern period is an act of theater history, a statement about
the past of theater practice, while the post-1660 form defines a continuum
of repertory practice even in those cases in which a play had sunk and would
not be revived. The accelerating closeness, after 1660, of publication to
première[17] is part of this reconnection of text to an immediate practice of
performance.

In one exceptional example the early modern play-text marks the continuities and processes of its own performance history. John Webster's *The Duchess
of Malfi* was first performed in late 1613 or early 1614. When the text was published in 1623, the list of "The Actors Names" carries for thirteen roles, including all the major parts, identifications of the actors who played them, the first
time any English play had been published with actors assigned to specific roles.
Even more remarkably, for three of the roles (Ferdinand, the Cardinal, and
Antonio), the list identifies two actors for each role, indicating the succession
of parts. The first names must relate to performances prior to December 1614
while the second must relate to a revival after 1619.[18] The text performs part
of the history of its own performances, making the succession of roles a matter
of record in recording its historical process as performance text.

II

In 1654 Richard Flecknoe, now remembered if at all only from the title to
Dryden's satire on Shadwell *Mac Flecknoe* (1682), published *Love's Dominion*,
announcing it as "a dramatique piece full of excellent moralitie; written as a
pattern for the reformed stage," dedicating it to Lady Elizabeth Claypole,
Cromwell's daughter, and using the dedication as an opportunity to try to

persuade Cromwell to allow theater performances.[19] In 1664 Flecknoe, having shifted sides as effectively as he could, republished the play, with the names of some of the characters changed, as *Love's Kingdom*, announcing on the title-page that it is "not as it was acted at the theatre near Lincolns-Inn, but as it was written, and since corrected."[20]

But now the play had an additional feature, also worth advertising on the title-page: "a short treatise of the English Stage." The extremely short treatise or "discourse," as Flecknoe also names it (sig. G4r), only nine pages long, is usually called "the first formal piece of theatrical criticism in our tongue," as Joel Spingarn dubbed it in 1908 when he reprinted it in his three-volume collection of *Critical Essays of the Seventeenth Century*.[21] Spingarn's possessive is conventional but the context is not. After its appearance in 1664 and its reissue in 1674, Flecknoe's discourse was reprinted by W. Carew Hazlitt in his collection of documents, *The English Drama and Stage under the Tudor and Stuart Princes 1543–1664*, printed, expensively, for the Roxburghe Library in 1869 and re-issued, only slightly more cheaply, in 1964 as part of that modern reprint series by Burt Franklin in which Genest also figured.[22] It is in the gap between Hazlitt and Spingarn, between documents for the history of drama and a collection of early examples of literary criticism, that the problems both of the text's definition and of the academic placing it has received become visible and the anxieties in the concept of theater history resurface.

Flecknoe's discourse is written from a recognition of the gap that separates the Restoration stage from the theater before the closure of 1642. Both memory and defense of that earlier form of theatrical culture, as well as a firm commitment to the theater as "a harmless and innocent Recreation" (sig. G7v), Flecknoe's little tract constructs the interaction of playwright and company in part as a defense of the pre-Restoration stage against the religious opposition that had closed it – Flecknoe was in a slightly odd position for this as an Irish Roman Catholic priest based at one time at Rome – but also in part as a validation of early modern drama for its lack of scenery:

> that which makes our Stage the better, makes our Playes the worse perhaps, they striving now to make them more for sight, then hearing; whence that solid joy of the interior is lost, and that benefit which men formerly receiv'd from Playes, from which they seldom or never went away, but far better and wiser then they came. (sig. G7v)

Flecknoe praises Shakespeare and Burbage, Jonson and Field, playwright and actor. He also praises a theater in which poets and actors work together: "It was the happiness of the Actors of those times to have such Poets as these to instruct them, and write for them; and no less of those Poets to have such docile and excellent Actors to Act their Playes" (sig. G7v).[23] A text that is concerned with dramatists and performers has, therefore, an ambiguous status: for Hazlitt a crucial part of the history of the early modern stage, for Spingarn a text of literary criticism and dramatic practice to be placed chronologically between the preface to Cowley's *Poems* (1656) and Sir Robert Howard's preface to his *Four New Plays* (1665). Spingarn seems almost apologetic for having included Flecknoe's piece: his hundred-page preface to the volumes devotes only two lines to Flecknoe's discourse, marking its significance as "theatrical criticism," itself an undefined category for him, while adding a contemptuous description of it: "poor thing as it is."[24]

Flecknoe's text comes then to be annexed to a particular and partial function (either as drama criticism or as theater history) and this is even more strikingly the case in the later of the two facsimile editions published in the early 1970s: from the Johnson Reprint Corporation in 1972, with an introduction by Peter Davison, and from Garland Publishing in 1973, with a preface by Arthur Freeman. Freeman's fifty-volume series, *The English Stage: Attack and Defense, 1577–1730*, inevitably means that, though the whole volume is reproduced, Flecknoe's play is as little regarded as in its own time and the volume exists for the sake of reproducing the "Short Discourse," seen by Freeman as "perhaps less a defense of theater than an epitome of its history and praise of its past."[25] The whole practice of such a reprint series, itself evidence of a pre-electronic time when university library budgets were significantly higher, is to align works so that Flecknoe's discourse can be perceived as a step in the artificially constructed chronological linearity of a sequence of argument for and against the stage.

III

In 1699, at the height of the first wave of the argument against the contemporary stage for its immorality and profaneness mounted by Jeremy Collier, William Haws published an anonymous short pamphlet called *Historia Histrionica*.[26] Extraordinarily, no piece of early theater history has been so often reprinted but it appears in three distinct and definable contexts, spaces within which it is given meaning. Usually identified as the work of James Wright, *Historia Histrionica*, subtitled "An Historical Account of the English Stage, shewing the ancient use, improvement, and perfection, of Dramatick Representations, in this Nation," is a dialogue between two playgoers: Lovewit, a young man about town, and Trueman, an old cavalier. The use of the dialogue form, unsurprisingly quite common in pamphlets on the stage at this time,[27] creates a structure for Trueman's memories about the early modern theaters, by then nearly sixty years before. Wright's preface identifies the reason for this further memorializing of earlier theater practice as a kind of historicizing of the argument that Collier represented, assenting to Collier's attack but wanting to describe "What it was in former Ages, and how used in this

Kingdom, so far back as one may collect any Memorialls" (sig. [A]3a). Wright was an antiquarian and essayist, author of *The History and Antiquities of the County of Rutland* (1684) and *Three Poems of St Paul's Cathedral* (1697). He was also noted as a collector of "old," i.e. early modern, plays,[28] and the preface notes that "Old Plays will always be read by the *Curious*" (sig. A3v). Wright's research must have been extensive: some of *Historia Histrionica* repeats material from statutes but Wright also quotes from John Heywood's *The Pardoner and the Friar* (printed 1533), from the Coventry cycle-drama and other early texts, using Sir Robert Cotton's great library as well as his own. But the extensive comments on early modern theater and its players, whom Trueman claims to have seen, are remarkable. Wright was born in 1643 but he had probably talked with pre-Civil War actors, like John Lowin. A combination of antiquarian research and oral history, *Historia Histrionica* is the only distinct account of early modern theater that has direct contact with the experience and few of its facts, masquerading as Trueman's memories, "can be challenged by any facts unearthed in the last two and one-half centuries," as G. E. Bentley noted in 1968.[29]

Bentley, indeed, found the material so important that he reprinted a major section of *Historia Histrionica* in the appendix to the first volumes of his great study of *The Jacobean and Caroline Stage*,[30] as part of a group of "certain contemporary documents which have been referred to so frequently in the body of the book that it was desirable to make them readily accessible."[31] By this point, Wright's pamphlet is being clearly identified as a crucial evidentiary source for the study of early modern theater, particularly for that period for which Wright can be assumed to have had a direct connection with an oral historical tradition. The motto on the title-page of the pamphlet, *olim meminisse iuvabit*, "it will some day be a joy to remember,"[32] hints at the function here of memory, memorializing theater itself, replaying its history as a performative act.

But the later history of the text, almost until Bentley's reprinting in 1941, often substantially dissociates the pamphlet from theater to define its importance in the history of drama, while at other moments it functioned as an articulation of a specific form of theatrical reminiscence, the pleasures of recalling performances. In 1743 Robert Dodsley, playwright and publisher, sought 200 subscribers for an edition of what he described as "old plays." Quickly successful in drawing up a list, in 1744 he produced the first ten volumes of his *Select Collection of Old Plays*, prefacing it with what he planned as "a short History of the rise & progress of the English stage till the Death of Charles the 1st."[33] He added two further volumes in 1745, reprinting in all sixty-one early modern plays. Dodsley's collection was and remains a major step in the investigation of early modern drama, the first significant attempt at surveying pre-Civil War plays. Its range is impressively wide. Dodsley drew on the collection of over 600 plays which had formed part of the Harleian collection and which he now possessed; many were later sold to Garrick and were left by him to what is now the British Library.[34] Dodsley's preface is significant in its own right as the first significant attempt to write something approaching a narrative of the pre-Restoration English stage. After a brief charting of the early history of the theater in other European countries, Dodsley moves through chronologically from William Fitz-Stephens's twelfth-century reference to performances in London to the closure in 1642. Where the post-Restoration stage had been briefly charted in *The History of the English Stage* ascribed to Betterton and printed in 1741, Dodsley's is a stride forward in attempting a more coherent account of earlier theater. It is part of what will become a crucial and often disabling tendency in theater history to provide nothing more than a chronological non-analytic history. Though Dodsley is concerned to trace "the Dramatic Muse thro' all her Characters and Transformations, till she had acquired a reasonable Figure,"[35] he is also interested in tracing the history of playhouses and companies, the practice of censorship and the attacks on the stage, the cultural placing of theater and work of individual actors. He has little or nothing to say about staging practices so that the historicized theatrical context is seen as external to the plays themselves in performance. But, within its limits, Dodsley's history was a brave attempt.

At the start of volume 11 of *A Select Collection*, Dodsley reprinted Wright's *Historia Histrionica* as "A Dialogue on Old Plays and Players," probably on the advice of William Warburton, then involved in his edition of Shakespeare which would appear in 1747.[36] Its function here is plainly to provide an addition to Dodsley's historical account. *A Select Collection of Old Plays* was a quite extraordinary and enduring success; it is still in print. In 1780 Isaac Reed re-edited the collection, adding, among other things an extensive supplement to Dodsley's history. Where Dodsley could state that he stopped at 1642 because "to pursue it farther, and take it up again at the Restoration . . . would be needless; because from that time the affairs of the stage are tolerably well known,"[37] Reed's supplement is offered for all its imperfections. Strikingly, Reed is surprised that narrative theater history is not more common and "to find that so little has been written on a subject from which so much of the amusement of life is derived"[38] but he also recognized the difficulty of such a project: "the materials for a history executed with such minuteness as the subject deserves are too much scattered, and too difficult to be obtained, to be readily brought together."[39] He goes on to identify where the materials for theater history could be found: in "the interior of the present playhouses; the neglected pamphlets of former times . . .; and the remembrance of many individuals."[40] Reed accurately identifies the resources for research in theater history. But this attempt to see how theater history might be constructed is to be undertaken because "The History of the Drama seems intitled to more regard than hath been bestowed upon it."[41] Reed's "slight view of the English theatres" was offered as part of a history of drama, a necessary but subordinate part of such a study. But there is also a surprising need to manifest a history now clearly irrelevant to the material for which it acts as preface. Reed never explains why a narrative theater history of the post-Restoration stage is an assistance in reading pre-Civil War drama. Instead the display of historical continuities becomes an end in itself, part of the display of learning.

Reed added a brief prefatory note to the text of *Historia Histrionica*, offering a sketch of Wright's biography. He moved the text to the end of volume 12, placing it as some kind of appendix, marking, in a way that Dodsley had not, its separation from the play-texts for which it offered a contextual primary source.[42] By the time Reed's edition in turn was revised and reissued in 1825, with yet further supplements to the stage history, *Historia Histrionica* had been identified by the editors as part of "the introductory matter"[43] and been moved from volume 12 to volume 1 where it was now paginated in roman numerals as part of the preface.[44]

If the long track of the presence of this brief pamphlet in the context of drama points to its status as nothing more than context, its second route is in a different configuration of a relationship with theater. In 1750 Robert Dodsley paid the substantial sum of 50 guineas for the copyright in Colley Cibber's autobiography.[45] Seeking to remarket a book which had been popular enough to have gone through two editions in ten years, Dodsley added to the end of the text both his own account of "The Rise and Progress of the English Theatre" written for *A Select Collection of Old Plays*, openly acknowledging its source, and the "Dialogue on old plays and old players," as *Historia Histrionica* had become known.[46] The pamphlet stayed attached to Cibber's autobiography through to the major nineteenth-century edition by R. W. Lowe in 1889, where Lowe identifies both what he calls the "historical value of this pamphlet" and "a peculiar propriety in prefacing [Cibber] by Wright's work" since "Cibber begins his account of the Stage . . . at the Restoration."[47] Where Dodsley's aim is little more than a marketing ploy of value added, what seems to be in Lowe's mind is stretching the history back through primary documentation. The narrative of theater needs the precursor to Cibber's work. Attached now to the genre of theatrical memoir, *Historia Histrionica* constitutes oral history testimony directly analogous to Cibber's. Cibber's forms of knowledge and Wright's are aligned, just as Cibber's is extended by Lowe's inclusion of Aston's supplement with further information about the actors Cibber discusses. It is this kind of connection that leads to its facsimile reappearances in the 1970s: introduced by Peter Davison and by Arthur Freeman, the former in the volume with Flecknoe, the latter with Downes.[48]

From a link to drama to a link with the later stage offers some kind of logic to these appearances of the pamphlet, but the third and last form of its manifestation is a dissociation from both the theater and drama and its insertion into the ragbag of generalized and barely focused antiquarian interest. The association of antiquarianism with theater history is itself an intriguing topic. Joseph Knight, John Doran and Edward Arber were all Fellows of the Society of Antiquaries, founded by royal charter in 1751 for "the encouragement, advancement and furtherance of the study and knowledge of the antiquities and history of this and other countries"[49] and James Wright himself, author of the *History and Antiquities of the County of Rutland*, is part of the same attitude towards theater history. As early as 1737 *Historia Histrionica* was summarized in one of the six numbers of William Oldys's journal *The British Librarian* which identified itself as exhibiting "a compendious review or abstract of our most scarce, useful and valuable books."[50] In 1872 Wright's pamphlet was reprinted in *Mr Ashbee's Occasional Fac-Simile Reprints* as pamphlet 30 of this series, printed by subscription and limited to 100 copies.[51] It appears irrelevantly (but what would be relevant in such a collection?) after a 1647 pamphlet about a Welsh prophet and is by far the latest work in the second volume of the series. Ashbee, bibliographer and collector of pornography, is simply marking its oddity as a kind of sample from an arbitrarily defined history, the chance accumulation of materials that represent that past.

Something of the same is true about the appearance of part of Wright's work in Edward Arber's consciously antiquarian collection *An English Garner*, subtitled "Ingatherings from our History and Literature," its eight volumes of randomly assembled materials published between 1877 and 1896.[52] So random and arbitrary is Arber's garnering that it necessitated a later edition that resequenced the collection; here, Wright appears in a volume called *Social England Illustrated*, edited by Andrew Lang, who apologizes for his incompetence: "Wright . . . is so valuable for the history of the stage that it needs a more expert commentator than I can pretend to be."[53] Arber's preface to *The English Garner* marks his collection as "the original materials out of which modern historians have culled the most graphic touches of their most brilliant pages," seeing it as "a Study on a large scale of detached areas of English history; and stands in the same relation to the general national Story, as a selected Collection of Parish Maps would do to the Ordnance Survey of English land."[54] Wright becomes a mark of a local mapping, a large-scale piece of historical cartography which the antiquarian has retrieved. From providing a context for the study of drama to being a useful supplement to a theater memoir to representing a fragment of the patriotic mapping of England's national past, the subsequent fates of *Historia Histrionica* define the ambiguities of finding a context for the work, rather than its being itself contextual.

IV

Mapping that history is precisely the process inaugurated by John Downes whose *Roscius Anglicanus, or An Historical Review of the English Stage* was published in 1708.[55] None of the reprints of Wright seeks to annotate the text. The editions of Downes become an intense site of accumulation of data. For, if

Wright is oral and antiquarian theater history, Downes represents the second British example of the theatrical memoir but the crucial inauguration of enumerative calendrical theater history. For the former, Downes had had one precedent, Tobyas Thomas's *The Life of the Late Famous Comedian, Jo. Hayns*, written probably by a minor actor just after and to capitalize on Hayns's death;[56] for the latter there was no theatrical precedent.

John Downes was a failed actor turned prompter who probably worked from early in the 1660s until his retirement in 1706. Ostensibly a kind of chronology, *Roscius Anglicanus* is an old man's random memories and documentation masquerading as an ordered sequence. He offers cast-lists and brief comments for dozens of plays, identifying the success and failure (from a primarily commercial perspective) and occasionally adding an anecdote. Downes is immensely valuable as a first-hand account of the economics of Restoration theater and he is also the unique source of many cast-lists and other details of production – hence Genest's description of it as consisting "chiefly of playbills" and his valuation of it as "the most valuable work of the sort that was ever printed."[57] But Downes's inaccuracies, possible or provable, over chronology and casting also result in the kind of blanket statement of Montague Summers, who edited the text, "that the chronology of John Downes must be regarded as utterly unreliable and uncertain"[58] or the more measured response of Downes's most recent editors, Judith Milhous and Robert D. Hume, that "if we accept the fact that chronology was of little or no interest to Downes . . . his assertions about casts, attributions, and popularity . . . stand up astonishingly well."[59]

There are, then, two characteristics of Downes's work that are highly significant: firstly that it is in a sense unreadable unless one likes reading lists and secondly that it encourages annotation. Lists of casts constitute a contribution towards what Dryden had called "annals" rather than "history properly so called";[60] they suggest a document that denies consecutive reading but invites consultation. Hence, for instance, it is striking that the 1969 facsimile edited by John Loftis for the Augustan Reprint Society at the Clark Library in Los Angeles, placing it away from theater history and into a historical context of the Augustan pamphlet, provided a rare addition in that series, an index, "of performers and plays," keyed to the pages of the facsimile, provided by David Rodes.[61]

Roscius Anglicanus was reprinted in 1789 as part of a series that would eventually become *The Literary Museum; or, Ancient and Modern Repository. Comprising Scarce and Curious Tracts.*[62] It sounds like a further example of antiquarian interest but its dedication to the actor John Philip Kemble as one "generally known to unite the elegant Antiquary with the accomplished Actor"[63] and its bringing together of plays, poems, specimens for Whalley's new edition of Ben Jonson and other such materials defines its literariness. The advertisement is concerned that books are read, not simply classed as vulnerable. The series was put together by Francis Godolphin Waldron, actor, playwright, poet and would-be man of letters. Waldron would go on to write *The Ancient and Modern Miscellany* in 1794, reissued as *The Shakespearean Miscellany* in 1802,[64] which includes a brief narrative history of the stage and a substantial series of biographies of early modern actors, each identified with a plate, a model he had explored across a broader chronological range in the three volumes of *The Biographical Mirrour* in 1795.[65]

Waldron's interest in *Roscius Anglicanus* had been sparked by having been loaned a set of notes beginning a commentary to the work written by Tom Davies, failed actor turned bookseller and author of a hugely successful biography of Garrick and a stage-oriented analysis of Shakespeare, with extensive commentary about contemporary actors' performances, both written after his bankruptcy in 1778.[66] Waldron interweaves Davies's notes with his own, creating a complexly annotated text that corrects errata, worries about Downes's meaning, adds analysis of the play-lists, supplements cast-lists and extends biographical detail on the actors, providing a first sketch in two hands of the kind of notes that would be extensively provided by Hume and Milhous two hundred years later in their edition.

At one point Waldron is worried by a matter of taste. One of Downes's most famous anecdotes describes Mrs Holden, acting in a revival of *Romeo and Juliet*, who

> enter'd in a *Hurry*, Crying, O my dear *Count*! She Inadvertently left out, O, in the pronuntiation of the Word *Count*! Giving it a Vehement Accent, put the House into such a Laughter, that *London* Bridge at low Water was silence to it.[67]

Waldron is embarrassed:

> in the Advertisement to this Edition, the Original is said to be faithfully followed; this silly and indecent passage had not been remarked when that was written, otherwise both would have been omitted: now there is a necessity to retain it.[68]

Scholarship and advertising truthfulness are the excuse to cover the lapse of taste.

Nonetheless Waldron's display of scholarship is substantial and he states in a final epistle to the reader that he "might have swell'd the book considerably by extracts from" an enormous range of texts including periodicals, biographies, stage-tracts, editions of the dramatists, Edmond Malone's history of the stage, and Dodsley's collection but "I have been very sparing of quotations from books in every body's hands,"[69] even though he goes on to print twenty-seven pages of additional notes and a memoir of Nell Gwyn.

Waldron's edition is thus dependent both on the availability of Davies's notes and on his own peacock-proud display of his own scholarship. It was also driven by his awareness of the high price copies of the original attracted, "a copy of it in Mr. Henderson's collection, was sold for 1*l*.5s."[70]

The tension between scholarship and price remained a crucial problem in subsequent editions. Joseph Knight's edition in 1886 is polite about Downes ("A just but timid critic"[71]), discriminating on his worth ("On matters concerning the theatre under his own immediate supervision he is moderately accurate. In respect of the other house . . . he is not always trustworthy"[72]) and mocking of his previous editors ("Neither . . . is much more accurate than Downes"[73]). A review of Knight's edition in *The Athenaeum* complained both that Knight was restrained in his commentary but, more significantly, that the nature of the edition was wrong-headed: "It has somehow been decided that Downes is not a popular author, and that he may command none save a private and peculiar circulation." After pointing out that there are only 135 copies of Knight's new edition for sale, the reviewer complains that "It is obvious that, even in his new guise, he is intended not nearly so much for the student as for the collector."[74]

The same exclusivity was characteristic of the next edition of Downes, edited by Montague Summers in 1928 with "Fifty copies on Alton Mill hand-made paper . . . and six hundred copies on Arnold unbleached hand-made paper"[75] and, to some extent, of the Augustan Reprint Society edition and that by Milhous and Hume for the Society for Theatre Research. If the last was unquestionably intended for students rather than collectors it came from a backwater of publishing, for all its institutional importance as the UK's oldest grouping for theater history studies, the place where, as it were, study of John Downes might be seen as belonging.

Summers admired Downes's work as "a document of incalculable value,"[76] not least, I suspect, for the opportunity Downes provided for the display of Summers's erudition. He annotates by giving full biographies for all actors Downes names so that one page of Downes can require thirty pages of notes.[77] Summers is by far the oddest of all theater historians: a fake Catholic priest with a special interest in Restoration drama, witchcraft and the works of de Sade and a man reliably reported to have celebrated black masses.[78] His edition of Downes is an uncontrolled display of his reading and enthusiasm, itself a kind of scholarly achievement as appropriate to its date as the scrupulous care by Milhous and Hume, the major historians of Restoration theater in the 1980s, accurately represents a different era of theater history, a different mode of scholarship but still underpinned by the same belief that Downes can only exist within the control of the annotation, that the text becomes a site of scholarly exposition and the scholarship a sign of a progressive discipline.

Downes's mode of theater history as enumeration had direct progeny from within the theaters. In 1749 Robert Dodsley published *A General History of the Stage* by William Rufus Chetwood, for many years prompter at Drury Lane.[79] There was also *The History of the Theatres of London and Dublin* printed in 1761[80] and continued in *The History of the Theatres of London from the year 1760 to the present time*, printed in 1771,[81] both the work of Benjamin Victor, treasurer of Drury Lane from 1759 to 1778. Outside the theater there was *The British Theatre*, probably by Dodsley himself, published in 1750, primarily a collection of biographies of playwrights,[82] reprinted by Dodsley as *Theatrical Records* in 1756.[83] Theater history as an enumerative chronicling, the creation of annals, continued in numerous late eighteenth- and nineteenth-century works, including Genest, until the publication in the 1960s of *The London Stage*, charting the day-by-day activity of theaters and concert-halls in London from 1660 to 1800, just as the collection of theater biographies that Waldron offered for the early modern period would become for 1660 to 1800 the sixteen volumes of the *Biographical Dictionary* published between 1973 and 1993.[84]

V

These massive successes of enumerative theater history owe much to the work of Allardyce Nicoll, founder of the Shakespeare Institute. Nicoll's series of historical studies of English drama began in 1923 with *A History of Restoration Drama, 1660–1700*[85] and eventually constituted, in their revised form, the six volumes of *A History of English Drama 1660–1900* by 1959[86] with their tailpiece, *English Drama 1900–1930* published in 1973, a year before Nicoll's death at the age of 85. Nicoll was often awkwardly unsure whether he was writing about drama or theater: his book *British Drama: an Historical Survey from the Beginnings to the Present Time* announces its scope in the preface: "This book . . . attempts to trace the history of our theatre."[87] His analysis of drama and of the evidence for theater are unremarkable but the archival work that documented the history of theater was prodigious. Nicoll also offered what he called "Hand-lists" of the plays for each period, recording not only publication history but also every performance of each play for which he had found evidence within the volume's period. As he acknowledged, "[I]n the preparation of this work I have received great assistance from my wife, who has aided me in the arduous and not always interesting task of collecting the theatrical records."[88] Mrs Nicoll, the first woman I have mentioned in the context of theater history, laboured doggedly to assemble the tedious data; the interpretative work was Nicoll's alone. The lengthy and largely pointless lists of performance, hardly ever used by subsequent theater historians, represent the mechanical limits of chronicling. While Nicoll's archival work turned up prodigious quantities of documents and transcribed or summarized them with scrupulous accuracy, he often seems to have little idea what the documentation might do. There is a plaintive irrelevance in the last document he lists for the Restoration stage, after more than forty pages of "Documents Illustrative of the History of the Stage": "Order to Sir Christopher Wren to inspect the Duke's Theatre in Salisbury Court as the King has heard that there is a wall defective. Nov. 29, 1671. (L.C. 5/14, p. 73.)"[89]

I may have sounded harsh about Nicoll's work. Its significance lies not only in the organization of primary material evidence for play after play, theater after theater. It lies also in Nicoll's fundamental and necessary comprehension that

> The drama belongs, of course, partly to literature and partly to the theatre. Part of the work necessary for its proper evaluation must be carried out in this area of bibliography and the analysis of texts; the other part of the work lies within the field of investigation into stage conditions.[90]

For Nicoll there could be no study of drama without the study of the theater, no history of drama without an accompanying history of theater. If theater history is still, in Nicoll's work, essentially a subservient tool for the analysis of drama, the result was an exceptional emphasis on drama as theater, as performance, as text in process.

In the preface to the fifth edition of his *The Development of the Theatre*, published in 1966, nearly forty years after it first appeared, Nicoll could note that "during the past twenty-five or thirty years . . . theater history, as an independent subject of investigation, has fully come into its own,"[91] a recognition of a discipline which enables the work of this volume and its successors, work which will often owe much to Allardyce Nicoll.

What Nicoll accomplished – and failed to accomplish – for British theater history from 1660 to 1930 is strikingly similar to the work of E. K. Chambers for the early modern period. Chambers, by occupation a civil servant, used his leisure to compile reference works that remain central to the discipline: *The Elizabethan Stage*, published in four volumes in 1923,[92] has not been superseded. Yet as F. P. Wilson, himself no mean theater historian, noted, this was "more a work of consolidation than discovery for he had little time to search for the information which lay dormant in the Public Record Office and elsewhere," for all that Chambers displayed his brilliance "in the acuteness with which he balances complicated evidence."[93] Chambers's work, acute in its judgement but responsive rather than innovative, continued to use a parallel model of theater history to Nicoll's. Like Nicoll, Chambers "was convinced that any history of drama . . . must start from a study of the social and economic facts upon which the drama rested."[94] Yet even here there is a slide, a slipperiness between "drama" and "theater" that is troubling, for his histories were of theater, as much as of drama.

VI

But Nicoll's or Chambers's search for documentation, their concerns and methodologies, are all present in the work which seems to me effectively to inaugurate theater history as an analytic discipline, a field of study which takes a properly scientistic and sceptical approach to the material evidence.

On 29 November 1790 Edmond Malone published his ten-volume edition of *The Plays and Poems of William Shakspeare* [sic].[95] As with Chambers's work which seems in some respects to move towards *William Shakespeare: a Study of Facts and Problems*,[96] so for Malone theater history is at the service of the study of Shakespeare, the same tension between theater history and literary analysis that would resurface so often later, and yet there is something distinctive and unprecedented about Malone's accomplishment. The first volume of Malone's edition was divided into two parts: the first contained the prefaces by his predecessors as editors and Malone's commentary on Rowe's life of Shakespeare; the second contained Malone's "An historical account of the rise and progress of the English stage, and of the economy and usages of our ancient theatres," 331 pages of narrative and analysis. The account had grown out of the 65-page version Malone had published in 1780 as part of his two-volume "Supplement" to the Johnson–Steevens edition of 1778, including the poems.[97] In the Boswell–Malone edition of 1821, including more of Malone's researches, it will have grown again to 550 pages.[98]

It is not simply the scale of the study and its extraordinary detail that marks its crucial importance in defining the discipline. Nor is it simply that Malone had found innumerable crucial documents, including the records of Sir Henry Herbert and the Henslowe papers. Nor is it simply the impressively wide range of topics he works on, including playbills and benefits and the sale of plays, prices of admission, profits and the size of the companies, enabling him to survey the whole mode of operation of this theatrical "economy." It is rather that Malone scrupulously and thoughtfully and critically analyzes the evidence to begin to understand its possibilities and implications, refusing to see the writing of theater history as a mere narrative and an uncritical response to the lure of the document and seeking instead to draw on as many disparate sources as possible in order to evaluate the truth of assertion, the validity of hypotheses.

When, for instance, Malone confronts the major puzzle for his contemporaries, the question whether the early modern stage had scenery, he takes thirty pages to review the evidence. He considers the phrasing in stage directions, the comments in prologues and epilogues, the remarks in other contemporary writings, the use of movable scenery at Christ Church, Oxford, in 1605, the novelty of Davenant's *The Siege of Rhodes* in 1656, the way Shakespeare refers to shifting of scene as an imaginary space, the possible use of sign-boards, traps, wax-lights, the heavens, the different kinds of meaning the word "scene" might have, the opinions of those who, like Steevens, held views opposite to his own. Cumulatively he is able to reach a decision:

> The various circumstances which I have here stated, and the accounts of the contemporary writers, furnish us, in my apprehension, with decisive and incontrovertible proofs that the stage of Shakspeare was not furnished with *moveable painted scenes*, but merely decorated with curtains, and arras or tapestry hangings, which, when decayed, appear to have been sometimes ornamented with pictures: and some passages in our old dramas incline me to think, that when tragedies were performed, the stage was hung with black.[99]

In its contorted syntax and awkward connectives, Malone's account is the tentative statement of a scholar who understands the sheer difficulty of his project, the limitations of his evidence and the need to find ways of understanding how conclusions might be drawn. In this, if in nothing else, Malone inaugurates the practice of a discipline.

Notes

1. James Wright, *Historia Histrionica* (London: William Haws, 1699), 32.
2. C. Hooper, "Rev. John Genest," *Notes and Queries*, Series 2, Vol. 9, 28 Jan 1860: 65.
3. C. P. R., "Rev. John Genest," *Notes and Queries*, Series 2, Vol. 9, 11 Feb 1860: 108–9.
4. *DNB*, 998.
5. "National Biography" in *National Review*, 27 (1896): 51–65, reprinted in Leslie Stephen, *Studies of a Biographer*, 4 vols (London: Duckworth, 1898), 1: 1–36. See also Stephen's earlier article on "Biography" in *National Review*, 22 (1893): 171–83, reprinted in Leslie Stephen, *Men, Books, and Mountains*, ed. S. O. A. Ullmann (London: Hogarth Press, 1956), 128–44.
6. C. P. R., "Rev. John Genest," 109.
7. John Genest, *Some Account of the English Stage from the Restoration in 1660 to 1830* (Bath: H. E. Carrington, 1832).
8. John Doran, *"Their Majesties' Servants": Annals of the English Stage*, rev. edn, ed. Robert W. Lowe (London: John C. Nimmo, 1897), 1: v.
9. Quoted in James Fullarton Arnott and John William Robinson, *English Theatrical Literature 1559–1900: a Bibliography* (London: The Society for Theatre Research, 1970), 90.
10. Robert W. Lowe, *A Bibliographical Account of English Theatrical Literature from the Earliest Times to the Present Day* (London: J. C. Nimmo, 1888).
11. Doran, *"Their Majesties' Servants"*, 1: v–vi.
12. Doran, *"Their Majesties' Servants"*, 1: v.
13. Doran, *"Their Majesties' Servants"*, 1: 312 n.1.
14. Colley Cibber, *An Apology for the Life of Mr. Colley Cibber*, 2 vols, ed. Robert W. Lowe (London: John C. Nimmo, 1889).

15. Robert W. Lowe, *Thomas Betterton* (London: Kegan Paul, Trench Trübner and Co. Ltd., 1891).

16. See R. W. Vince, "Theatre History as an Academic Discipline," in Thomas Postlewait and Bruce A.McConachie, eds, *Interpreting the Theatrical Past: Essays in the Historiography of Performance* (Iowa City: University of Iowa Press, 1989), 1–18. See also R. W. Vince "Comparative Theatre Historiography," *Essays in Theatre*, 1 (1983): 64–72; and, of especial relevance to the material in this paper, Ronald W. Vince, *Renaissance Theatre: a Historiographical Handbook* (Westport, Conn: Greenwood Press, 1984).

17. See Judith A Milhous and Robert D. Hume, "Dating Play Premières from Publication Data 1660–1700," *Harvard Library Bulletin*, 22 (1974): 374–405.

18. Ostler died in December 1614 and is listed first for Antonio. Burbage died in March 1619 and is listed first for Ferdinand. For further details see John Webster, *The Works of John Webster*, ed. David Gunby, David Carnegie, and Antony Hammond (Cambridge: Cambridge University Press, 1995), 1: 423–7, 468.

19. Richard Flecknoe, *Love's Dominion* (London: n.p., 1654). See J. Douglas Canfield, "Richard Flecknoe's Early Defense of the Stage: An Appeal to Cromwell," *Restoration and 18th Century Theatre Research*, Series 2, 2: 2 (1987): 1–7.

20. Richard Flecknoe, *Love's Kingdom* (London: R. Wood, 1664).

21. Joel E. Spingarn, ed., *Critical Essays of the Seventeenth Century* (Oxford: Clarendon Press, 1908–9), 1: lxxii.

22. W. Carew Hazlitt, *The English Drama and Stage under the Tudor and Stuart Princes 1543–1664* (London: For the Roxburghe Library, 1869), reprinted *Research and Source Works Series*, 48 (New York: Burt Franklin, 1964).

23. For Flecknoe's sustained preference for pre-Restoration drama, see his poem "Former Playes and Poets Vindicated," in *Epigrams of All Sorts* (1671), 51–2, quoted in Paul Hammond, "Flecknoe and *Mac Flecknoe*," *Essays in Criticism*, 35 (1985): 318–19.

24. Spingarn, *Critical Essays*, 1: lxxii.

25. Arthur Freeman, "The English Stage: Attack and Defense, 1577–1730," preface to Richard Flecknoe, *Love's Kingdom*, (New York: Garland Publishing Inc., 1973), 5. The "Short Discourse" also appears as part of totalizing reprinting: in the Wing microfilm series which aims to reproduce all printing between 1642 and 1700 and in the microcard series, *Three Centuries of English Drama*, which aimed to include all texts printed between 1500 and 1900.

26. It was announced in the *Term Catalogues* for June 1699; see Edward Arber, ed., *The Term Catalogues, 1668–1709 A.D.*, 3 vols (London: Edward Arber, 1903–6), 3: 143. It was advertised in *The Post Boy* for 4–6 July 1699; see John Dennis, *The Critical Works*, 2 vols, ed. Edward Niles Hooker (Baltimore: Johns Hopkins University Press, 1939), 1: 469.

27. Hooker notes, for example, *Animadversions on Mr. Congreve's Late Answer to Mr. Collier* (1698), *The Stage Acquitted* (1699), Oldmixon's *Reflections on the Stage* (1699) and *The Comparison between the Two Stages* (1704); see Dennis, *Critical Works*, 1: 436.

28. *DNB* (s.v. Wright, 1021) quotes Hearne that Wright was "one of the first collectors of old plays since Cartwright." Freeman quotes this as "one of the finest collections of old plays": Arthur Freeman, ed., *"Historia Histrionica" and "Roscius Anglicanus"* (New York: Garland Publishing Inc, 1974), 5–6.

29. Gerald Eades Bentley, ed., *The Seventeenth-Century Stage* (Chicago: University of Chicago Press, 1968), viii.

30. Gerald Eades Bentley, *The Jacobean and Caroline Stage*, 7 vols (Oxford: Clarendon Press, 1941–68), 2: 691–6.

31. Bentley, *Jacobean and Caroline Stage*, 1: vi.
32. Virgil, *Aeneid*, Book 1, line 203.
33. Quoted by Harry M. Solomon, *The Rise of Robert Dodsley* (Carbondale: Southern Illinois University Press, 1996), 94. On Dodsley see also Ralph Straus, *Robert Dodsley: Poet, Publisher & Playwright* (London: John Lane, The Bodley Head, 1910).
34. See George M. Kahrl, *The Garrick Collection of Old English Plays: a Catalogue* (London: British Library, 1982).
35. Robert Dodsley, ed., *A Select Collection of Old Plays*, 12 vols (London: R. Dodsley, 1744–5), 1: xxi.
36. *DNB* (s.v. Wright, 1022) identifies the adviser as Warburton. Arthur Freeman, in his edition of *"Historia Histrionica" and "Roscius Anglicanus"* (6), identifies him as Thomas Wharton but Wharton seems improbable and Thomas Warton the younger was far too young.
37. Robert Dodsley, *A Select Collection of Old Plays*, rev. Isaac Reed (London: J. Nichols for J. Dodsley, 1780), 1: lxix.
38. Isaac Reed, in Dodsley, *A Select Collection*, rev. edn (1780), 1: xxiii.
39. Ibid., 1: cxxxii.
40. Ibid., 1: cxxxii.
41. Ibid., 1: cxxxii.
42. See James Wright, *Historia Histrionica*, in Dodsley, *A Select Collection*, rev. edn (1780), 12: 337–63.
43. Robert Dodsley, *A Select Collection of Old Plays*, revised Isaac Reed, Octavius Gilchrist, and "The Editor," 12 vols (London: Septimus Prowett, 1825), 1: iv.
44. James Wright, *Historia Histrionica*, in Dodsley, *A Select Collection*, rev. edn (1825), 1: cxxxix–clxix. The text is moved back to the fifteenth in the 4th edition, ed. W. Carew Hazlitt (London: Reeves and Turner, 1876), 15: 399–431. It was also included in *The Old English Drama*, 3 vols (London: Thomas White, 1830).
45. See James E. Tierney, ed., *The Correspondence of Robert Dodsley 1733–1764* (Cambridge: Cambridge University Press, 1988), 32.
46. See Colley Cibber, *An Apology for the Life of Colley Cibber, Comedian*, third edn, (London: Robert Dodsley, 1750), 489, 521. I take it that the renaming of *Historia Histrionica* is the consequence of Dodsley's having access to a copy of the 1699 text without title-page or preface, since the preface was not included in *A Select Collection* until 1825. The half-title at the head of the dialogue in 1699 is "A dialogue of plays and players"; *Historia Histrionica* (1699), 1.
47. Colley Cibber, *An Apology for the Life of Mr. Colley Cibber*, 2 vols, ed. Robert W. Lowe (London: John C. Nimmo, [1889]), 1: vi–vii.
48. *"Historia Histrionica" and "A Short Discourse of the English Stage,"* introd. Peter Davison (New York: Johnson Reprint Corp, 1972), and *"Historia Histrionica" and "Roscius Anglicanus,"* ed. Arthur Freeman (The English Stage: Attack and Defense, 1577–1730. New York: Garland Publishing Inc, 1974). I have not been able to see a copy of the third 1970s facsimile of *Historia Histrionica* (New York: AMS Press, 1974).
49. Website of the Society of Antiquaries of London, 8 March 2002, http://www.sal.org.uk/.
50. William Oldys, *The British Librarian* (London: T. Osborne, 1737).
51. James Wright, *Historia Histrionica*, in *Mr Ashbee's Occasional Fac-Simile Reprints*, Pamphlet 30 (London: for subscribers only, 1872).
52. Edward Arber, ed., *An English Garner*, 8 vols (London: E. Arber, 1877–96), 2: 272–82.
53. Andrew Lang, ed., *Social England Illustrated* (Westminster: Archibald Constable and Co, 1903), xxix. The text is on 421–32. The whole collection was edited by Thomas Seccombe in 1903–4. See also *An analytical catalogue of the contents of the two editions*

of *"An English Garner,"* compiled by Edward Arber *(1877–97)*, & rearranged under the edit-orship of Thomas Seccombe *(1903–04)* (Manchester: Manchester University Press, 1909).

54. Edward Arber, *An English Garner*, 1: 10.
55. John Downes, *Roscius Anglicanus* (London: H. Playford, 1708).
56. Tobyas Thomas, *The Life of the Late Famous Comedian Jo. Hayns* (London: J. Nutt, 1701).
57. Genest, *Some Account*, 1: 27.
58. John Downes, *Roscius Anglicanus*, ed. Rev. Montague Summers (London: The Fortune Press, 1928), ix.
59. John Downes, *Roscius Anglicanus*, ed. Judith Milhous and Robert D.Hume (London: The Society for Theatre Research, 1987), xvi.
60. Quoted by Downes, ibid., p. xv.
61. John Downes, *Roscius Anglicanus (1708)*, Augustan Reprint Society Publication 134, introd. John Loftis (Los Angeles: University of California, William Andrews Clark Memorial Library, 1969), 53–76 (its pagination continuing that of the pamphlet).
62. Francis Godolphin Waldron, ed., *The Literary Museum; or, ancient and Modern Repository: Comprising Scarce and Curious Tracts* (London: for the Editor, 1792).
63. Ibid., 3.
64. *The Ancient and Modern Miscellany* (London: E and S Harding, 1794); *The Shakespearean Miscellany* (London: Lackington, Allen and Co, 1802).
65. Francis Godolphin Waldron, *The Biographical Mirrour* (London: Silvester Harding, 1795).
66. Thomas Davies, *Memoirs of the Life of David Garrick, Esq.* (London: for the Author, 1780); Thomas Davies, *Dramatic Micellanies* [sic] (London: for the Author, 1785).
67. Downes, *Roscius Anglicanus* (1708), 22.
68. John Downes, *Roscius Anglicanus*, in Waldron, *The Literary Museum*, 31.
69. Waldron's comment in ibid., 71.
70. Ibid., advertisement, p. ii.
71. Joseph Knight, in John Downes, *Roscius Anglicanus*, ed. Joseph Knight (London: J. W. Jarvis, 1886), viii.
72. Ibid., xxii.
73. Ibid., xxii.
74. Anonymous review in *The Athenaeum*, 25 December 1886, n.p.
75. Quoted Arnott and Robinson, *English Theatrical Literature*, 87.
76. Downes, *Roscius Anglicanus*, ed. Summers, vii–viii.
77. See, e.g., Summers's notes to his edition of Downes, *Roscius Anglicanus*, 2, 71–99.
78. On Summers see especially Joseph Jerome, *Montague Summers: a Memoir* (London: Cecil and Amerlia Woolf, 1965); Timothy D'Arch Smith, *Montague Summers: a Talk* (Edinburgh: Tragara Press, 1984); Frederick S. Frank, *Montague Summers: a Bibliographical Portrait*, The Great Bibliographers Series 7 (Metuchen, New Jersey: Scarecrow Press, 1988).
79. William Rufus Chetwood, *A General History of the Stage* (London: W. Owen, 1749).
80. Benjamin Victor, *The History of the Theatres of London and Dublin*, 2 vols (London: T. Davies et al., 1761).
81. Benjamin Victor, *The History of the Theatres of London from the year 1760 to the present time* (London: T. Becket, 1771).
82. *The British Theatre* (Dublin: Peter Wilson, 1750) is often ascribed to Chetwood but Chetwood is thanked in the preface (1750, sig. A2r) in a melancholy passage: "who, from a State of Affluence, is now reduced to almost a State of Indigence, and has

nothing in view but the melancholy Prospect of ending the Residue of Life within the Walls of a Prison, where Ill-Fortune has already thrown him."

83. *Theatrical Records* (London: R. and J. Dodsley, 1756).
84. E. L. Avery et al., eds, *The London Stage 1660–1800*, 11 vols (Carbondale, Ill: Southern Illinois University Press, 1960–68); Philip Highfill, Kalman Burnim and Edward Langhans, eds, *A Biographical Dictionary of Actors, Actresses, Musicians, Dancers, Managers and Other Stage Personnel in London, 1660–1800*, 16 vols (Carbondale, Ill: Southern Illinois University Press, 1973–93).
85. Allardyce Nicoll, *A History of Restoration Drama, 1660–1700* (Cambridge: Cambridge University Press, 1923).
86. Allardyce Nicoll, *A History of English Drama 1660–1900* (Cambridge: Cambridge University Press, 1952–9).
87. Allardyce Nicoll, *British Drama: an Historical Survey from the Beginnings to the Present Time* (George G. Harrap & Co, 1925), 1.
88. Allardyce Nicoll, *A History of Early Eighteenth Century Drama 1700–1750* (Cambridge: Cambridge University Press, 1925), viii.
89. Allardyce Nicoll, *A History of Restoration Drama 1660–1700*, 4th edn, revised (Cambridge: Cambridge University Press, 1952), 385.
90. Allardyce Nicoll, *A History of English Drama 1660–1900*, 3rd edn, Vol. 2: *Early Eighteenth Century Drama* (Cambridge: Cambridge University Press, 1969), 409.
91. Allardyce Nicoll, *The Development of the Theatre*, 5th edn, revised (London: George G.Harrap & Co. Ltd., 1966), v.
92. E. K. Chambers, *The Elizabethan Stage* (Oxford: Clarendon Press, 1923).
93. E. T. Williams and Helen M. Palmer, eds, *The Dictionary of National Biography 1951–1960* (London: Oxford University Press, 1971), 205.
94. Ibid.
95. Edmond Malone, ed., *The Plays and Poems of William Shakspeare*, 10 vols., (London: J. Rivington, 1790). On this edition see Margreta de Grazia, *Shakespeare Verbatim* (Oxford: Clarendon Press, 1991), which barely mentions the "Historical Account" in passing (101–2), and Peter Martin, *Edmond Malone Shakespearean Scholar* (Cambridge: Cambridge University Press, 1995) which gives it a little more attention (e.g. 125–7).
96. Sir E. K. Chambers, *William Shakespeare: a Study of Facts and Problems*, 2 vols (Oxford: Clarendon Press, 1930).
97. Edmond Malone, *Supplement to the Edition of Shakspeare's Plays Published in 1778*, 2 vols (London: for C. Bathurst and others, 1780).
98. James Boswell, *The Plays and Poems of William Shakspeare*, 21 vols (London: F. C. and J. Rivington, 1821). The "Historical Account" appears in volume 3.
99. Malone, *Plays and Poems of William Shakspeare*, vol. 1, part ii: 84–9. Compare the version of the statement in the *Supplement*: "All these circumstances induce me to believe that our ancient theatres, in general, were only furnished with curtains, and a single scene composed of tapestry, which appears to have been sometimes ornamented with pictures: and some passages on our old dramas incline me to think, that when tragedies were performed, the stage was hung with black" (1: 19).

2

Confessions of an Encyclopedist

Dennis Kennedy

My topic is *The Oxford Encyclopedia of Theatre and Performance*, a work that I edited and that was published by Oxford University Press in February 2003. It was a dauntingly large adventure, as some numbers will indicate: two volumes, twelve advisory editors, 100 illustrations, 320 contributors, 1600 pages of print, 4300 main entries, 8000 typed sheets of copy, and about 1.3 million words. I was engaged with it in some form from 1996 to 2002: a couple of years of proposals and negotiations, more than a year on planning the contents and creating the controlling database, two years on commissioning, another two (partly overlapping) on editing, six months on peripheral material, copy editing, and proof reading. At the height of the labor I was editing as many as 60 000 words a week, the size of a small book, and later proofing 40 000 words a day. I had five research and editorial assistants in Dublin, while a project manager in Oxford maintained the database, handled formal correspondence, arranged contracts and payments, wrote deadline reminders, and kept the budget. One of the advisory editors withdrew, a number of contributors silently moved or fell ill, four defaulted at the very last minute, and two, regrettably, died.

It was my principal project for three years and my full-time work for the final fourteen months of preparation, usually amounting to about sixty-five hours a week. It led me to think like Aesop: slow and steady wins the race, he works best who works longest. It caused enormous heartache and headache, affected my sleep and my health. When I detail this my overriding emotions are not pride, satisfaction, or even relief, but dismay, regret, and mental exhaustion. As a lad of about ten I had a recurring nightmare in which I was forced to accomplish a large and difficult task – most commonly undertaking an arduous trip around the world for some specified but forgotten purpose – and discovering on its completion that I had to do it all over again. That dream lately reappeared. And it has been real, for every time the project seemed finished, some new trouble or new task arose. In retrospect, I must have been out of my mind. Perhaps there should be an international register of encyclopedists, so residents can protest when one tries to move into the neighborhood. Why did I do it? No doubt it would take years of psychoanalysis to discover the answer. But among insalubrious reasons like flattery, status, and self-esteem, there was an important positive one: an opportunity to make a work that would be useful for some time and might affect how the field is perceived outside the discipline itself.

Encircling knowledge

The Greek word *enkyklopaideia* means a circle of learning, or a complete system of knowledge – what we might call an all-round education. The classical age produced many examples of compendiums designed in one way or another to further that goal, most of them of limited scope. The mapping of nature and thought characteristic of Aristotle, who himself demonstrated the taxonomic side of the encyclopedic urge, no doubt influenced a range of works that appeared in late antiquity that ventured to present useful information in accessible forms. In the medieval and early modern periods the emphasis shifted to what readers might do with the information provided. As early as 1244 the scholar Vincent of Beauvais, in *Speculum majus* or *The Great Mirror*, claimed his work reflected the world both as it is and as it should become, an idea picked up by the Spanish humanist Juan Luis Vives in *De disciplinis* in 1531. Francis Bacon's incomplete *Instauratio magna* (1620) for the first time laid out a plan for containing knowledge that was comprehensive and scientific. So influential was Bacon's concept that Diderot acknowledged him 130 years later in the prospectus to the *Encyclopédie*.[1]

That work, one of the major documents of the Enlightenment, is widely regarded as establishing the modern concept of the genre. The text of the *Encyclopédie* was published between 1751 and 1765, the plates in the decade from 1762, amounting in all to thirty-three large folio volumes, including two volumes of analytical index. Its range and confidence was without precedent. But the impulse to rationalize information and thought had of course been central to the Enlightenment project of both the Académie Française (founded 1635) and the Royal Society (1662), and important predecessors had been published in French and English starting in 1690. Its nature had been affected as well by Ephraim Chambers's *Cyclopedia* (London, 1728); in fact André Le Breton, the publisher of the *Encyclopédie*, originally planned only a French translation of Chambers. The eventual editors, Denis Diderot and Jean Le Rond d'Alembert, provided much more, of course: in length, about seventeen times more. They set out to create a "dictionaire raisonné des sciences, des arts et des métiers" by encircling all that was known, a comprehensive and engaged account of the world in history and in the present, a presentation of "*the interrelation of all knowledge*," as Diderot put it in his famous entry on "Encyclopédie." The object of the work, he wrote, is de rassembler les connoissances éparses sur la surface de la terre . . . que nous ne mourions pas sans avoir bien mérité du genre humain.[2]

(to collect all the knowledge scattered over the face of the earth . . . that we will not have died without gaining the high regard of the human race).

This article, some 40 000 words long, often discursive and pointedly political, aligns itself with the larger project of the *Encyclopédie* to reform France with the principles of the *philosophes* as basis, both a prefiguring of the Revolution and an intellectual alternative to it.

Fascinating as it is, it would take too long to trace the history of dictionaries and encyclopedias further, but I do want to emphasize a relevant point about identification of authors. One characteristic of the *Encyclopédie* is its legend of alphabetical letters to identify contributors. Given the importance of some of them, it would have been a huge loss had they remained anonymous; in fact Diderot called attention to his own contributions by placing an asterisk in front of most of the articles he wrote. But the practice of attribution did not extend to all parts of the *Encyclopédie*. To take a case near to home, excellent explanatory plans are included in the plates under the heading of "Machines de Théâtres," large-scale drawings of transformation effects on stage, some of which fold out. But nowhere do these note that they are the designs that the Italian scenographer Giacomo Torelli made for the Petit-Bourbon more than 100 years earlier. Nor did attribution continue for subsequent universal works. The *Encyclopaedia Britannica*, for instance, first published between 1768 and 1771, a little more than a decade after Diderot, stopped using signatures of any type. Even today, when many reference works acknowledge authorship, identity is normally partly obscured by the use of initials rather than names. Though designed to save space, this practice nonetheless contributes to the false sense of objectivity that encyclopedias foster.

Fact and fiction

The opening of Voltaire's entry on history in the *Encyclopédie* reads:

> HISTORY, f. n., is the recital of facts represented as true. Fable, on the contrary, is the recital of facts represented as fiction.

Facts: the hard cold evidence: the central problem of the historian, whether she thinks of history as truth, fiction, or an uncertain blend of the two. All historical documents are partial and in some sense false. In an extreme statement of the position, Jacques le Goff insisted that "there is no such thing as an objective, innocent, primary document . . . In the end, there is no documentary truth. Every document is a lie. It is up to historians not to feign innocence."[3] For theater and performance history the issue of fact has been intensely problematic, for two chief reasons. First, the low cultural status of the theater in most periods did not encourage detailed record keeping; second, the matter under investigation in performance history was never material (or embodied) for more than a few hours, even if repeated with variations on subsequent days and nights. There are forms of cultural memory that are not dependent on objective fact, as Joseph Roach and others have shown, some of which can give important insights into the nature of the performative modes of the past.[4] Yet on a crucial level it remains true that performance history is memory engaged with the traces of the disappeared, the act of calling up that which cannot be completely recalled, a conjuring trick practiced on the dead. Marco de Marinis put it this way: "on close inspection one is not producing theatre history but only a history of theatrical documents."[5]

Performance historians have been made well aware of this conundrum in a variety of ways, and it is not my task to review them. Instead I want to ask some questions about how a theater reference work touches on the methods, presentation and evidence of theater history. Though the historiographic implications of a book in dictionary format may not be immediately apparent to a general reader, on a moment's reflection it is obvious that huge assumptions about value, inclusion, approach, theoretical stance, range of coverage, and definition of the field lie behind the planning such a work – even if these assumptions have not been foregrounded or even conscious on the part of the editors. A reference work presents the field of its investigation as coherent: what is contained herein, the book always implies, is what is important. But important how? For the facts? A volume that is printed alphabetically works by virtue of cross references, pointers in one entry guiding the reader to related entries, which are probably discrete topics in themselves but which touch in some way upon the initial enquiry. (One of Diderot's most notable interventions comes in the entry on "Creation," which was written by a believing cleric. At the end of a standard Christian account of the topic, the editor inserted a cross reference: "See Freaks.") Most readers are likely to treat cross referencing as the accumulation or interrelationship of facts: did Shakespeare die before Richard Burbage, when was the Comédie-Française founded, what does "kabuki" mean, which actor assassinated Abraham Lincoln, what is kathakali, who is Robert Wilson? But for the curious the answers always create new queries, and could lead to an almost endless turning of pages.

Suppose, for instance, you are interested in the theater of the absurd. Once you discover whether it is under T or A, you should find therein a treatment of existentialism and the intellectual and artistic climate of postwar Paris, the nature and theme of exile, the characteristics of the absurdist style, why and how it got named, as well as a critique of the idea of lumping disparate artists under its banner. Standard stuff. But you will also be pointed elsewhere, to

entries on playwrights like Adamov and Ionesco and Beckett and Pinter, directors like Roger Blin, perhaps to period issues like modernism. If the entry is
good, you also should see references to Jarry, Artaud, Sartre and Camus, as well
as to symbolism, dada and surrealism, and – if you are reading the *Oxford
Encyclopedia* – pointers to tangents like dialogue, the construction of character,
the nature of dark comedy or tragicomedy, the status of the dramatic text, and
its relationship to directing. Let us imagine that you follow all of these cross
references, thus putting together a scattered but personal view of absurdism.
Does this amount to a minor treatise on the subject? Obviously not. It is a
hypertextual adventure, a reader's saga without an aware or self-conscious historiography, and is not the same as the interpretation of fact and incident by
an engaged historian. At the same time, however, the adventure represents a
more active intellectual participation on your part, not only because you have
been given the freedom to fill in the inevitable gaps but also because you are
almost forced to construct a history of your own in so doing.

   For me the primary issue is how a reference work acknowledges its awkward
position relative to fact and history. Most of the models in theater studies have
a neutralist approach: they present their material as factual, important in itself,
and unproblematic. To a certain extent this goes with the territory, for a dictionary or encyclopedia, almost by definition, proposes itself as comprehensive, objective and authoritative. A government health warning would defeat
its purpose. Clearly the implication of objectivity has ramifications for sales,
since it would be intensely counterproductive to note on every page that the
information offered is faulty, incomplete or subject at any moment to post-
structuralist revision. To problematize everything is to solve nothing, to be
trapped in Derridian cycles of inexpressivity. If we are going to have reference
works at all, ultimately one must simply get on with it.

   But does getting on with it mean that the concerns I have outlined must be
obliterated in the tyranny of an alphabetic presentation of facts? Let's look at
the results. There are a number of handy references on theater in print, but
three dominate: *The Oxford Companion to the Theatre*, edited by Phyllis Hartnoll;
The Cambridge Guide to Theatre, edited by Martin Banham, which are both in
dictionary form like my work; and the massive *The World Encyclopedia of
Contemporary Theatre*, edited by Don Rubin and others in five volumes, limited
to the period after 1945.[6] All have global range and large virtues as reference
works; even Hartnoll, which is seriously out of date (and which my work will
replace), remains a useful source, especially for British topics and for its 211
illustrations. But the appearance of objectivity of these volumes, which of
course is illusionary anyway, is achieved chiefly by what is not present, for
none includes articles that attempt to define the field or its sub-fields,
much less problematize it, or treat theoretical issues overtly, or address the
contentious expectations of the wide range of potential readers.

I will take one example only. A feature of all three is the inclusion of relatively lengthy national histories of theater. This is most true of Rubin, which divides its volumes by continents and normally treats each country as a separate entity. But both Hartnoll and Banham do something similar, despite their alphabetical design, devoting by far the largest number of their overall words to the topic of nations. For example, Hartnoll gives 4000 words to a theater history of Japan and 11 000 to England, while the somewhat larger Banham volume gives 14 000 to Japan and 15 000 to England. This an admirable redressing of Hartnoll's cultural bias, though Banham has its own bias, inexplicably allotting 19 000 words to the US and only 8000 to France. But what can articles of those lengths say about the complexities of a country like France with a thousand years of theatrical history? Revealingly, almost none of these entries, even in the nationally arranged Rubin, seriously interrogates the idea of nation, the formation of states, or the part theater and performance play in the growth of nationalism. Nor does any of them look overtly at the convoluted ways that national notions of theater are challenged by the post-colonial, by the internationalizing of commerce and culture, by diaspora, immigration, race, or global television. Even if they had been inclined to such issues, there simply would not be room for reasonable discussion. But neither do these works include general or theoretical entries that might address such issues on a larger or synchronic scale.

A matter of principle

I began from that point, persuaded that a reference work about theater and performance needs to ground itself in contemporary theater and performance studies. In part this merely reflects the sea-change in self-consciousness about the methodologies of arts and humanities subjects of the past two decades; in part it registers a professionalizing of the discourse of the reference book model; and in part my own desire to move away from the biographical approach that has so often dominated general or popular works about theater. I sought advisory editors with international perspectives, who are theoretically sophisticated, and of course who have deep connections to their own areas.[7] The advisors were crucial in planning the entries and in suggesting contributors. Most also wrote major articles for the work, helped out in crises, and reviewed the texts of longer entries in their specialties. No one knows enough to edit a book like this, least of all me, and thus the quality of the advice received in planning, commissioning and execution is central to the enterprise.

The operating premise was that while objectivity is impossible, balance is achievable. In practical terms balance meant that contributors were free to express opinions and maintain points of view, even the occasional idiosyncratic one, but they were asked to note in the entry when their outlooks were contentious or uncertain. The advisors and I agreed that biographical and purely literary issues should be de-emphasized in favor of performative ones; that the work should contain discursive articles on concepts, as well as on historical forms and movements; that it should see the field as enlarged and enriched by the discoveries and developments of performance studies; and that it should strive for an international outlook so that, for example, major theoretical articles did not choose their instances solely from Western cases.

Convinced that entries on national theater traditions were inevitably oversimplified and misleading, we made what is probably our most controversial decision and eliminated them. There are no entries on Western nations, not even for Ireland, where theater is normally conceived in nationalist terms – as it is in a number of smaller states, especially post-colonial ones. Some people will see this as a loss, but when I read the national entries in Hartnoll or Banham, even those written by very good commentators, they seem to me if not weary and stale, then flat and unprofitable. In place of national articles we commissioned entries on cities and regions that are theatrical centers, encouraging the authors to write social histories of performance that draw upon the political and cultural backdrop of the locale. There are 110 of these, and they take up 10 percent of the work. Some, like Paris and London, are relatively long, running to over 9000 words; New York is half that; others are briefer. But because urban theatrical centers are a new development in many areas of the world where performance has been chiefly traditional in nature, we expanded the notion to regional areas and linguistic traditions. In effect this meant that for some areas and countries in Asia and Africa we actually do have summary entries. We were careful not to make these national theater histories but rather introductions to the complexity of performance in the local circumstance.

Take India, where the idea of a national tradition is completely obliterated by the continued existence of numerous local forms and eighteen official languages. The work has an overview entry of some 4000 words on India by Rustom Bharucha which, among other ambitions, points to the series of entries on performance in the linguistic traditions of South Asia: Bengali theater, Manipuri theater, Marathi theater, Telugu theater and so on. Because of their importance, there are also entries on Bombay and Calcutta as centers of performance (listed under their new names, Mumbai and Kolkata). But performance in other parts of the globe does not fit the Indian model, particularly in Africa. So we have a major overview entry on sub-Saharan Africa by David Kerr, which is mostly about pre-colonial performance, and four entries on colonial and post-colonial theater organized by colonial language area: anglophone, francophone, lusophone (Portuguese-speaking), and one on the three contemporary Horn of Africa countries of Eritrea, Ethiopia and Somalia. Because of their unfamiliarity to many likely readers, there are short articles on the countries of East Asia and Southeast Asia, in general pointing to further entries on specific theater forms and people.

The largest conceptual difficulty by far related to biographies. Theater and performance have been dominated by artists and personalities; people make theater, and their records and remnants are the major part of its history. More to the point, I imagine that readers are frequently inclined to use a work like this for a quick reference about those people: their dates, their work, something of their importance. But as the limitation on the total extent of the volumes remained implacable, in the end the solution adopted was to include a large number of biographical entries – actually more than either Banham or Hartnoll – but to make their average length shorter. We further asked contributors to pay especial attention to issues of performance; in playwrights' entries, for instance, to attend more to production history than to literary issues or pleasing biographical anecdotes. We planned out the lengths of biographies in advance by decisions about relative importance, which is always difficult and contentious but as a method of resolving magnitude is probably better than that used in Banham, where the extent of the biographical entries seems to have been determined by the contributor.

To take illustrations from more substantial cases: in Banham, Max Reinhardt gets 250 words while Aleksandr Tairov has 700, which is a curious situation when we consider that their international reputations are parallel, with Reinhardt generally viewed as more influential; in my work they both have 750. In Banham, Anton Chekhov has only 200 words more than his nephew, the actor and director Michael; in my work Anton has 1000 and Michael 300. Reaching to some non-Western cases, Banham gives Bhasa 160 words and Zeami 275, I give them 300 and 500 respectively. But to achieve balances like these in terms of significance and worldwide equity, and yet to include many names, it was necessary to reduce the allotments of lesser figures drastically, persons in some categories getting only 100 words, some 175 words, some 250, etc., and only a very few extremely influential people going to 1000 or above: Aeschylus (1100), Lope de Vega (1025), Molière (1900), Garrick (1000), Brook (1300). At 3800 words, Shakespeare gets by far the longest biography, but crucially that is the result of emphasizing the extensive and complicated history of his performance rather than bardolatry. Contributors often found lengths of less than 175 words very difficult, as might be expected, and it is possible that readers will as well.

I believe that the most important innovation in the work is the series of entries on concepts and theories. These outline the nature of the field, provide speculative frameworks for the historical and biographical topics and, more concretely, give the general reader an introduction to terminology, genre and methods. This part of the work, which takes up another 10 percent of the total text, is a major departure from the systems employed by Hartnoll, Banham, and Rubin. In this respect only it is similar to the highly useful *Dictionnaire du Théâtre* by Patrice Pavis, since translated into English,[8] though Pavis wrote that book on his own while our entries were divided among a variety of contributors, who sometimes expressed conflicting views.

Organizing the world

No one thinks alphabetically, so the first task in planning an encyclopedia is to systematize potential entry topics according to some reasonable plan – what Diderot and d'Alembert might have called an outline *raisonné*. To accomplish this I prepared a broad topical guide for further thinking, for consulting the advisers, and ultimately for determining of the headwords of entries. Presented here as a table, it shows the relative weight given to each area for planning purposes. (The actual length of entries varies in some cases, and in the result the total extent of the work crept up to about 1.3 million words, including considerable peripheral material, such as a timeline, general bibliography and an index of dramatic titles.)

Analysis of coverage by topic – main entries (figures are rounded)

Topic category	Words	% of text	No. of entries	Avg. length	% of entries
1 Concepts and theory	120 000	10	135	875	3
2 Styles and movements	155 000	13	391	400	9
3 Other historical themes	96 000	8	131	725	3
4 Cities, regions, linguistic traditions	120 000	10	127	925	3
5 Biographies	530 000	45	2910	180	68
6 Organizations and institutions	94 000	8	516	180	12
7 Buildings/material elements	60 000	5	80	700	2
8 Media issues	25 000	2	6	4185	0.1
Totals for work	1 200 000	100	4300	275	100

Each of these of these eight areas was further divided to account for the numerous subsidiary topics they raise. It would be unprofitable to list the entire outline here, but a sample of the first three topics should be useful.

Outline sample, topics 1–3

1. Concepts and theory
    1.1. Theories of theatre and performance
        1.1.1. Origins
        1.1.2. Theories of drama (dramaturgy)
        1.1.3. Social theories and issues
        1.1.4. Theories of acting, directing, design

1.2. Genres and synchronic forms
1.3. Critical concepts and methods
2. Styles and movements
  2.1. Antiquity
  2.2. Middle ages in Europe
  2.3. Europe 1500–1700
  2.4. Europe and the Americas 1700–1800
  2.5. Europe and the Americas 1800–1900
  2.6. Europe and the Americas since 1900
  2.7. East Asia
    2.7.1. China
    2.7.2. Korea
    2.7.3. Japan
  2.8. South Asia
    2.8.1. India
    2.8.2. Pakistan, Bangladesh
    2.8.3. Sri Lanka, Nepal
  2.9. Southeast Asia
 2.10. Africa and Middle East
    2.10.1. North Africa and Middle East
    2.10.2. Anglophone Africa south of Sahara
    2.10.3. Francophone Africa south of Sahara
    2.10.4. Africa, other (lusophone, Eritrea, Ethiopia, Somalia)
3. Other historical themes
  3.1. Character and performer types
  3.2. Popular entertainment
  3.3. Audiences
    3.3.1. Gestures and behaviour
    3.3.2. Class, gender, age
    3.3.3. Riots and control
  3.4. Publishing, law and the state
    3.4.1. Play publishing
    3.4.2. Censorship
    3.4.3. Regulations on performance
    3.4.4. Safety
    3.4.5. Copyright and licensing
  3.5. Finance
  3.6. Systems of organization
  3.7. Organizational personnel

It is necessary to stress again that the outline was merely a memorandum for conceptualizing and researching what the actual headwords should be. Since there are 4300 main entries, I can give only a brief tasting of what these are. But the entire list of headwords, organized thematically, is printed in the preliminary pages of the first volume as a guide of what entries exist in the work. Since the list is topical, it overcomes the tyranny of the alphabet while encouraging readers to browse among the main concerns of theater studies. It most clearly reveals the premises of the encyclopedia, its biases, and its limitations. Since it is impossible in a work of this length to treat all the people and subjects of potential significance, the thematic table of contents also carries the seeds of its own deconstruction. Fortunately this is not a major worry, for few readers have the intellectual arrogance of the *philosophes* and expect that all knowledge can be encircled in print. *The Oxford Encyclopedia of Theatre and Performance* is not the best of all possible books in the best of all possible theater worlds. As a sample, here is the full listing for topic 1.

Sample of thematic listing of entries

Longer, more discursive entries are listed first.
1. Concepts and theories
   1.1. Origins
        origins of theatre
        religion and theatre
        ritual and theatre
        ****
        civic festivals
        dreams and theatre
        impersonation
        mimesis
        theatre
   1.2 Dramatic concepts and terms
        criticism
        dramaturgy/dramaturg
        theories of drama, theatre and performance
        ****
        act
        action
        anagnorisis
        book
        catastrophe
        character
        chorus
        complication
        coup de théâtre

crisis
decorum
deixis
denouement
deus ex machina
dialogue
didascalia
drama
epilogue
exposition
hamartia
hubris
illusion
monologue
peripetia
playwright
plot
prologue
recitative
scenario
scene
scène à faire
soliloquy
stage directions
stock character
text
theatricality
unities
verse
1.3 Social theories and issues
agitprop
carnival
catharsis
diaspora
dramatis personae
gender and performance
mass media
play
politics and theatre
pornography and performance
race and theatre
realism and reality

Verfremdung (distancing or alienation)
women and performance
1.4 Acting, directing, design
acting/actor
directing/director
scenography
training for theatre
****
agon
audition
casting
doubling
mask and masking
mise-en-scène
performance
rehearsal
subtext
understudy
vision and the visual
1.5 Genres and synchronic forms
amateur theatre
comedy
dance and dance-drama
melodrama
musical play
opera
puppet theatre
tragedy
tragicomedy
****
acrobatics
ballet
bourgeois theatre
closet drama
didactic theatre
executions, public
farce
folk and folklore
genre
historical drama
mime
monodrama

      moresca
      music in the theatre
      Native-American performance
      one-act play
      operetta
      parades and processions
      parody
      Purim play
      rasa
      revue
      sainete
      satire
      shadow-puppet theatre
      slapstick
      spectacle
      state displays
      tableau vivant
      zarzuela
1.6 Critical concepts and methods
      anthropology, theatre
      feminism
      historicism
      historiography
      materialist criticism
      metatheatre
      myth studies
      performance studies
      performativity
      post-colonial studies
      psychoanalytic criticism
      queer theory
      reception
      semiotics
      structuralism and post-structuralism
      theatre studies

Entries under other headings are highly various. Interesting topics in category 3 (other historical themes) include character, families in the theater, female impersonation, hero (heroine) and antihero, lines of business, male impersonation, and villain; circus, amusement arcades, animal baiting, freak shows, sport, tango, and waxworks; applause, audience, riots, audience dress, laughter, and women in audiences; censorship, licensing acts, publishing of plays, safety, fires in theaters, and royalties; arts councils, finance, benefit perform-ance, festivals, playbills and programmes, posters, prompter, publicity, and touring. Topic 7 (buildings and material elements) treats issues such as play-houses, toilets, environmental and site-specific theater, open-air performance, proscenium, and thrust stage; costume, lighting, masks, scenography, scene painting and scene shifting, perspective, properties, hell mouth, *hanamichi*, and footlights; sound effects, special effects, flying actors, and traps. Some of these – playhouses, scenography, lighting, costume, for example – are quite long entries. As a final set of examples, topic 8 (media issues) includes film and theater, radio, television, cyber theater, media and performance, and multi-media performance.

The devil and the details

When Oxford University Press proposed the book the intention was that it would be a completely new work in the Oxford Companion series that would replace Hartnoll. The reason was clear: since the publication of Banham's *Cambridge Guide to Theatre* the sales of Hartnoll had dropped considerably, and OUP decided that book was too old-fashioned to merit revising. From the Press's standpoint, the undertaking was about recovering market share by virtue of a better product. OUP is of course a non-profit organization. It has UK charitable status, and the equivalent around the world. It has no separate legal identity from the University of Oxford, to whom it is ultimately answerable – and to whom 30 percent of its post-tax surplus belongs. The rest of the surplus, one supposes, is reinvested in the Press's activities, since by law the profits can-not be distributed. In the past few years, around £20 million per annum has been turned over to the general funds of the university. But this charitable sta-tus should not confuse us about OUP's operation. It is the world's largest uni-versity press, and the world's largest publisher of reference books. According to its own official statement, "it publishes more than 4,500 books a year, has a presence in over fifty countries, and employs some 3,700 people worldwide." Its publishing program "includes scholarly works in all academic disciplines, bibles, music, school and college textbooks, children's books, materials for teaching English as a foreign language, business books, dictionaries and refer-ence books, and journals." Thus the work of a typical university press, the pro-duction and distribution of scholarly books that would be not be handled by commercial publishers, is only a small part of the OUP enterprise. In my under-standing its reference division, which publishes hundreds of volumes annually, functions as a commercial publisher, being required to recapture expenses on each book within a year of publication, and hopefully make a profit thereafter.

It is revealing that trouble arose when the Oxford commissioning editor did his sums. The book in the Companion series he proposed was to be only

750 000 words long, sold at a trade price of about £35 (or $60). A work of that limited extent had no hope of equaling Banham's, much less bettering it. But a larger work would cost so much more to commission and produce that the Companion model was discarded in favor of an academic encyclopedia in two volumes that would sell more limited quantities to libraries and specialists, and at a much higher price: £150 ($250). Book publishing is a long-term business. Once in print, the Encyclopedia could be reduced to a Companion size in a couple of years; later the Companion could be further reduced to a Concise Companion in paperback; then it would be time for a new edition of the original, starting the cycle over again. Perhaps that explains the return of my recurrent nightmare.

I go through these somewhat sordid details to remind us of the material conditions of academic publishing. Despite the incursions of web-based and other electronic methods, the great majority of scholarship in our field is printed in books and journals by university presses. In the context of rampant global capitalism, the economy of this undertaking is extremely curious. With few exceptions, academic authors receive very little direct financial return for their writing, and accept this as a condition of employment by universities. In paying the authors' salaries and providing research grants and time for research, the universities and funding bodies are subsidizing a non-profit publishing industry. As a result the universities are able to insist that academics publish regularly because the presses will print what they write, so that all three entities – the professorate, the press and the institutional academy – are locked in a circular and perpetual dance.

It would be naïve to think that these conditions do not affect the nature of what is published. While there have been periodic crises with regard to monographs, in the past decade there has been a noticeable increase in the number of compendiums, compilations, anthologies, and reference works from academic presses, which have safe sales at a time when scholarly monographs do not. And commercial publishers have tapped into this market as well, creating a dense ecology of works that seek to provide approximately the same service. For example, a new one, *The Continuum Companion to Twentieth Century Theatre*, was published in spring 2002, 900 pages at £100.[9] It is often remarked that we live in an age where information is required on demand, its value determined by its speed of delivery; yet at the same time facts are reduced to game-show trivia. Whether on the web or in a traditional book, the compendium of information seems to offer the illusion of completeness, the world in your hands, finger-tip slave for intellectual irritations. Perhaps the rush towards reference works represents nothing more than the packaging of recycled knowledge in tune with the economic conditions of postmodernity.

Obviously I hope that the *Oxford Encyclopedia* is more than that. But in ending, I must again note what it is not: it is not a history of theater. At best it provides a ready source or starting point for further investigations, guided by bibliographies and a timeline and cross references and the thematic table of contents. Yet it intervenes historiographically nonetheless. First, by de-emphasizing essentialist biography the work suggests that historical forces larger than individuals have been at work over time in creating theater and performance and the academic enterprises that examine them. Second, by avoiding nationalist histories it hopes to highlight the significance of cities and regions in creating theater, as separate from any grand narrative of nation that has often been imposed on local expression. And third, by wrapping its information inside extended articles on theory and critical methods, it aims to provide a more sophisticated context for general readers as well as for specialist ones.

Whether it succeeds in these goals is not for me to say. What I can say, deeply and unconditionally, is that I hope I will not have to repeat my nightmare and do it all over again.

Notes

1. The entry on "Encyclopaedias and Dictionaries" in the fifteenth edition of *The New Encyclopedia Britannica* (2002) has a useful summary of their history; see 18: 257–86.
2. *Encylopédie*, vol. 5 (Paris, 1755).
3. Jacques le Goff, "Documento/Monumento," *Enciclopedia Einaudi*, 4 (1978): 44–5.
4. See Joseph Roach, *Cities of the Dead: Circum-Atlantic Performance* (New York: Columbia University Press, 1996). I am grateful to Roach for the Diderot anecdote in the next paragraph.
5. Marco de Marinis, " 'A Faithful Betrayal of Performance': Notes on the Use of Video in Theatre," *New Theatre Quarterly*, 1 (1985): 383.
6. Phyllis Hartnoll, ed., *The Oxford Companion to the Theatre*, 4th edn (Oxford: Oxford University Press, 1983, with subsequent corrected reprintings). Martin Banham, ed., *The Cambridge Guide to Theatre* (Cambridge: Cambridge University Press, 1995; 1st edn published as *The Cambridge Guide to World Theatre*, 1988). Don Rubin, et al., eds, *The World Encyclopedia of Contemporary Theatre*, 5 vols (London: Routledge, 1994–8); subsequently four of the volumes have been published in paperback (2001). A reference of considerable worth is Mark Hawkins-Dady and David Pickering, eds, *International Dictionary of Theatre*, 3 vols (New York: St. James Press, 1992–6), but as this is a guide to people and plays only, it is in a different historiographical category.
7. The Advisory Editors for the project are: Rustom Bharucha, Jacky Bratton, Edward Braun, Marvin Carlson, John Conteh-Morgan, David Kerr, Kate McLuskie, Brooks McNamara, Kirstin Pauka, Thomas Rimer, Adam Versényi and Ronald W. Vince.
8. Patrice Pavis, *Dictionaire du Théâtre* (Paris: Dunod, 1996); in English as *Dictionary of the Theatre: Terms, Concepts, and Analysis*, trans. Christine Shantz (Toronto: University of Toronto Press, 1998).
9. Colin Chambers, ed., *The Continuum Companion to Twentieth Century Theatre* (London: Continuum Press, 2002).

3

The Criteria for Evidence: Anecdotes in Shakespearean Biography, 1709–2000

Thomas Postlewait

> "There is no limit to the odd things people will say about Shakespeare."
> E. K. Chambers, *Sources for a Biography of Shakespeare*[1]

I

As many of us know, Shakespeare played the role of the Ghost in *Hamlet*, which premièred at the Globe Theatre, possibly between 1599 and 1601. How do we know this? Nicholas Rowe told us so in the brief biography affixed to his 1709 edition of Shakespeare's plays. Rowe explained that he made enquiries and, though unable to discover anything else about Shakespeare's acting, he heard, from an unidentified source, "that the top of his Performance was the Ghost in his own *Hamlet*."[2] Thus, 110 years after the supposed event, a piece of hearsay evidence entered the biographical record on Shakespeare.

Since Rowe's initial report, the story has been repeated often, not only in the eighteenth century, when anecdotes were often accepted without question, but also in the modern age. For example, *The Reader's Encyclopedia of Shakespeare* (1966) begins its stage history on *Hamlet* with the explanation that "tradition credits Shakespeare himself with originating the part of the Ghost."[3] Recent biographers continue to support this tradition (e.g. Russell Fraser and Peter Levi).[4]

Park Honan, in *Shakespeare: a Life* (1998), also credits Shakespeare with the role, but he identifies a second intermediary as a source:

> When Shakespeare accepted roles in his own works, he seems to have played old Adam in *As You Like It*, or the Ghost in *Hamlet* – elegiac, affecting voices; small parts – and, says [John] Aubrey in the seventeenth century, he "did act exceedingly well". Aubrey could have heard that from the son of Christopher Beeston of the Chamberlain's Servants.[5]

But Honan misleads us, for Aubrey's statement in 1681 actually says nothing about any role. In Aubrey's words: "This Wm. being inclined naturally to Poetry and acting, came to London I guess about 18. and was an Actor at one of the Play-houses and did act exceedingly well."[6] Aubrey's unspecific statement thus requires a conditional spin from Honan: "seems to have" and "could." There is no documented evidence – as Honan himself admits later in his biography: "Facts are another matter: . . . so far, at best, we have frail hints as to his acting roles – not proof" (204). And in a footnote Honan admits that "so far, no one can be sure as to the poet's roles in his own, Jonson's or other plays" (439). This is the basic point that E. K. Chambers made in 1930 in *William Shakespeare: a Study of Facts and Problems.*

Undeterred by the lack of evidence, John Southworth recently claimed in *Shakespeare the Player: a Life in the Theatre* (2000) that the "probability" of Shakespeare playing the Ghost "is strengthened by the indications we have already uncovered of Shakespeare having played similar spectral roles in Kyd's [*The*] *Spanish Tragedy*, and . . . *Julius Caesar*."[7] The "we" in this statement is Southworth himself. He has no evidence that Shakespeare acted in these other plays, but because he believes that Shakespeare played the Ghost in *Hamlet*, he supposes (then quickly surmises) that Shakespeare played other spectral roles as well. So, even though Southworth acknowledges that most of Rowe's anecdotes are "little better than gossip – dubious at best, some demonstrably false" (185), he develops a circular argument without any supporting documentation (45). He thereby compounds failures in deductive reasoning with those in inductive analysis. His argument, lacking even a hint of contingent or circumstantial evidence, is nothing but a series of notions, suppositions, and dubious conjectures.

Thus, in the long tradition of Shakespearean biography, from Rowe to Southworth, this spectral anecdote, appearing on demand, haunts the documentary record. Of course, suspect anecdotes are pervasive in all historical scholarship. The challenge, then, is not simply to reject them but to analyze anecdotes carefully in order to establish their historical authenticity. Granted, it is often difficult to establish the truth of statements in documents because historical testimony, both written and spoken, is often based upon recollections – the vagaries of human memories (and storytelling skills). But historical scholarship, even in our postmodern era, requires some basic guidelines for analyzing sources. Potential evidence should be subjected to not only internal criticism for its credibility but also external criticism for its reliability.[8] In brief, the evidence should be evaluated in terms of the concepts of possibility, plausibility, probability, and certainty.

What, then, can we say about the evidence for Shakespeare playing the role of the Ghost? We know that between 1599 and 1613 the Lord Chamberlain's Men and the King's Men performed well over 100 plays (and perhaps even

200–300) at the first Globe Theatre. Most of these plays apparently had over a dozen speaking characters (and often closer to two dozen), so there were likely 2000 or more roles performed at the first Globe. Shakespeare, a shareholder in these two companies, was one of the players. The 1623 First Folio lists him as one of the "Principal Actors in all these Plays."[9] So, of the many roles available to him, both in his own plays and the many other plays, Shakespeare may have selected or been assigned the role of the Ghost (just as he may have played many other roles). Rowe's anecdote thus meets the preliminary requirement of historical evidence: the rule of possibility.

Yet in spite of extensive archival research over the centuries, no one has discovered a piece of supporting evidence from Shakespeare's lifetime that places him in any of his plays.[10] The anecdote lacks, therefore, any contemporary warrant that might serve as probable evidence. Even if we assume that Shakespeare acted regularly in the Globe productions of his plays, this assumption, which may seem plausible but cannot be proved, does not locate him in any specific role. At best, then, Rowe's anecdote is an unsubstantiated oral report, gathered by the actor Thomas Betterton on a trip to Stratford-upon-Avon, as Rowe noted.[11] Betterton apparently heard the anecdote from a person who heard it from someone else who, in turn, may have heard it from someone else. And so on.

And to complicate matters, the anecdote may have nothing to do with Shakespeare's acting career and lifetime. Instead, it may derive from an event at Dorset Garden Theatre in 1679, when Thomas Betterton, identifying himself as Shakespeare, came on stage, "Representing the Ghost of Shakespeare,"[12] to deliver the prologue for Dryden's version of *Troilus and Cressida*. We must wonder: did Betterton's representation help launch the anecdote about Shakespeare playing the Ghost? Did Betterton himself initiate the anecdote, then credit it to someone else in order to warrant it?[13] Or was the decision to portray Shakespeare in this role influenced by the knowledge or belief that Shakespeare had played the role at the beginning of the century?

Given these uncertainties, there is no justification for proclaiming that Shakespeare played the Ghost. This anecdote, three generations removed from the original staging of *Hamlet* (and one generation after the Dryden event), fails to satisfy basic standards of internal criticism (credibility) and external criticism (reliability). By giving it the status of "tradition," and then presenting it as received truth, biographers have misled their readers (and perhaps themselves). Repetition does not make it true.

Of course, anecdotes, both reliable and unreliable, have always contributed to the history of theater. From the unverifiable anecdote about the death of Aeschylus, who supposedly was struck dead (by chance or fate) when an eagle dropped a tortoise onto his head, to the current stories about the misadventures of Kathleen Battle at the Metropolitan Opera House in New York City, anecdotes have been irresistible sources of information for writers and read-ers.[14] They provide interesting, fascinating, bizarre, and sometimes definitive details about theatrical lives and events. Indeed, a well-chosen anecdote can carry the authority of a thousand dry documents. Yet despite the appeal and charm of many anecdotes, they are usually suspect historical sources; as a recent guide to research methods reminds us: "Anecdotes enliven sociological explanations but usually do not count as good evidence."[15]

What, then, are the criteria for "good evidence," and, more to the point, how, why and when do anecdotes qualify, if at all? Shakespearean biographies, from Rowe's *Life* (1709) to the present, offer us a series of test cases on the prob-lems that attend the use of anecdotes as evidence. In general terms, these numerous biographies, across the three centuries, reveal a three-part historical development: (1) the rapid, expansive spread of anecdotes in the seventeenth and eighteenth centuries; (2) the attempts since the latter half of the eigh-teenth century – beginning especially with Edmond Malone and carrying for-ward to E. K. Chambers and Samuel Schoenbaum – to establish a documentary method for historical evidence and writing, thereby putting in doubt most anecdotal sources; and (3) the return and defense of anecdotes in contempo-rary scholarship, often in tandem with critiques of positivism and the concept of historical objectivity.

Perhaps the key issue to be considered here is the historical development since the late eighteenth century of a basic distinction between what E. K. Chambers called "mythos" and "records" and what Samuel Schoenbaum called "legendary anecdotes and ascertainable facts."[16] In making this two-part division, Chambers and Schoenbaum were attempting to follow well-established procedures and principles in historical scholarship which treat most anecdotal stories as unreliable and most archival documents as reliable. For the most part the historical caution that guides this categorical antithe-sis has proved to be quite appropriate, though establishing and enforcing the principle in Shakespearean biography has been most difficult (and not just in the case of the anecdote about the Ghost in *Hamlet*). But beyond the failures in vigilant historical criticism, there are recurring problems with the categorical assumptions that posit a division between "legendary anec-dotes and ascertainable facts." As I wish to show, these problems appear not only in the scholarship of the documentary researchers such as Malone, Chambers and Schoenbaum but also in the post-positivist histori-ans who offer critiques of the documentary traditions of objectivity and authenticity.

II

After Shakespeare's death in 1616 a series of "apocryphal anecdotes and episodes" began to multiply. "These trends," Samuel Schoenbaum notes, "culminate in 1709 in the first full-dress biography, Nicholas Rowe's *Some Account of the Life, &c. of Mr. William Shakespear.*[17] Rowe gets some factual details wrong on Shakespeare's family (e.g. number of children), so what should we make of his collection of anecdotes?

In the *Account*, Rowe put forward the following claims, without identifying any sources, excepting Betterton in general and William Davenant in one case:[18]

(a) as a young man Shakespeare had to leave Stratford-upon-Avon because he was caught in the act of poaching a deer from the estate of Thomas Lucy of Charlecote;

(b) in consequence of the writing of *Venus and Adonis*, Shakespeare received £1000 from the Earl of Southampton who was supposedly his patron (Davenant is the source);

(c) when the Chamberlain's Men rejected Ben Jonson's early play *Every Man In His Humour* (1598), Shakespeare interceded and convinced his fellow players to perform it;[19]

(d) Queen Elizabeth commanded Shakespeare to remove the name of Oldcastle from *Henry IV*, apparently in order to placate the Lord Chamberlain, William Brooke, the seventh Lord Cobham, whose family descended from Sir John Oldcastle;

(e) Elizabeth requested, in turn, a play about Falstaff in love, thus causing Shakespeare to write *The Merry Wives of Windsor*;

(f) by means of the character of Justice Shallow in *Merry Wives*, Shakespeare satirized Thomas Lucy, from whom he had poached a deer ten years earlier;

(g) upon retiring to Stratford, Shakespeare wrote a satiric epitaph for John Combe, a Stratford-upon-Avon neighbor who foolishly sought to know how he would be eulogized upon his death; and

(h) as noted already, Shakespeare played the role of the Ghost in *Hamlet*.

None of these anecdotes can be proved; they all lack sufficient supporting evidence except possibly the deer-poaching story which has more than one source. It is true, for instance, that Shakespeare changed the name of Oldcastle to Falstaff (as internal evidence within the play's text and epilogue suggests). It is possible, perhaps even plausible, that someone complained. But there is no direct or indirect evidence that Queen Elizabeth involved herself in this matter.[20] Nonetheless, throughout the eighteenth century this anecdote about Queen Elizabeth was repeated by various writers on Shakespeare.

In addition, several other key stories emerged during the seventeenth and eighteenth centuries.[21] For example, the actor Charles Macklin (c. 1700–97) claimed to have had a document – subsequently lost in the Irish Sea – that included anecdotes about Ben Jonson's ingratitude to Shakespeare. Edmond Malone later demonstrated convincingly that Macklin was lying.[22] Likewise,

Edward Capell (1713–81), who edited the plays and later published *Notes and Various Readings to Shakespeare* (1779–83) at the end of his life, circulated a story, derived apparently from William Oldys (1696–1761), that Shakespeare played the role of Adam in *As You Like It*. The basis of the story was the weak memory of a very old man in Stratford (supposedly a brother of Shakespeare's in one version of the anecdote) who very late in his life remembered something about Shakespeare being carried onto the stage in a production.[23] No doubt, then, Shakespeare must have played the role of Adam.

Most intriguingly, William Davenant (1606–68), the playwright, theater manager and poet laureate, is responsible for some of the most resilient anecdotes. He claimed, for example, that Shakespeare began his London career by holding horses outside the playhouse, a story repeated by various people, including Dr Johnson.[24] In the following century James Orchard Halliwell-Phillipps, the leading Victorian antiquarian on all things Shakespearean, argued that there must be at least "a particle of truth in it" because Davenant told Betterton, who told Nicholas Rowe, who told Alexander Pope, who passed the story on to Dr Johnson.[25] With such a line of pedigree how could the story be false?

Davenant is also the source of an anecdote that slandered his own mother, for he claimed to be the natural son of Shakespeare. The anecdote was passed on by several people who heard it from Davenant, including John Aubrey who recorded in his diary:

> Sr William Davenant Knight Poet Laureate was born in — street in the City of Oxford, at the Crowne Taverne . . . His father was John Davenant, a Vintner there, a very grave and discreet Citizen: his mother was a very beautifull woman, & of a very good witt and of conversation extremely agreable . . . Mr William Shakespeare was wont to goe into Warwickshire once a yeare, and did commonly in his journey lye at this house in Oxon: where he was exceedingly respected . . . Now Sr. Wm [Sir William] would sometimes when he was pleasant over a glasse of wine with his most intimate friends e.g. Sam: Butler (author of *Hudibras*) &c. say, that it seemed to him that he writt with the very spirit that [inspired] Shakespeare, and was *seemed* contentended [*sic*] enough to be thought his Son: he would tell them the story as above (in which way his mother had a very light report, whereby she was called a whore).[26]

This fanciful anecdote, which Davenant may have meant only in a poetical sense, has been a source of many repetitions, rumors, and conjectures.[27] Rare is the Shakespeare biography that does not repeat and enhance this anecdote, even when raising doubts about it. For example, James Orchard Halliwell-Phillipps, in the process of investigating and analyzing the anecdote in his *Outlines of the Life of Shakespeare* (1882), devoted eighteen pages to the docu-

ments and issues.[28] After careful analysis he expressed doubts about its reliability, but he blamed Jennet Davenant, not her son, for the continuing circulation of the anecdote. Because she was a beautiful woman, Halliwell-Phillipps
points out, she attracted such stories. Apparently, if she had been ugly, the
story would not have appealed to the many people who repeated it. Circulate
it did, right up to present times (e.g. a recent essay in, of all things, a book
in honor of Samuel Schoenbaum).[29] Also, additional anecdotes about
Mrs Davenant circulated. By the eighteenth century she was rumored to be the
out-of-wedlock daughter of John Florio, the writer and translator. And by the
twentieth century she was put forward as the "dark lady" of Shakespeare's
sonnets.[30]

The relation between Shakespeare and Ben Jonson generated a dozen or so
anecdotes, often about the two of them in rivalry.[31] Some stories also have
them drinking together. For example, since the early nineteenth century, various biographers, including Georg Brandes and Sidney Lee, have placed the two
of them in their cups together at the Mermaid Tavern or Club, drinking with
many of the famous people of the Jacobean era (including Sir Walter Raleigh,
despite the fact that he was locked up in the Tower).[32] And Joseph Quincey
Adams not only celebrated the drinking at the Mermaid but even claimed that
Shakespeare got his drinking buddy Jonson out of jail after Jonson had killed
an actor.[33] The anecdote has been proven false by I. A. Shapiro and
Schoenbaum,[34] but it continues to appear in biographies of Shakespeare, for
who can resist the sentimental evocation of great men drinking together?[35]

Another drinking anecdote has also appeared regularly in the biographies,
despite the lack of any documentary proof. In this story Shakespeare drank
himself to death. The story began with John Ward, who was Vicar of Stratford
between 1662 and 1681. In his diary of 1661–3 Ward recorded the following
statement: "Shakespear, Drayton, and Ben Jhonson, had a merry meeting, and
itt seems drank too hard, for Shakespear died of a feavour there contracted."[36]
This story lacks the appeal of the Mermaid Tavern anecdote, but it still continues
to be told.

For example, Richard Dutton, though acknowledging that the anecdote was
"written down some half a century later" (157), argues that it may be reliable
because Ward knew Shakespeare's daughter Judith. This conjecture is in the
realm of possibility, but how dependable is Ward, who also believed, based
upon a rumor, that Shakespeare annually spent one thousand pounds, an exor-
bitant amount?[37] He also proclaimed that John Milton was a papist, even
though Milton had actively participated in Cromwell's government just a few
years earlier. Confused about Milton, Ward hardly seems a reliable source for
events two generations earlier.

Nonetheless, his anecdote lives on. Russell Fraser, who published *Young
Shakespeare* (1988) and *Shakespeare: the Later Years* (1992), begins the second

book with an appeal to the favorite source of Shakespearean biographers: "If tradition has it right, a drinking bout finished off Shakespeare" (1).[38] Fraser then returns to the story at the end of the book (274):

> Shakespeare died on his birthday, April 23, 1616. The story goes that he and his friends, Michael Drayton and Ben Jonson "had a merry meeting and it seems drank too hard." Death followed from "a fever there contracted." Some [people] jib at this – "no ground for imputing to him an excessive indulgence in 'hot and rebellious liquors'" – but the story originates with a student of medicine who became Stratford's vicar while Shakespeare's kin still lived there. Drayton, of Warwickshire, wrote at least one great poem, Jonson more than a few, and Shakespeare, if drink killed him, was lucky in his companions.

Although this anecdote cannot be grounded in any death records, Fraser and others are obviously drawn to the idea of these three men drinking together. But the logical ellipses and evasions in this statement make for questionable history.

John Southworth, in *Shakespeare the Player* (2000), goes Fraser one better, for he insists that the drinking had to occur in London, most likely "on the evening of Shrove Tuesday [12 February] or quite shortly afterwards."[39] Racked with fever, Shakespeare then hurried home to Stratford-upon-Avon, but death caught up with him. With this detailed scenario in place, we are almost ready for the filming of *Shakespeare in Death*.

III

Of course, there have been some major efforts to anchor Shakespearean biography in documentary evidence, beginning with Edmond Malone (1741–1812), the editor, biographer, and theater historian.[40] In a life committed to archival research, book collecting, the writing of biographies, literary editing, and theater history, Malone established himself as the leading scholar of his time on Shakespeare and English theater history. He was the first scholar to provide a documentary basis for the chronology of Shakespeare's plays. He was the first scholar to delve into the Stratford records for information on Shakespeare.[41] And he was the first scholar to investigate the Henslowe papers, which provided valuable information for his "A Historical Account of the English Stage" (1790). He also successfully exposed the forgeries of William Henry Ireland. And in 1790 he produced his major edition of the plays, including his history of the stage. In the process of providing commentary on the edited plays, he rather systematically challenged almost every factual error and anecdote that Nicholas Rowe had put forward. His aim, as his recent biographer Peter Martin points out, was "to demonstrate the spuriousness of popular anecdotes."[42]

Although Malone worked on a biography of Shakespeare throughout his life, this task remained unfinished. The incomplete manuscript, which stops soon after Shakespeare arrives in London, was edited and published by James Boswell, Jr. in the 1821 edition of the *Plays and Poems*, the third Variorum. Over the years Malone had collected many documents on Shakespeare, but he obviously had difficulty in turning this evidence into an extended, unified narrative. Perhaps he was unable to bridge the gap between his commitment to the documentary record and his impulse to write the biography of genius. His two Shakespeares – of the facts and of the imagination – failed to merge into one figure. Malone did succeed, however, in establishing the documentary foundation for Shakespearean scholarship. His commitment to the archive and its documentary records provided the guiding principle for the scholars who came after him, including Halliwell-Phillipps, Charles William Wallace, E. K. Chambers, G. E. Bentley and Samuel Schoenbaum.

For example, Chambers, an independent scholar like Malone, was deeply suspicious of most anecdotes.[43] In *William Shakespeare: a Study in Fact and Problems* (1930), Chambers separates documentary records from unreliable sources, placing various unreliable allusions to Shakespeare in the category of "problem" or what he calls "mythos." This term refers to the anecdotes and tales that were transmitted from the time of Shakespeare's death until the mid-nineteenth century.[44]

Like Malone, Chambers spent much of his career preparing to write the biography of Shakespeare. But he did not succeed in writing a narrative life. Instead, he gathered together the documentary archive that could serve as the basis for a biography. In volume one of *William Shakespeare: a Study in Facts and Problems*, he presents a preliminary review of the evidence for Shakespeare's life, but he then gives over most of the volume to an analysis of the theater companies, the printing and publishing of plays, the textual history of the quartos and folios, the textual history for each of the plays, and a chronological history of the productions between 1588 and 1642. The second volume is primarily a collection of the many documents, both reliable and unreliable, on Shakespeare.

Yet despite Chambers's vigilance in separating anecdotes from the factual records, he did not dismiss all anecdotes out of hand. For example, he remained intrigued by the possibility that Queen Elizabeth had requested a Falstaff play. In the main, though, even more than Malone, he tried to maintain the two-part division between mythos and records. Toward the end of his life, in *Sources for a Biography of Shakespeare* (1946), he reiterated his critique of anecdotes or what he called the "tradition" of stories about Shakespeare:

What then are we to think of tradition as an element in the making of a biography? It is obviously far less reliable than record, which may be misinterpreted, but at least gives a germ of fact, which has to be worked in at its appropriate place. Tradition is attractive. It may deal with more picturesque and intimate matter than record. On the other hand, it may be due to invention, either to decorate the dull narrative of a book or to satisfy the persistence of inquiries with tips in their pockets. In any case there is room for errors of transmission, either through inexact memories, or through the human instinct to leave a story better than you found it. Nevertheless, tradition cannot be altogether disregarded.[45]

The "tradition" of anecdotes, though always tempting, must be treated with great skepticism.

This measured assessment, so typical of Chambers, also guides the scholarship of Samuel Schoenbaum who at times seems to be echoing Chambers directly. For example, in an essay on the facts and myths about the relation between Shakespeare and Jonson, he states: "It is the nature of traditions that they are more picturesque than facts; hence the image formed by posterity would in large measure be fashioned by the mythos."[46]

In *Shakespeare's Lives* (1970; rev. edn, 1991), after reviewing various legends, traditions, relics, and anecdotes about Shakespeare, Schoenbaum presents his assessment: "As a whole they make a contribution to the Shakespeare-Mythos – in E. K. Chambers's terms – rather than to biography proper. Yet historians have not been able to dismiss them all out of hand, for in some may reside a kernel of truth."[47] And in *Shakespeare: a Compact Documentary Life* (1977, rev. edn, 1987), he writes:

> I have viewed my domain as being spacious enough to include the apocryphal anecdotes and legendary feats that have a way of springing up around the memory of great men in the times following their death. So I devote some of my pages to the deer-poaching escapade at Charlecote, the Bidford toping contest, the bruited amour of Mrs. Davenant, and the other curious episodes that make up the Shakespeare mythos. Much of this material is quite simply good fun, but the workings of myth have a place in the historical record, and may sometimes conceal elusive germs of truth.[48]

Germ of truth, kernel of truth – this is the specific language of Chambers; Schoenbaum, however, seems slightly more receptive to – or intrigued by – the mythos.

He is bemused by the various stories generated by Davenant, though he expresses doubts about them. As for the deer-poaching story, Schoenbaum states that "in modern times most (but not all) responsible scholars would reject the entire episode as traditionary [*sic*] romance."[49] Yet like Chambers he is prepared to claim that there is "plausibility to the tradition" of Rowe's story about Queen Elizabeth requesting Shakespeare to write a play about Falstaff in love.[50] The original source for this anecdote is John Dennis in 1702. Rowe took it up from Dennis and passed it on in 1709. Schoenbaum is not prepared to dismiss it, even though Chambers and others thought that it was apocryphal. Also, while Schoenbaum grants that John Ward's story about Shakespeare drinking himself to death "cannot be trusted as fact," he notes that "it remains a possibility."[51] In accord with Malone and Chambers, then, Schoenbaum sets up a basic distinction between records and anecdotes, facts and fabrications. Yet, uneasily, he also entertains the possibility that a few traditions might carry a germ of truth.

Schoenbaum's commitment to this basic historical concept of "possibility" is understandable, even admirable, for it allows him on occasion to recognize that the basic two-part division between fact and mythos (or objectivity and subjectivity) does not always hold in historical study. But this openness also creates a tension, even a contradiction, in his critique of biographers. Indeed, in *Shakespeare's Lives* he has two basic arguments to make, and they tend, on occasion, to pull in opposite directions. On the one hand, he wants to anchor all scholarship in the documentary record. He is most disdainful, for example, of the various anti-Stratfordians. And he is a strong critic of biographers who fail to follow rigorous documentary procedures. On the other hand, he repeatedly proclaims that all biographies are necessarily an expression of the biographers' own perspectives, values, experiences and time periods. Each biographer "admires Shakespeare in his own image." As illustration, Schoenbaum quotes Halliwell-Phillipps's statement: "There's a point of resemblance in Shakespeare's personal story and my own personal story."[52] This basic insight, which acknowledges the unavoidable interpretive, even subjective, nature of historical writing, provides part of the analytical strength and value of *Shakespeare's Lives*. It also complicates the positivist principle of documentation that Schoenbaum sets up as the basis of historical writing.

Thus, his own biography, *Shakespeare: a Documentary Life* (1975), is full of documents and illustrations that serve as both a demonstration and a justification of the documentary method. Schoenbaum insists that he has resisted the kinds of speculations, conjectures, and anecdotes that have flawed previous biographies:

> Were I to claim any novelty for my narrative, that claim would have to rest on its lack of novelty . . . I have no new theories respecting the genesis or first performance of any of the plays. In fact, I have no interesting theories at all to offer. These I leave to more adventurous spirits. Of speculation, sometimes masquerading as evident truth, there has, I feel, been sufficient, though it is mostly harmless enough. The present moment is perhaps as reasonable as any for a summing up of knowledge. So I have examined all the

documents again, at first hand, and set forth (I hope without special pleading) what they tell us.[53]

Having declared his method and aim, Schoenbaum then, by way of preface, pays homage to the scholarly tradition that guides him, specifically Malone, Halliwell-Phillipps and Chambers. And he also praises his contemporaries, including G. E. Bentley and Stanley Wells, who, likewise, are scholars committed to this scholarly tradition, a tradition that can be traced in a fairly straight line from Malone to the present.

IV

So, we have two abiding – and apparently contending – traditions at work in the history of Shakespearean biography: the tradition of popular anecdotes and the tradition of documentary scholarship. Malone, as the father figure of the documentary tradition, carries a major responsibility for creating what is now called "the Shakespeare industry." Held in high esteem by Chambers and Schoenbaum, he served as the model for their scholarly research. But of course this status, in all of its historicist authority, makes him a suspect figure in our anti-authoritarian age. To the extent that he represents the scholarly commitment to documentary method, objective analysis, and authentic texts, he occupies a precarious place in scholarship today. In recent years, the new scholarship has "interrogated" established assumptions and procedures, from the independent status of the subject to the stability of the text.[54] Accordingly, traditional scholarship, including the historicism that Malone helped to develop, has invited a timely critique.

In *Shakespeare Verbatim: the Reproduction of Authenticity and the 1790 Apparatus*, Margreta de Grazia presents Malone as the leading spokesman for an Enlightenment project that not only enshrined Shakespeare as the national poet (a campaign led, of course, by David Garrick) but also sanctioned the scholarly ideals of the objective researcher, the authentic text and the intentional author (who, in Shakespeare's case, is to be revered as both a respectable man of his time and a genius for all times).[55] Malone was thus largely responsible, she argues, for the historical "construction" of the textual works and the transcendental identity of Shakespeare that we have inherited from the eighteenth century.[56]

Of special relevance here, de Grazia criticizes Malone for creating a dichotomy between reliable documents and unreliable anecdotes. In her analysis of Malone, de Grazia focuses primarily on his documentary method, which she calls the "apparatus" that guided his textual and biographical construction of Shakespeare in the 1790 edition of the *Plays and Poems* (10 vols). As de Grazia points out, Malone challenged the textual and biographical methods of his predecessors (including the editing and commentary of Dr Johnson, whom

Malone revered). He was "the first to emphasize the principle of authenticity in treating Shakespeare's works and the materials relating to them . . . the first to depend on facts in constructing Shakespeare's biography" (2). This may be an overstatement that slights the methods of Malone's predecessors (for he did not emerge in a vacuum), but his achievement was foundational for subsequent scholarship. And de Grazia quite correctly notes that Malone's approach to the works and life was founded upon an "overwhelming preoccupation with objectivity" (5). Thus, de Grazia's aim is to examine the apparatus that he put in place "in order to reveal its operations, to weaken its authority, to expose the schema" (13). The authority of Malone's scholarship, especially his documentary method that guided his textual editing and his biographical research, must be shown to be flawed.

Malone was obsessed with *authenticity*, a word and standard that he used like a weapon to assault other editors and biographers. The problem, as de Grazia sees it, is that Malone, in the process of trying to authenticate the works and the life, created not only an impossible model of objective scholarship but also a principle of authority that established Malone himself as the master arbiter of Shakespeare. In consequence, the concepts of "authenticity and inauthenticity (forgeries and counterfeits) subscribe to the same underlying principle of authority" (11) – an authority that de Grazia assails (just as Malone had assailed the authority of Rowe).

For example, whereas Rowe had depended upon the Fourth Folio (1685) for his edition of the plays, Malone insisted that his edition would be based upon the First Folio (1623). Malone argued that he was attempting to avoid the many editorial mistakes which had accumulated in the later folios. But de Grazia sees this as a sign that Malone was committed to a false or impossible idea of editing: the recovery of the original, authentic text. He invested the First Folio with an authority that it cannot deliver, as de Grazia demonstrates in her analysis of it. So, Malone's textual aim – to discover the author's intended text – reveals a naïve idea of authenticity. Although he succeeded in developing the basic model of the copy text, which became the textual norm for W. W. Greg and others in the twentieth century, this model has lost its hold on recent editors of Shakespeare. Today, an editor of Shakespeare's plays, if attuned to revisionist bibliography, does not believe that any such intention is retrievable. Or even desirable. Renaissance play-texts express the multiple voices, economics and politics of the theatrical and publishing communities, not the lone voice of genius.

Moreover, de Grazia criticizes Malone's critical, textual, and biographical "apparatus" because it not only imposed a false authority on the texts but also controlled the reception of them. This constraining apparatus, with its detailed editorial footnotes, "predisposes the reader to specific modes of reading and understanding" (11). A new prison-house of language and understanding thus

emerged with Malone's edition of Shakespeare. As readers, we have been confined within this editorial system ever since. (It is not clear, though, if de Grazia
believes that this authoritative system has also operated in the theaters of the
last 200 years, dictating how to stage and watch the plays).

In her critique of Malone's scholarly methods, de Grazia is especially critical
of his failure to see any value in the stories that Rowe and others pass on. In
Malone's biographical apparatus, "factual accounts discredited traditional anecdotes" (6). Without question, Malone campaigned vehemently against Rowe
and his anecdotes. Countering Malone, de Grazia makes the case that these
anecdotes, even though they may not be true, still offer an era's version of
Shakespeare. Instead of rejecting Rowe, we should honor him. In this spirit, de
Grazia makes the case for the return of anecdotes in our study of Shakespeare:
"Rather than individuating Shakespeare by amassing particulars corroborated
by facts residing in documents, the anecdotes set him in relation to the community, frequently in a public place of exchange – a shop, theater, or tavern"
(75). She suggests that the early anecdotes, when considered together, portray
an appealing or intriguing man of roguish behavior. "While the anecdotes may
not have conformed with facts, they clearly conformed with how Shakespeare
was perceived, as early as the Folio's influential characterization: short on education, original rather than imitative, natural rather than artful, spontaneous
rather than industrious" (76). Thus, the earlier versions of Shakespeare deserve
our serious attention, for they offer an alternative to Malone's radical "reconsti-
tution of the subject" (7). Malone tried to confine Shakespeare within documentary records, but in the process supposedly turned him into the isolated
genius of bardolatry; de Grazia will liberate him from this solitary imprisonment
by returning him to his public community of shops, theaters and taverns.

This defense of the anecdotes correctly suggests that by attending to the
storytellers of the seventeenth and eighteenth centuries, we can construct a
social history of the idea of Shakespeare. Well and good, for, as Schoenbaum
insisted, the figure of Shakespeare that biographers have given us, from 1709
to the present, is not one person but a variable figure who answers in part to
our changing cultural perspectives. Shakespeare has many lives, not one (hence
the title of Schoenbaum's book). Even if we resist the postmodern argument
that history writing is always determined by controlling narratives (e.g.
Hayden White's historiography), we recognize that the playwright, like the
plays, is always being reconceived and reconstituted (in the study and on the
stage). Perhaps there are as many Shakespeares as there are Hamlets. But does
this recognition put in doubt all attempts at documentary scholarship, including the authority of reliable evidence?

Unfortunately, de Grazia's opposition between the social construction of
Shakespeare (our open-minded project, by way of anecdotes) and the documentary construction of the man (Malone's closed-minded historicism, by way

of facts) sets up a misleading, even a false dichotomy. Malone, Chambers and Schoenbaum struggled to distinguish between "legendary anecdotes and ascertainable facts" (or mythos and records) because they recognized just how difficult the task is. Perhaps that is part of the reason that the biographical project was always in process for them, as they kept documenting the life (yet never quite writing a complete biography). Unlike many biographers, they knew that between truth and falsehood there exists a muddled middle ground of possibility, plausibility and probability that always has to be negotiated.

But de Grazia, in the process of celebrating anecdotes, constructs a rather romanticized, even Edenic, world of storytellers who imaginatively created versions of Shakespeare before Malone the documentary serpent appeared. In this prelapsarian world people like Nicholas Rowe were free to gather and pass on the various anecdotes about Shakespeare that had developed during the seventeenth century. "The validity of these accounts depended not on their factual accuracy as verified by documents, but on the circumstances of their having been accepted and transmitted from generation to generation" (72). From de Grazia's perspective the early biographers and editors of Shakespeare, before the arrival of Malone, were guided by "principles of decorum and taste, not facts" (73). These principles (which seem to be a formulaic version of eighteenth-century society and culture) allowed them to construct Shakespeare in a freely interpretive manner, without being imprisoned within the constraining demands of authenticity, fact, and objectivity. Before Malone arrived on the scene, people were free to speculate about Shakespeare and the plays, but Malone's new rules not only attack these speculations but "render them obsolete" (6). Thus Malone imposed a constricting authority on the free flow of interpretation and imagination. In Malone's approach to scholarship, "information pre-empted evaluation, factual scholarship phased out literary judgement" (70).

In this opposition between the anecdotal storytellers and the documentary Malone, de Grazia posits an overly neat division between free interpretation, which is good, and constricted factuality, which is bad. Thus she announces that the basic principles of "factual accuracy and inaccuracy appeal to the same criterion of truth" (11), and this truth, because it is wedded to the suspect ideas of objectivity and authenticity, is apparently a false standard. Accordingly, de Grazia reverses the evaluative registers of Malone's apparatus by subverting the factual, the objective, and the authentic in order to privilege the anecdotal, the interpretive, and the communal. Yet despite this reversal, she is still confined within the dualism that supposedly controlled Malone.

There is real value, of course, in writing a history of the cultural idea of Shakespeare, as represented by the storytellers. But Malone was taking on a different task. Attempting to discover what could be learned about Shakespeare, Malone sought to place Shakespeare in his own time, not in the subsequent periods. Biography can take up both of these projects, but a distinction needs to be made.[57] At the end of the eighteenth century, unreliable anecdotes and forgeries defined much about the record on Shakespeare's life. In order to get back to the late sixteenth and early seventeenth centuries, Malone had to expose the forgeries and strip away the anecdotes, with their accumulated meanings, in order to determine, for the first time, what the rather limited evidence reveals to us. At that time and in his situation, he was developing procedures and justifying practices that began to clarify for Shakespearean scholars the historical issues and problems in the life, the texts, and the possible chronology for composition and production. Perhaps, as de Grazia argues, Malone was overly insistent in his commitment to the principles of authenticity, fact, and documentation, but at that time those very principles made scholarship possible (not merely as a constricting apparatus). And those principles still justify historical research, even though the ideal of certainty cannot be achieved.

So, while there is substantial merit in some aspects of de Grazia's examination of Malone, including her critique of historicism or positivism (a well-rehearsed topic in modern historiography), her faulting of Malone's certainties (for at times he could be authoritarian, not just authoritative), her demonstration that the First Folio does not deliver an "authentic" text, and her commitment to multiple social histories, we may still reject the version of Malone that she constructs. In her telling, he becomes somewhat of a caricature of himself – a demon of the apparatus.

Also, despite de Grazia's critique of the "apparatus" of objectivity, including the demands of "logic and evidence" (13), she cannot avoid these traits of argument in her own analysis, as she has to acknowledge in her introduction. By appealing to logic and evidence, she quite skillfully shows that he developed an effective weapon in his battle against falsehood. The more she succeeds in her argument, the more she sanctions Malone's agenda and aims. For example, to her credit, in a careful documentary analysis, she questions the supposed factuality of various statements in the First Folio – that is, the truth and falseness of these statements. She illustrates how and why aspects of the Folio provide unreliable evidence about Shakespeare and his plays. Thus, in an attempt to offer a critique of Malone's decision to give priority to the First Folio over the Fourth, she uses his own analytical methods based upon the criteria of authenticity and factuality.[58] He found fault with the Fourth Folio; she in turn finds fault with the First Folio. Basically, she applies the same tactic that Malone had used against Rowe. But if we are to take her analysis of the First Folio seriously, as it surely deserves, we should honor Malone's critique of the Fourth Folio.

Beyond the logical traps in her own analysis, the key problem here is that de Grazia gives us an incomplete historical perspective on Malone. As a materialist historian, she insists upon the importance of surrounding and shaping conditions. She thus accuses Malone of insulating and enclosing Shakespeare within his own "autonomous self" and genius (10, 78, 148, 172, 225), apart from the social and material culture that produced him. Yet in her analysis of Malone she separates him from the specific aspects of his career and age, making him a singular, obsessive figure, basically enclosed within his campaign for authenticity. In order to take the historical measure of Malone, we need to attend to his cultural and social worlds (including the publishing world), for he was hardly alone in the campaign for authenticity. Consider his colleagues. We only have to look at Edward Gibbon's grand historical project, the writings of Edmund Burke, and the discourses on painting by Joshua Reynolds to see a similar commitment to a powerful idea of authenticity. And James Boswell, in his own way, was just as obsessively committed to presenting the authentic Dr Johnson as Malone was in discovering the authentic Shakespeare. No doubt we can offer modern critiques of certain aspects of their commitment to authenticity, but the achievements of Gibbon, Reynolds, Boswell, Burke and Malone need to be seen in relation to one another, as part of the history of that time. In turn, their achievements were part of the development of the writing of history.[59] Constructing Malone alone, apart from his community, creates a misleading biography of the man and an equally distorted picture of his historical ideas and campaigns.

Likewise, when de Grazia insists that Malone was adamantly opposed to all anecdotes and literary judgements, she strangely ignores the fact that he made literary judgements throughout his writings.[60] Indeed, his decisions to edit Shakespeare, Dryden, Pope and Goldsmith were all based upon his deeply held and carefully articulated judgements about the quality and importance of these writers and their imaginative works.[61] Malone was not some kind of dry archivist, worshipping at the shrine of facts. Instead, his commitment to documentation and his commitment to literary evaluation went hand in hand. We may be uncomfortable today with a romantic heritage that seemed to lift Shakespeare into a realm beyond criticism, but Malone's commitment to Shakespeare derived from his deep pleasure in English poetry and the lives of the poets. In this commitment, he was, like Dr Johnson, a person of his time. And both were quite capable of making critical distinctions.

Perhaps the most interesting illustration of Malone's complex, often ambiguous relation to anecdotes can be seen in his friendship and partnership with James Boswell, with whom he worked closely on the writing of the *Life of Johnson*. With Malone's editorial guidance during hundreds of hours together, Boswell finished the book in 1790. Then, after Boswell's death in 1795, Malone, as literary executor, edited four more revised and expanded versions of the *Life of Johnson*, the last two undertaken in partnership with Boswell's son, James Boswell, Jr. So, at the very same time in the late 1780s that he was busy finishing his major edition of Shakespeare's plays, including his history of the

English theater, he was also working closely with Boswell on the *Life*, anecdote by anecdote.

What we discover, then, when placing Malone back in his time and activities, is, on the one hand, a strong critic of the pervasive eighteenth-century industry of anecdotes, including anecdotal essays and books, yet, on the other hand, an editor and biographer committed to a defense of what he called "genuine anecdote."[62] The contradictions, both real and apparent, are important to keep in mind. Malone developed his idea of "genuine anecdote" in response to Hester Thrale Piozzi's *Anecdotes of the Late Samuel Johnson* (London, 1786), a book that greatly irritated both Malone and Boswell because they felt that it misrepresented Johnson.[63] What he and Boswell sought, then, were genuine or authentic anecdotes – an oxymoron only if we reduce Malone to a version of Dickens's Thomas Gradgrind in *Hard Times*. In his various projects Malone could not avoid anecdotal evidence. In fact, when doing research on Alexander Pope, he depended upon an unpublished manuscript of Joseph Spence's titled "Anecdotes," which was full of stories about Pope. And T. Glover's essay "Authentic Anecdotes" (1774) on Oliver Goldsmith served as the basis for Malone's memoir of Goldsmith in his edition of the plays and poems (1777).[64] Also, one of Malone's last scholarly activities was to edit Joseph Spence's *Observations, Anecdotes, and Characters, of books and men, arranged with notes by the late Edmond Malone.*[65]

Anecdotes defined the age and the archive. From Malone's perspective, in an age when hundreds of people published articles and books of anecdotes,[66] the historical challenge was to develop rigorous methods for discovering which anecdotes were genuine. When he was working on his biography of John Dryden, for example, he was very suspicious of various stories and anecdotes, which, he stated, "confirmed and increased my distrust of traditional anecdotes, many of which, on a close examination, I have found, if not wholly false, yet greatly distorted by ignorance, or inattention, or willful misrepresentation, of those by whom they have been transmitted from age to age."[67] This caution, in turn, guided Malone when he took up the anecdotes on Shakespeare. He assaulted Rowe's *Account*, but he was prepared to accept some anecdotes about Shakespeare in John Aubrey's manuscript, which he studied in the Ashmolean Museum at Oxford University.[68] He thus passed on Davenant's story about his mother and Shakespeare. Apparently if Malone discovered an anecdote in the archive, it carried more weight for him than one transmitted by Rowe. He tried to hold this evidence to a rigorous standard, but like all biographers of Shakespeare, he was sometimes tempted to accept a piece of information without sufficient supporting evidence. The historical struggle was not simply between facts and anecdotes but between the reliable and unreliable aspects of anecdotes, as he note ruefully in 1802: "half the stories running around the world are partly true and partly false."[69] In all of his endeavors, as a full reading of his many works and letters reveals, Malone never found a documentary position outside of anecdotal evidence, despite his campaign against these stories.

V

Thus, in the 300-year history of Shakespearean biography, the two traditions, the documentary and the anecdotal, have achieved a certain logical division, as basic rules of evidence prescribe. Scholars since the time of Malone have attempted to distinguish between facts and anecdotes. Yet despite their best intentions, all scholars, including Malone, Chambers, and Schoenbaum, have found themselves drawn to certain anecdotes which provide supporting evidence for their assumptions and arguments. In those cases the scholars, despite their rigorous principles, often modify or abandon the normal rules of evidence. Just as importantly, even the most diligent scholars have recognized that the distinction between facts and anecdotes (or records and legends) is impossible to maintain consistently in any examination of historical documents; many records are not factual; many anecdotes not only contain a kernel of factuality but also express representative truths.

The problem that I began with – an overly neat division between records and mythos – cannot be resolved, not even by cunning reversals that attempt to displace the documentary frame of mind with the imaginative reconstruction of the past. The choice is not really between fact and fiction – objectivity and subjectivity – in the handling of evidence. The two traditions are our heritage, and our abiding struggle. So, perhaps Malone deserves one last statement here:

> There is, certainly, a great difference between traditions; and some are much more worthy than others. Where a tradition has been handed down, by a very industrious and careful inquirer, who has derived it from persons most likely to be accurately informed concerning the fact related, and subjoins his authority, such a species of tradition must always carry great weight along with it.[70]

This authority that Malone attempted to establish, not always successfully, is basic to historical research. Of course, the biographer's task is to know both traditions and to do justice to each of them. Malone had learned, year by year, that the two traditions, despite his effort to separate them, are not just intertwined but mutually constitutive. Perhaps Malone came to see that they shared, despite their logical opposition, a kind of doppelgänger relationship. This recognition may lie behind his inability to finish his biography: the evidence for Shakespeare the man and Shakespeare the genius would not come together into one perspective nor separate into neat, understandable categories. Perhaps, even more than Chambers or Schoenbaum (who also had difficulty in writing a life of Shakespeare rather than compiling a documentary catalogue of records and mythos), Malone, at the origin of historical study, recognized the dark, troubling mutuality between anecdotes and facts. What indeed is the nature of a "genuine anecdote"?

Notes

1. E. K. Chambers, *Sources for a Biography of Shakespeare* (Oxford: Clarendon, 1946), 40.
2. Nicholas Rowe, *Some Account of the Life &c. of Mr. William Shakespeare* (1709); reprinted in *Eighteenth Century Essays on Shakespeare*, ed. D. Nichol Smith, 2nd edn (Oxford: Clarendon Press, 1963), 3. This short biography by Rowe served as the introduction to his six-volume edition of the plays, the first edition to appear after the publication of the four folios in the seventeenth century. They were published in 1623, 1632, 1663 (and reprinted in 1664 with seven additional plays) and 1685. Rowe's edition, published in 1709 by Jacob Tonson, was reasonably successful, and thus was reprinted in 1714. But it was soon superceded by the new editions by Alexander Pope, Samuel Johnson, Johnson and George Steevens, and Edmond Malone. Indeed, by 1790, when Malone published his twelve-volume edition (which was based upon the First not the Fourth Folio), Rowe's contributions as an editor had been completely displaced.
3. Oscar James Campbell, ed., Edward G. Quinn, assoc. ed., *The Reader's Encyclopedia of Shakespeare* (New York: MJF Books/Thomas Y. Crowell, 1966), 288.
4. Russell Fraser, *Young Shakespeare* (Columbia University Press, 1988), 91; Peter Levi, *The Life and Times of William Shakespeare* (London: Macmillan, 1988), 218.
5. Park Honan, *Shakespeare: a Life* (Oxford: Oxford University Press, 1998), 110–11. Page references are to this edition.
6. E. K. Chambers, *William Shakespeare: a Study of Facts and Problems* (Oxford: Clarendon Press, 1930), 2: 253.
7. John Southworth, *Shakespeare the Player: a Life in the Theatre* (Gloucestershire: Sutton Publishing, 2000), 185.
8. On historical methodology, see Marc Bloch, *The Historian's Craft*, trans. Peter Putnam (New York: Random House, 1953); J. H. Hexter, *The History Primer* (New York: Basic Books, 1971); Louis Gottschalk, *Understanding History: a Primer of Historical Methods*, 2nd edn (New York: A. Knopf, 1969); Robert Jones Shafter, ed., *A Guide to Historical Method*, 3rd edn (Homewood, IU: Dorsey Press, 1980); and Peter Achinstein, ed., *The Concept of Evidence* (Oxford: Oxford University Press, 1983). On probability, see Ian Hacking, *An Introduction to Probability and Inductive Logic* (Cambridge: Cambridge University Press, 2001).
9. The First Folio names twenty-six actors. It does not identify any roles, and it does not provide dates. So it cannot clarify who acted often, who acted occasionally; nor can it help us with who took on the major roles, who played minor roles. Yet despite the suggestion that all the named players performed in "all these plays," we know that some of them were not at the Globe during all of the fourteen years. So this statement is not reliable. Moreover, there are many factual and interpretive problems with various aspects of the First Folio, as recent textual analysis has shown; so a historian should proceed with caution and skepticism. See, for example, Leah Marcus, *Puzzling Shakespeare: Local Reading and Its Discontents* (Berkeley: University of California Press, 1988).
10. For example, in the 1616 edition of Ben Jonson's plays, Shakespeare's name is listed as one of the "principall Comoedians" for the 1598 production of *Every Man In His Humour*. And he is listed as a player in Jonson's *Sejanus* in 1603. No specific role is

identified in either case. As for Shakespeare's own plays, the record is blank. There is, though, another unreliable anecdote from William Oldys (1696–1761) that suggests the possibility of Shakespeare playing Adam in *As You Like It*. But E. K. Chambers dismisses it as yet another "fabrication." See *William Shakespeare* (1930), 2: 274–82.

11. Rowe notes that Betterton made a trip to Stratford-upon-Avon "on purpose to gather up what Remains he could of a Name for which he had so great a Value." Nicholas Rowe, *Life*, 19.

12. John Dryden, "The Prologue Spoken by Mr. Betterton," *Troilus and Cressida* (1679); reprinted in Brian Vickers, ed., *Shakespeare: the Critical Heritage, Volume One: 1623–1692* (London: Routledge & Kegan Paul, 1974), 249.

13. Here, too, we have at least a possibility, if not a probability.

14. See, for example, Johanna Fiedler, *Molto Agitato: the Mayhem Behind the Scenes at the Metropolitan Opera* (New York: Doubleday, 2001).

15. Wayne C. Booth, Gregory G. Colomb and Joseph M. Williams, *The Craft of Research* (Chicago: University of Chicago Press, 1995), 147.

16. S. Schoenbaum, *Shakespeare's Lives*, new edition (Oxford: Clarendon Press, 1991), 89; E. K. Chambers, *William Shakespeare: a Study of Facts and Problems*, 2 vols (Oxford: Clarendon Press, 1930), 1: xii–xiii (and passim).

17. Schoenbaum, *Shakespeare's Lives*, 41. For a comprehensive gathering of all allusions, anecdotes and references before 1700, see *The Shakespere Allusion Book: a Collection of Allusions to Shakespere from 1591 to 1700. Original complied by C. M. Ingleby, Miss L. Toulmin Smith, and by Dr. F. J. Furnivall, with the assistance of the New Shakespere Society; re-edited, revised, and re-arranged, with an introduction by John Munro (1909), and now re-issued with a preface by Sir Edmund Chambers*, 2 vols (London: Humphrey Milford; Oxford University Press, 1932).

18. He also mentions John Dryden and Ben Jonson, but not in relation to a specific anecdote; it is quite likely, though, that he picked up some information from John Dennis, who claimed in 1702 that Queen Elizabeth commanded the writing of *Merry Wives of Windsor*. See E. K. Chambers, *William Shakespeare*, 2: 263.

19. James Shapiro, for example, passes on this unsubstantial story in *Rival Playwrights: Marlowe, Jonson, Shakespeare* (New York: Columbia University Press, 1992), 2; but then on p. 137 he raises doubts about its reliability.

20. See, though, the statement in 1625 by Dr Richard James, the librarian for Sir Robert Cotton. James states "that offense being worthily taken by personages" who were descended from Sir John Oldcastle, "the poet was put to make an ignorant shift of abusing Sir John Falstaff, a man not inferior of virtue." Quoted in S. Schoenbaum, *Shakespeare's Lives*, 49. Schoenbaum speculates (p. 50) that the complaint "most likely" came from either William Brooke, seventh Lord Cobham, or his successor, Henry, eighth Lord Cobham, who descended, on the mother's side, from Oldcastle.

21. E. K. Chambers gathers together the various anecdotes, legends, and traditions in *William Shakespeare*, vol. 2, under the category of "mythos."

22. As E. K. Chambers noted, Macklin "published some anecdotes on Shakespeare which were certainly fabrications." *Sources for a Biography of Shakespeare* (Oxford: Clarendon Press, 1946), 42. See, also, Schoenbaum, *Shakespeare's Lives*, 128–9.

23. E. K. Chambers, *William Shakespeare*, 2: 274–8, 289.

24. Schoenbaum, *Shakespeare's Lives*, 65–6.

25. J. O. Halliwell-Phillipps, *Outlines of the Life of Shakespeare* (London, 1882; reprint, New York: AMS Press, 1966), 53. See also, S. Schoenbaum, *Shakespeare's Lives*, 65.

26. E. K. Chambers, *William Shakespeare*, 2: 254; derived from the manuscript at the Bodleian library, Oxford University. As Chambers points out, the last clause, placed here in parentheses, was scored out in the manuscript, perhaps by Anthony Wood.

27. The Davenant story may remind us of an oft-repeated French anecdote, equally suspect, that identifies Flaubert as the father of Guy de Maupassant.

28. J. O. Halliwell-Phillipps, *Outlines*, 139–43; 487–99.

29. Mary Edmond. "Yeoman, Citizens, Gentlemen, and Players: the Burbages and their Connections," in *Elizabethan Theater: Essays in Honor of S. Schoenbaum*, ed. R. E. Parker and S. P. Zitner (Newark: University of Delaware Press, 1996), 38.

30. Arthur Acheson, *Mistress Davenant: the Dark Lady of Shakespeare's Sonnets* (London: Bernard Quaritch, 1913).

31. On the supposed rivalry, see G. E. Bentley, *Shakespeare and Jonson: their Reputations in the Seventeenth Century Compared*, 2 vols (Chicago: University of Chicago Press, 1945); James Shapiro, *Rival Playwrights: Marlowe, Jonson, Shakespeare* (New York: Columbia University Press, 1991); S. Schoenbaum. "Shakespeare and Jonson: Fact and Myth," in *The Elizabethan Theatre II*, ed. and introd. by David Galloway (Toronto: Macmillan, 1970), 1–19; T. J. B. Spencer. "Ben Jonson on his beloved, the Author Mr. William Shakespeare," *The Elizabethan Theatre IV*, ed. George Hibbard (Toronto: Macmillan, 1974): 22–40; and E. K. Chambers, *William Shakespeare*, 2: 202–11.

32. On the origin of story see Schoenbaum, *Shakespeare's Lives*, 215, and his *William Shakespeare: a Compact Documentary Life*, 2nd edn (Oxford: Oxford University Press, 1987), 259. It began with William Gifford, who published an edition of *The Works of Ben Jonson* (London, 1816).

33. S. Schoenbaum, *Shakespeare's Lives*, 363, 507.

34. I. A. Shapiro. "The Mermaid Club," *Modern Language Review*, 45 (1950): 6–17; S. Schoenbaum, "Shakespeare and Jonson: Fact and Myth," 1–19. See, also, David Riggs, *Ben Jonson: a Life* (Cambridge, Mass: Harvard University Press, 1989), 160–3, 193.

35. Park Honan, for example, raised doubts about the Mermaid anecdotes, yet he basically resurrects the tavern for another round of wit-combat; *Shakespeare: a Life*, 253–4.

36. E. K. Chambers, *William Shakespeare*, 2: 250.

37. On Shakespeare's likely income, which Chambers places at no more than a third of the one thousand figure, see Schoenbaum's *William Shakespeare: a Compact Documentary Life*, 211–12.

38. Russell Fraser, *Shakespeare: the Later Years* (New York: Columbia University Press, 1992), 274. Fraser gives Sidney Lee's *A Life of William Shakespeare* (1898), 481, as the source for "no ground for imputing to him an excessive indulgence in 'hot and rebellious liquors'."

39. John Southworth, *Shakespeare the Player: a Life in the Theatre*, 275.

40. Malone receives pride of place in S. Schoenbaum's *Shakespeare's Lives*, only matched by the attention and praise Schoenbaum gives to E. K. Chambers.

41. We should note, though, that he often got other people to do the archival digging at Stratford for him. He also convinced the city authorities to loan the city records to him, and for years refused to return the records, despite many requests.

42. Peter Martin, *Edmond Malone, Shakespearean Scholar: a Literary Biography* (Cambridge: Cambridge University Press, 1995), 123.

43. Both Malone and Chambers were independent scholars not tied to a university, both dedicated themselves to Shakespearean scholarship, both were archivists, both

turned themselves into theatre historians, both edited the plays, both compiled and published documents, both were determined critics of forgery, and both tried to write biographies of Shakespeare that proved to be short on narrative and long on documentation.

44. In Appendix D, which covers sixty-four pages in volume 2, Chambers reproduces many of these unreliable sources.

45. E. K. Chambers, *Sources for a Biography of Shakespeare*, 66.

46. S. Schoenbaum. "Shakespeare and Johnson: Fact and Myth," 5. This statement, which repeats some words and phrasing of Chambers, is a case of homage and close affinity.

47. S. Schoenbaum, *Shakespeare's Lives*, 49.

48. S. Schoenbaum, *William Shakespeare: a Compact Documentary Life*, ix.

49. S. Schoenbaum, *Shakespeare's Lives*, 72.

50. S. Schoenbaum, *Shakespeare's Lives*, 51–2.

51. S. Schoenbaum, *Shakespeare's Lives*, 78.

52. S. Schoenbaum, *Shakespeare's Lives*, 91, 283.

53. S. Schoenbuam, *William Shakespeare: a Documentary Life* (New York: Oxford University Press, with The Scholar Press, 1975), xii.

54. The origins for these new developments are various (and debatable, of course), but in Shakespeare studies the revisionist scholarship surely arrived by 1980: Stephen Greenblatt, *Renaissance Self-Fashioning: From More to Shakespeare* (Chicago: University of Chicago Press, 1980); Steven Urkowitz, *Shakespeare's Revision of King Lear* (Princeton, NJ: Princeton University Press, 1980). Of course, behind these developments stand the writings of key figures such as Jacques Derrida, Roland Barthes, Michel Foucault and Raymond Williams; and the textual revolution was carried forward by G. Thomas Tanselle, D. F. McKenzie, Jerome McGann, Peter W. M. Blayney, Randall McLeod and many others.

55. Margreta de Grazia, *Shakespeare Verbatim: the Reproduction of Authenticity and the 1790 Apparatus* (Oxford: Clarendon, 1991). Page references appear in the text and are to this edition.

56. For some other critiques of the Shakespeare industry, see R. W. Babcock, *The Genesis of Shakespeare Idolatry 1766–1799* (Chapel Hill: University of North Carolina Press, 1931); Ivor Brown and George Fearon, *Amazing Monument: a Short History of the Shakespeare Industry* (London: Heinemann, 1939); F. E. Halliday, *The Cult of Shakespeare* (London: Duckworth, 1957); Arthur Sherbo, *The Birth of Shakespeare Studies: Commentators from Rowe (1709) to Boswell–Malone (1821)* (East Lansing, MI: Michigan State University Press, 1986); Marjorie Garber, *Shakespeare's Ghost Writers: Literature as Uncanny Causality* (London: Methuen, 1987); Jonathan Bate, *Shakespearean Constitutions: Politics, Theatre, Criticism 1730–1830* (Oxford: Clarendon Press, 1989); Gary Taylor, *Reinventing Shakespeare: a Cultural History from the Restoration to the Present* (New York: Weidenfeld and Nicolson, 1989); Michael Bristol, *Shakespeare's America, America's Shakespeare* (New York: Routledge, 1990); Michael Dobson, *The Making of the National Poet: Shakespeare, Adaptation, and Authorship* (Oxford: Clarendon Press, 1992).

57. See, for example, how Rachel M. Brownstein makes this distinction in her study of the construction of the French actress Rachel: *Tragic Muse: Rachel of the Comédie Française* (New York: Knopf, 1993).

58. "There are, then, substantial discrepancies in the Folio between signs and what they signify: between portrait and subject, ascription and author, imprint of printers and printers, table of contents and contents, list of actors and actors" (de Grazia,

Shakespeare Verbatim, 28). Apparently de Grazia misses the irony of her Malonean methodology here.

59. There is extensive scholarship on the development of history writing in the eighteenth century; Malone was at the center of these historiographic projects. For a quick survey, see Ernst Breisach, *Historiography: Ancient, Medieval, and Modern* (Chicago: University of Chicago Press, 1983).

60. In her bibliography de Grazia only lists three works by Malone, excepting the 1790 and 1821 editions. Her study remains focused on textual matters, so she has some difficulty, as a historian, placing him in his time and cultural context, both biographically and socially. See Peter Martin's biography for a fuller perspective on his career and values, flaws and accomplishments.

61. He produced major editions of Shakespeare, Dryden and Goldsmith, but he failed to complete the Pope project. He did, though, also publish the works of Sir Joshua Reynolds. See the bibliography in Peter Martin, *Edmond Malone*.

62. See Martin, *Edmond Malone*, 146.

63. Ibid., 146; they also had great difficulty accepting that a woman had published a biography on Dr Johnson.

64. Ibid., 17.

65. Joseph Spence, *Observations, Anecdotes, and Characters, of Books and Men, arranged with notes by the late Edmund [sic] Malone* (London: John Murray, 1820). The anonymous advertisement, crediting Malone as the editor, claims that "it is well known that his taste for literary anecdotes was keen, and his skill in literary history excelled that of any man of letters of his day" (iv).

66. Malone was taking on the unregulated outpouring of anecdotes that operated at all levels of society, not simply the biography of Shakespeare. As even a random sample of publications reveal, the anecdote was the primary mode of representation: John Nichols, *Biographical and Literary Anecdotes* (London, 1782); John Nichols, *Literary Anecdotes of the Eighteenth Century*, 9 vols (London, 1812–15); Horace Walpole, *Anecdotes on Painting in England* (London, 1762–71).

67. Edmond Malone, *The Critical and Miscellaneous Prose Works of John Dryden . . . an Account of the Life and Writings of the Author*, 3 vols (London, 1800), 1: 148; quoted in Peter Martin, *Edmond Malone*, 233.

68. In a potential misleading statement, de Grazia suggests that Aubrey's *Brief Lives* circulated as a published text like Ben Jonson's *Timber* and Thomas Fuller's *Worthies* (*Shakespeare Verbatim*, 71). Actually, it remained unpublished until the nineteenth century, though a few selected passages circulated in the eighteenth century. With the aim of editing and publishing it, Malone transcribed the whole manuscript; but he never finished the task. However, he did publish, for the first time, all of Aubrey's comments on Shakespeare in his 1790 edition of the *Plays and Poems*.

69. Unpublished letter, 30 November 1802; quoted by S. Schoenbaum, *Shakespeare's Lives*, 171.

70. Malone, *Plays and Poems of William Shakespeare*, ed. J. Boswell, Jr. and E. Malone (London, 1821), 1: 119; quoted in Schoenbaum, *Shakespeare's Lives*, 175.

4
Decomposing History (Why Are There So Few Women in Theater History?)

Susan Bennett

By the end of the twentieth century, expansion of the canon of dramatic literature and proliferation of revisionist history-making practices had led to far more inclusive, and definitely more interesting, theater histories. And, not surprisingly, one crucial aspect of this reformation has been a new familiarity with dramatic work written by women. Aphra Behn and Caryl Churchill have become mainstays of the canon, their work almost certain to be featured somewhere in the curriculum studied by drama and theater students, and the roster of women playwrights likely to be encountered in period and/or national surveys has significantly increased. Yet, overall, knowledge of the full range of women dramatic writers from the medieval to contemporary periods remains, at best, limited. For example, how many of us know even a few of the names of the more than 500 women who, according to Beverly Davis and Gwenn Joyce's bibliography of American and British women dramatists,[1] wrote plays in the period 1876–99? The reality is that we still do not have anything resembling a comprehensive account of women's dramatic production or any full sense of what these women have contributed, in their own historical moments and beyond, to the history of theater. This is despite the very real labor of many scholars working in different periods and different geographies on women playwrights and so it seems that the problem may be less one of identification and more one of categorization. This chapter, then, is concerned with the frequency and density of theater history's blind spots and what this continues to mean for women.

The example of the hundreds of women writing plays at the end of the nineteenth century is an important one. In many ways, what happens in Western drama in this period still sets the stage for how we write our histories of modern theater. For British theater history-making, this has thus been a period where we focus on the impact of continental European drama on the emergence of a modern, realist theater in England. Allardyce Nicoll (in his foundational series of five volumes on the history of British drama) takes Henry Arthur

Jones, Arthur Wing Pinero, Oscar Wilde and George Bernard Shaw as exemplary playwrights of the 1880s and 1890s. Nicoll asserts, too, that the publication in 1882 of William Archer's *English Dramatists of To-day* was evidence of "the new living interest which had been awakened among thinking people in the fortunes of the English drama."[2] What both Archer and Nicoll mean here is the emergence of a group of male English playwrights whose work relied more on the realist precepts of continental drama than on the conventions of melodrama that have been typically said to characterize nineteenth-century English theater, and whose work also relied on the presence, just offshore, of Henrik Ibsen, standing as he does at the forefront of all progressive developments in the modern drama. As Katherine Kelly has pointed out in the introduction to her landmark anthology of *Modern Drama by Women 1880s–1930s*, "[c]ritics and historians turned a blind eye to the thousands of plays, some of them distinguished and commercially successful, written by women."[3] Kelly suggests, among other things, that cosmopolitanism, "the dominant ideological shaper of 'Modern Drama,' proved hostile to any but the most 'universal' of playwrights" and that this reinscription of "male-only, English-only culture in the context of a universalist view of human nature – promoted a new conservatism in the canon that precluded the eruption of voices speaking from multiple positions within a nation's borders."[4] Certainly this can be said to apply to Nicoll's approach and it is just this ideological impetus that affords him the preposterous claim of "Tom Robertson" as "the Giotto of the English theatre in the nineteenth century, and translated Ibsen . . . its Raphael."[5]

The very structure of Kelly's revisionist anthology points up one of the most resilient assumptions underlying the making of history for modern drama. She divides the text's dozen plays into two selections of six, one labeled "Realisms" and the other "Departures." She notes: "In dividing these plays into two groups . . . I am both documenting the variety of realisms in the emerging modern drama and simultaneously demonstrating the non-realist (or 'modernist' or 'avant-garde') dramatic writing that flourished in small, coterie theaters."[6] In a single strategic move, then, this anthologist has reminded us both of the far from monolithic practice of the genre we commonly refer to as "realism" and of the diversity of genre practices that necessarily coexist at any historical moment including the one we commonly refer to as "modern." A careful reading of Kelly's selections (their authors drawn from a variety of geographical locations ranging beyond Europe to the United States, Argentina, and Japan) cannot fail to pose all kinds of difficult questions for our received understanding of canonical plays of this period. This, it seems to me, enacts precisely the kind of revisionism proposed in Adrienne Rich's seminal definition:[7] we can read those women's plays anthologized by Kelly so as to look back at a well-known and well-defined period and set of texts with fresh, critical points of entry. Kelly's work on the modern theater insists that we rethink the parameters and presumptions for the period and, indeed, theater scholars have, in recent years, provided this kind of revisionist project for almost all conventional periods of theater history.[8]

In the short term, there can be no question that revisionist work – whether on behalf of women or any other previously minoritized group of dramatic writers – has effected significant shifts in who we think of as the canonical figures of Western theater as well as in what we consider the story told by theater history. But it is time, I think, to question the long-term benefits of this strategy, one that, among other things, consistently fails to tell the full story of women's contributions. The problem is with revision, a process committed to the act of correction, improvement and updating. Theater history-making needs a much more thorough overhaul, what I am calling here "decomposing history." I want to address the potential for the now more inclusive theater histories to become much more inclusive, by breaking up our practices of history-making, by separating into basic components our categories of organizing those narratives we recognize as theater history, by measuring those categories' effects. The question then becomes how might theater history be composed so as to account for the extensive production of dramatic writing by women.

Clifford Siskin has ably demonstrated the links between disciplinarity, professionalism and Literature as "*historical* categories – categories constituted through acts of classification – acts that select hierarchically, and thus empower, particular kinds of knowledge, particular kinds of work, and particular kinds of writing."[9] He continues: "That empowerment has, in turn, entailed the naturalizing of those hierarchies, such that disciplinarity became the proper path to truth, professionalism became an unavoidable product of economic development, and the selection we know as Literature became the transcendent output of the human imagination – simply the best."[10] To recast Siskin's project in the theater, as it were, requires very little amendment of the process he sets out. Theater histories have, too, naturalized the hierarchies upon which they depend. My concern is to point up some of those historical categories that underpin a selection of particular kinds of plays to constitute the "best" representative theatrical work of any period and place, and how significantly our knowledge – which is to say, our lack of knowledge – of women playwrights is produced by and through that network of categories. Ultimately a different composition for theater history should not merely be more inclusive, but should allow us to make more effective use of the research that has already been undertaken in the realm of women's dramatic writing. All the time revisionist archival and critical work is anchored to conventional theater history-making, it can only (as it certainly does) prove that there have been women writing for theater just as there have been men writing for theater and illustrate, in that connection, how women have often struggled to gain the same access to the public stage as their male counterparts. What I am arguing, for, however, is that theater history itself will need a different composition if it is to record a full range of dramatic writing both by men and by women. And, in this way, gender is an axis on which questions of theater history inevitably turn.

My earlier reference to the conceptualization of modern drama within a standard history of English drama was to mark the inclusion of only a very few dramatists of the late nineteenth and early twentieth centuries, inevitably all of them men, as well as the effects of a casual consignment to the generally derogatory category of nineteenth-century melodramatists of so many of the women writers contemporary to these literary mainstays of modern drama. Fully 50 percent of the women playwrights listed in the Davis and Joyce bibliography produced and published their plays in the final twenty-five years of the nineteenth century and, according to Donald Mullin's compilation of *Victorian Plays: a Record of Significant Productions on the London Stage, 1837–1901*, 20 percent of the plays performed on the London stage in this period were authored by women.[11] We might agree, then, with Kelly that "it took a sustained effort on the part of critics, historians, and producers to create the ghost effect."[12] Kelly's own project takes on the category of "realism," to unpack its gendered history and the exclusions that it has insisted upon in its occupation of such a prominent place in the history of British and other Western theaters. The formation, more generally, of period categories has rightly been held up to increasing scrutiny in many of theater studies' cognate fields. New "micro- and macro-periodizations . . . open our eyes to schema that are occluded by old paradigms of periodization," notes Lawrence Besserman, and such critical inquiry has demonstrated the various ways "how and why traditional 'megaperiod' labels like 'Medieval,' 'Renaissance,' and 'Modern' are now . . . suspect."[13]

With standard arguments for maintaining received period categories come, inextricably, standardized genre practices. For example, traditional theater history has seen "the Renaissance" as the finest period of dramatic literature in English, setting the standards for tragedies and comedies of any historical moment, and where that period, "the Renaissance," has, until very recently, insisted on more or less the complete absence of women from public performance of any kind. Margaret Ezell notes of *The Norton Anthology of Literature by Women*, "[t]he entries imply that the values used to construct the male canon that has graciously included women writers come into force" to determine who are the "best" women writers of a period.[14] Ezell goes on to note rather wryly that "Lady Mary Wortley Montagu, Anne Finch, and Katherine Philips have never been completely 'lost' although they may have been thoroughly patronized. Enduring critical notice, therefore, even negative, seems to be one unacknowledged criterion of 'value.' "[15] This last comment is particularly instructive, for it reminds us of how some of the first "revisions" of the canon to include women writers took place. The "lost" texts that were most easy to find and then to accommodate were those where the women were making dramas that most closely resembled, though did not quite so much excel as, their male counterparts in the same period as it was commonly understood, for the same performance conditions, and within the same genre practices insofar as those genres were considered fundamental to the overarching genre of theater.

Genre is, without question, one category that begs interrogation and historicization, if not decomposition.[16] It remains a commonplace to observe that men have written all the great tragedies and that women have fared better in the arena of comedy. Linda Kintz has clearly accounted for the fact that "[t]ragedy enforces its own privilege in a way made most obvious by the gendered hierarchy that can always be found in a list of those genres supposedly inferior to tragedy: comedy, melodrama, sentimental fiction, soap operas, sitcoms and so forth."[17] Davis and Joyce observe that "[c]omedy in all its forms, comedy, comedietta, farce, is the dominant form" in their list of women's plays as "it accounts for 40 to 45 percent of the works."[18] That categorization and analysis, I would suggest, may not necessarily be true. It may be that comedy, as we have historically understood that category, most easily accommodates many of the plays authored by women. Here we might consider the comment of Anne Shaver, editor of a collection of Margaret Cavendish's plays: "Two of her plays are tragedies; most of the rest could be called comedies, though her work often challenges traditional categories."[19] Moreover, as Susan Carlson claims for much more recent comic dramas by women, these works exploit theater's potential to "provide a way around the traditional limitations of the genre," limitations that insist on the negation of women's power, agency and self-definition.[20]

The very sedimentation of genre, then, demands more than simply stated revisioning. Indeed, I would reiterate that women's plays have become "categorized" or "categorizable" only in as much as the few – the exceptional – can be demonstrated to meet, or at least come close to, the criteria that men's plays and genre theory have laid down, through history, as exemplary in a given moment or for a particular trajectory of dramatic genre. But what about those dramas by women who have failed to attract critical notice, positive or negative, then or now? And what, too, of those women playwrights that have been categorized and criticized as not writing for the stage at all? I have written elsewhere about the application of the category "closet drama" to the plays of Joanna Baillie[21] and how, despite her determined and continuous efforts to consider how and where her own plays might be produced, she has always remained, for theater historians and drama critics alike, someone whose "plays were written to be read" – as Adrienne Scullion puts it, "being closer to the genre of 'closet' plays that the era allowed for and celebrated than to active engagements in the theater industry."[22] Yet, this is hardly true: Baillie's "Introductory Discourse," first published in 1798 as the preliminary materials to the *Plays on the Passions*, did the crucial work of introducing a readership to her playwriting even before she attempted to find a theater that would consider producing any of them. Baillie was at pains, from the outset, to underscore that readers should not imagine "that I have written [the plays] for the closet rather than the stage."[23] Some six years later, the first page of her preface to *Miscellaneous Plays* includes the statement, "It has been and still is, my strongest desire to add a few pieces to the stock of what may be called our national or permanent acting plays."[24] Her authorial intention is, again and again, expressed in these prefaces; and, crucially, she looks for a stage that suits her plays' theatrical shape and purpose.

Both plays and prefaces demonstrate a deft understanding of how the theater works as a craft *and* as an institution. Baillie's response is not – most definitely not – a retreat into the closet, but an imagination of what might better work as dynamic theatrical experience to meet the ideas and, of course, the passions that she imagined three-dimensionally. As late as the preface to the three-volume *Dramas* published in 1836, Baillie writes of a desire to see some of her work produced in "the smaller theatres of the metropolis, and thereby have a chance, at least, of being produced to the public with the advantages of action and scenic directions, which naturally belong to dramatic compositions."[25] To define Joanna Baillie, still, as a closet dramatist, against her career-long discussions of theatrical production as well as the actual performance histories of those of her plays that made it to the stage, seems to deliberately miss the point. Revisioning what we mean by "closet" does not solve the situation. Instead, we should abstract from the particular case of Baillie's categorization (the result of her reception history) the need for a much more rigorous and systematic interrogation of both major and minor genre categories as to the specificities of their histories and the interlaid condition of gender. Classifying Baillie's work as closet drama is, in the end, a deft strategy for diminishing its contribution to theater history of the period and in general.

Furthermore, genre practices are often inextricably tied to the practical aspects of theatrical production. So it was in the rapid expansion of theaters in the nineteenth century, when, as Marvin Carlson puts it, "spectators did not know what specific play was being performed at a certain theater, they could predict with reasonable assurance the *type* of play offered there, with all the attendant generic expectations – whether it be a nautical melodrama, a vaudeville, a burletta, a domestic comedy, or a fairy spectacle."[26] We might more carefully analyze the availability of particular performance venues to women dramatists and the impact this would have on their choice of form and genre.

The category of performance venue has obviously been fundamental, like genre, to the composition of theater history. Theater histories pay a great deal of attention to where a play is staged, and the architectural plans and the actual dimensions of a theater are accorded extraordinary relevance in how we understand what a play from a distant historical past might have been like in performance and how its spectators might have responded to the experience of seeing it in that theater space. Histories of theater buildings have tended to focus almost singly on performance venues located in metropolitan centers, the first and second tier cities of major European countries and the United States. They have, too, concentrated, by way of a commitment to the major theater buildings, on public performance. If we want to understand women's participation rates as playwrights whose work was performed on those best-known stages of our theater histories, then we need, most certainly, to examine more rigorously and comprehensively the history of women's access to those same stages. At some historical moments, women simply could not get their work produced, and at other moments, it has been notoriously difficult – and has often required persistence and ingenuity on a writer's part to see her work produced at all. Ellen Donkin's monograph on women playwrights in London in the period 1776–1829 provides a detailed and often chilling account of just that struggle.[27]

But to return to my earlier example of the end of the nineteenth century and the hundreds of plays written then by women, part of what we have not generally added to our theater histories for that period is the breadth of performance venue that women sought for their dramatic writing. Yes, many of them wrote for the public stage and with much success since this was a time of rapid growth in the number of theaters available to stage their work. But other women chose very different venues indeed, sometimes with significant commercial success. Their dramatic writing consisted of amateur theatricals, home theatricals, plays for children, as well as tableaux and pageants for street and other informal performance, often around particular social issues (temperance and suffrage perhaps being the best known). Sarah Annie Shields was a best-selling playwright in America in the 1860s and 1870s, the author of volumes such as *Amateur theatricals and fairy-tale dramas. A collection of original plays, expressly designed for drawing-room performance* (published in New York by Dick & Fitzgerald in 1868), *Dramatic proverbs and charades, containing a collection of original proverbs and charades, some of which are for dramatic performances, and others arranged for tableaux-vivants* (1866), and *New book of dialogues, designed for performance at school anniversaries and exhibitions* (1872). In the preface to another volume, *Parlor Charades*, Shields suggests her plays "are intended solely for performance by small circles of friends, in private parlors or saloons, and require but little trouble or expense to make them effective. The plots are simple and intelligible, although sometimes a striking dramatic situation, or strong contrast of character, has been attempted."[28] As Davis and Joyce so aptly put it, "[h]er work is for amateur players; she was not an amateur playwright."[29]

Thus, we need to look long and hard at the privilege borne by public performance venues in the composition of our theater histories and to consider what happens when the kinds of venues that Shields anticipates (and which made her a successful professional playwright) come in to the picture: the drawing room, the saloon, the school, the exhibition. Shields's corpus raises the question, too, of intended and actual audiences for women's plays. In her case, the audience and the actors might be identical or at least intimately connected with each other, although in some cases it may be that the amateur performance has much the same spectator–stage dynamic as the relationship for any main stage in a major city. We know little, of course, of actual audiences and we know that intended audiences, as with those Joanna Baillie sought for her plays, are often ignored or disregarded. Much of the time we have only scant information about the demographics for particular theaters and only a few accounts of the success or otherwise of a play produced. In the latter case, this is generally in the form of the play review written for a print publication – the views of a single spectator and one whose economic livelihood can be tied to the commentary provided. Those reviewers, through history, have been predominantly male – a fact that has changed somewhat, though slowly, over the last while.

We are attentive to theater reviewers and critics because their discourse is formative in our understanding of theatrical production in a particular period and their knowledge and perception of the "theater scene" often plays a significant role in informing what becomes theater history. Notwithstanding the predominance of male reviewers and critics, women have written extensively on the theater – often with a significant audience for their writing – and a more thorough knowledge of their commentary on the theatrical productions of their own historical moments would open up our histories to a wider range of accounts not just of the plays themselves but, more crucially, of what these reviewers *see* in these productions. Furthermore, there seems to me a necessary alliance between scholars interested in a critical practice that pays specific attention to questions of gender and those women who, in other historical moments, did much the same thing. It might be argued, in fact, that the institutionalization of feminist scholarship – certainly in arts disciplines and arguably more broadly – makes today's task a great deal easier than it was for these women who, earlier, put their critical perspectives into the public domain. This, above all else, is a compelling reason to compose theater history anew. In this spirit, then, I want to dwell on two eighteenth-century women critics of the theater, Frances Brooke and Elizabeth Inchbald. We have come to know them (somewhat) as playwrights – and as good examples of writers whose plays have been more or less forgotten – but here I want to focus on what they said about the theater of their time and how this imposes challenges for traditional theater history-making and directions for a new historiography.

Frances Brooke had sent her first play *Virginia* to David Garrick for consideration for production at Drury Lane and also to Christopher Rich for consideration for Covent Garden, and had had it rejected by both; as Donkin observes, "who can hope to get their first script accepted and produced?"[30] Without success for her first play, Brooke turned to another popular medium to reach her audience, the weekly periodical. For thirty-seven weeks (1755–6) and at a cost to the subscriber of two pence an issue, Brooke wrote the six-folio page weekly, "The Old Maid." Its essays were accounts of the life of Mary Singleton, Spinster[31] – as the header would have it – a 50-year-old woman and her experiences in London, often in the company of her niece Julia and her niece's friend, Rosara. Brooke was indeed unmarried at the time of writing "The Old Maid," but she was a relatively youthful 31 rather than Mary Singleton's more mature (and more hopeless!) 50. What is interesting in particular is that "The Old Maid" takes the theater as its subject from time to time. In one issue (Saturday, 13 March, 1756), Mary Singleton goes to see *King Lear*: "I went with three of my six critical virgins, into a party of the house, where we enjoyed the double advantage of seeing the play, and observing the audience; and I had the satisfaction of finding we were accompanied in our tears, by almost the whole house."[32] Her review provides a detailed analysis of the strengths of Mr Barry's performance in the lead role, as well as of several of the other actors. She takes the opportunity, too, to enter what was already a significant debate on which was the better *King Lear*, Shakespeare's or Nahum Tate's. "It has always been matter of great astonishment to me," writes Brooke,

> that both the houses have given *Tate's* wretched alteration of *King Lear*, the preference to *Sheakespear's* excellent original; which *Mr. Addison*, the most candid, as well as judicious of critics, thinks so infinitely preferable, as to bear no degree of comparison; and one cannot help remarking particularly, and with some surprise, that *Mr. Garrick*, who professes himself so warm an idolater of this inimitable poet . . . should yet prefer the vile adulterated cup of *Tate*, to the pure genuine draught, offered him by the master he avow's to serve with such, fervency of devotion.
>
> As to *Mr. Barry*, I think he was perfectly right to take the *Lear* which is commonly play'd, that the competition between him and *Mr. Garrick* in this trying part, may be exhibited to the public upon a fair footing; I have not yet been so fortunate as to see the latter in it, whose performance, I doubt not, is no less justly, than generally, celebrated and admired; but the advantage *Mr. Barry* has from his person: the variety of his voice, and its particular aptitude to express the differing tones which sorrow, pity, or rage, naturally produce, are of such service to him in this character.[33] (Spelling and italicization as in original)

Brooke paid dearly both for her dislike for Tate's *Lear* and for her preference for Mr Barry's performance since one or both of these opinions caused Garrick to

do as much as he could to damage her active career as a translator and novel-
ist and later, of course, he again rejected the plays she submitted.[34] It is fair to
note, however, that she did not hesitate in publishing her opinions, the risks
of which would surely have been palpable to the author herself.

In another issue of "The Old Maid," Brooke/Singleton uses her negative
review of a stock character she has seen at one theatrical production during
that week to launch into what is a quite remarkable account of her visit to a
performance of Shakespeare's *Henry VIII*. Here she is not specifically interested
in the quality of the production – although she does provide some pointed
commentary on the interpretation of the King's role "most ridiculously bur-
lesqued in the representation, and that both *Shakespear* and the monarch are
very inhumanly sacrificed; to the polite taste, and elegant distinction of the
upper gallery"[35] – but instead she perseverates on a celebrity member of the
audience, the Moroccan Ambassador. The Ambassador was clearly already a
figure of notoriety in London society and the object, apparently, of an out-of-
control orientalism, but Brooke's moment-by-moment observations of his reac-
tions to the production of *Henry VIII* are not only fascinating in her
interpretation of spectatorial response but in her own comprehension of his
"otherness":

> Whatever neglect, his Moorish Excellency might discover of this Part [that
> of the King], he paid great attention to that of Queen Catherine; but noth-
> ing seemed to affect him so strongly as Miss Young's singing, at which he
> appeared quite collected, and listened to her with all the marks of rapturous
> admiration: his whole soul appeared touched, and at the end of the song, he
> joined the house in clapping, a mark of applause I did not observe him give
> at any other time.
>
> I thought upon the King's kissing *Anna Bullen*, that he appeared surprised
> and, offended, and looked about, to observe whether others, were not
> affected in the same manner.
>
> The procession was less marked by him than I had expected, but upon the
> *Champion's* entry on horse-back, he burst into such an immoderate fit of
> laughter, as to fall quite back in his seat.
>
> At the end of the Play he rose, as if to leave the House, but looked very
> well pleased upon being informed there was more entertainment to come.[36]

This is an extraordinary account of intra-audience interaction and provides a
rare example of a spectator measuring, from both the perspectives of gender
and race, the response of another audience member. Her conclusions are typically patriotic (and, interestingly, she wishes the Ambassador might see
Mr Garrick perform in *Richard*), but at the same time compellingly invested in
understanding how the actor–audience relationship works.[37]

Around the time "The Old Maid" ceased publication, Frances Brooke married and spent time with her husband in Quebec where he had garrison duties. She then turned to writing novels and translating others from French – both of which were successful occupations for her. The various issues of "The Old Maid" were published in collected form in 1764, the year after the appearance of her first novel, which had been published anonymously. On her return to London, she became involved again in the theater – she had her opera *Rosina* produced[38] – and in 1777 published a novel, *The Excursion*, in which one of the female characters has her play rejected by Mr Garrick. How should we categorize Frances Brooke for theater history? Perhaps that the most important concern is simply that we *should* categorize her for theater history and accord her the voice she was so determined to have. As Ellen Donkin finely argues, Brooke's career was absolutely tied to Garrick's extraordinary power in the London theater scene of the moment, yet Brooke herself did not give up against what seemed like defeating odds. She worked in a number of different genres to keep her theatrical interests vibrant and available to a London public – and to keep her own "career" in theater developing. Such multifaceted interests and investments in the theater of the eighteenth century can productively complicate the labor of theater historians and shed light on the omissions of more familiar accounts of theater in this period.

Similarly, Elizabeth Inchbald, some years later, had what we would now call a "diverse career pattern" that gave her a particular purchase on the theater history of the period. As is by now well known, Inchbald had moved to London at the age of sixteen to pursue a career as an actress. She married an older actor for what turned out to be a short, but nonetheless volatile marriage of seven years until her husband died unexpectedly. Many accounts of Inchbald's life suggest that she had little success as an actress, in part at least because of an unfortunate stutter, and that she only had a career at all by touring the provincial stages with her husband. The production in 1784 of her first play, a farcical afterpiece entitled *The Mogul Tale*, is often used as the culminating evidence of her lack of success as an actor. But, as Cecelia Macheski has pointed out, the financial rewards for moving from performer to writer were substantial. As an actress, Inchbald would have earned less than £1 a week; for *The Mogul Tale*, she made 100 guineas (£105). Neither did Inchbald give up acting when her play was a success. As Donkin describes her, "She straddled two careers for well over a decade, watching plays from the wings, both as the actress waiting to make an entrance, and also as the playwright, sizing up the moment-to-moment impact of her own work and other people's."[39] Donkin notes, too, Inchbald's savvy. After such a success with her first script produced by George Colman for the Haymarket's summer season, she took her next script to Thomas Harris at Covent Garden.[40] Her career, both inside and outside the theater, was a remarkable one for a woman: she wrote two novels, more than twenty plays (most of which were successful in production), and – the subject of my interest here – was a prolific theater critic. Her will, held in the Folger Shakespeare Library, reveals that she had an estate of more than £5000.[41]

Inchbald's career in drama criticism is constituted by the 125 prefaces she wrote for plays to be included in *The British Theater*. As well as establishing a canon of dramatic literature for her period, it is important to note that publishers put together various of the plays, each with its Inchbald preface, into original volumes so that her influence was widespread across a broad readership for dramatic texts. I want to refer here to some of these prefaces to illustrate some of Inchbald's remarkable contributions to thinking about theater. First, and very briefly, I want to cite her preface to *King Lear*, if only as a postscript to Frances Brooke's own dramatic criticism of Shakespeare's famous tragedy. Inchbald reproduces the arguments concerning preference for Shakespeare's original or Tate's amendment and comments with what is surely a sentiment many of us might echo: "It is curious and consolatory for a minor critic to observe, how the great commentators on Shakespeare differ in their opinions."[42] In her preface to another Shakespeare play, *As You Like It*, she comments, "This comedy has high reputation among Shakespeare's work; and yet, on the stage, it is never attractive, except when some actress of very superior skill performs the part of Rosalind."[43] Her preface concludes with high praise ("perfect exhibition") for Mrs Jordan's rendition of the role. Here is a critic, then, who is not shy to weigh in both on the quality of Shakespeare's dramatic writing and the quality of contemporary performance. It is hardly surprising that she demonstrates time and again in these prefaces a keen eye for an actress's contributions to a play's success.

Among the many other prefaces are those attached to her own plays – one of which is *Such Things Are*, written in 1786, some two years after the success of *The Mogul Tale*. Inchbald introduces *Such Things Are* thus:

> The writer of this play was, at the time of its production, but just admitted to the honours of an authoress, and wanted experience to behold her own danger, when she attempted the subject on which the work is founded. Her ignorance was her protection. Had her fears been greater, or proportioned to her task, her success had been still more hazardous. A bold enterprize requires bold execution . . .
>
> Such was the consequence on the first appearance of this comedy – its reception was favourable beyond the usual bounds of favour bestowed upon an admired play, and the pecuniary remuneration equally extraordinary.[44]

What is quite extraordinary to my mind is Inchbald's focus, albeit with a suitably modest tone, on the cultural conditions for a playwright. Unlike her preface to *King Lear* which opens "The story of this Tragedy has been told in many an ancient ballad, and other ingenious works" – in short, like most of her prefaces, about the work itself – Inchbald's preface to *Such Things Are* takes her own experience as a professional playwright as the required context for the own play. *Such Things Are* is a play set in the East Indies and based on the life of John Howard, a philanthropic traveler. Inchbald comments on the "elevated style of conversation and manners" of two of the play's characters, Sir Luke and Lady Tremor, making the point that this style "would assuredly have been much more pleasing; especially to those who may now sit in judgment, as readers, and cold admirers of that benevolence, no longer the constant theme of enthusiastic praise, as when this drama was first produced."[45] Again, then, we see her acute understanding both of the reasons for the play's success in the theater and the changed cultural sensibilities that will inform its print readership. Any contemporary reader of the prefaces cannot fail to appreciate her acumen in reading the preferences and passions of her historical moment.

Inchbald's preface to George Colman's *A Jealous Wife* has been of particular critical interest since it brought her the wrath of a theater manager – a fate resembling the attacks on Brooke by Garrick.[46] Inchbald writes:

> This comedy, by Colman the elder, was written in his youth; and, though he brought upon the stage no less than twenty-five dramas, including those he altered from Shakespeare and other writers, subsequent to this production, yet not one of them was ever so well received by the town, or appears to have deserved so well, as "The Jealous Wife."
>
> To this observation, "The Clandestine Marriage" may possibly be an exception; but, in that work, Mr. Garrick was declared his joint labourer. It therefore appears, that Mr. Colman's talents for dramatic writing declined, rather than improved, by experience – or, at least, his ardour abated; and all works of imagination require, both in conception and execution, a degree of enthusiasm.[47]

Once again we see the professional playwright's perspective on her subject and also witness the clarity and confidence with which she offers her assessment. Not surprisingly, perhaps, the comments infuriated Colman's son, a significant dramatist in his own right and, like his father, an author of a play satirizing women writers. (His *The Female Dramatist* had been produced in 1782 and had met with such disapproval that it had been immediately canceled.)[48] Colman wrote Inchbald an angry letter asking "Is it grateful from an ingenious lady, who was originally encouraged, and brought forward, as an authoress, by that very man on whose tomb she idly plants this poisonous weed of remark, to choke the laurels which justly grace his memory?"

Inchbald replies, "Let it be understood that my obligation to your father amounted to no more than those usual attentions which every manager of a theater is supposed to confer, when he selects a novice in dramatic writing as worthy of being introduced on his stage to the public."[49] Taken against the remarks she makes of her own novice playwriting career in the preface for *Such Things Are*, this exchange tells us a great deal about the professional resilience Inchbald had both developed and assumed by this time of this exchange of letters (1808).

Theater criticism, as we see it in Brooke's periodical "The Old Maid" and Inchbald's *Remarks for the British Theatre*, provides significant and informative points of entry into the experience of theater of the second half of the eighteenth century. Yet we have hardly remembered their contributions, either as dramatists or as critics, to the history of that period. Samuel Johnson, Joseph Addison, Oliver Goldsmith, and David Garrick are much more familiar to us as its arbiters. Criticism, then, as much as the other categories touched upon here, has been remembered selectively and hierarchically with that same effect of narrowing the field of study. There is a genealogy of women critics that needs to be as familiar to theater history and contemporary historians as the trajectory of male critics we have studied for their views on the theaters of their times. We might remember here historian Bonnie Smith's pointed comment that "studies of history as a profession often follow fantasies of male historiographic parthenogenesis, of an exclusively male subject of historical truth, and of the importance of male-defined procedures and topics."[50]

I have attempted here to chart a preliminary course through some of the primary markers for the making and understanding of theater history. I have argued, I hope, that elasticizing our existing histories to accommodate more women's plays and more generally speaking, women's writing about the theater will, in the end, do little to produce a comprehensive account of how women have inhabited, informed and developed theatrical practices across time. We have broadened the scope of our scholarship through an expanded corpus of plays and a different range of documents, but how we organize, value and archive materials has not much changed. Theater history is a repository of knowledge and we need to look to its very architecture in order to effect change. Siskin argues so effectively in showing us how, for the long eighteenth century, the "Great Forgetting" became "The Great Tradition" and he reminds us, too, that remembering is only one particular task.[51] Attention, more extensively, to "how we forgot" should make us determined, as theater scholars, to seek new articulations of theater history.[52] How did we forget these women dramatists and what composition of theater history will have us, fully and appropriately, remember?

Notes

1. Gwenn Davis and Beverly A. Joyce, compilers, *Drama by Women to 1900: a Bibliography of American and British Writers* (Toronto: University of Toronto Press, 1992).
2. Allardyce Nicoll, *A History of English Drama 1660–1900*, 2nd edn (London: Cambridge University Press, 1959), 5: 157.
3. Katherine E. Kelly, ed., *Drama by Women 1880s–1930s: an International Anthology* (London: Routledge, 1996), 4.
4. Ibid., 4, 5.
5. Nicoll, *A History of English Drama 1660–1900*, 5: 207.
6. Kelly, *Drama by Women*, 7.
7. Rich described "re-vision" as "the act of looking back, of seeing with fresh eyes, of entering an old text from a new critical direction." See her essay "When We Dead Awaken: Writing as Re-vision," in *On Lies, Secrets, and Silence* (New York: W. W. Norton, 1979).
8. Recent studies aimed at revising theater history to include the dramatic production of women include S. P. Cerasano and Marion Wynne-Davies, *Renaissance Drama by Women* (London: Routledge, 1996); Margarete Rubik, *Early Women Dramatists 1550–1800* (London: Macmillan, 1998); Ellen Donkin, *Getting into the Act: Women Playwrights in London 1776–1829* (London: Routledge, 1995); John Franchescina, *Sisters of Gore: Seven Gothic Melodramas by British Women, 1790–1843* (New York and London: Routledge, 1997); Tracy C. Davis and Ellen Donkin, *Women and Playwriting in Nineteenth-Century Britain* (London: Cambridge University Press, 1999); Kelly, *Modern Drama by Women 1880s–1930s*; Elaine Aston and Janelle Reinelt, *Cambridge Companion to Twentieth-Century British Women Playwrights* (London: Cambridge University Press, 2000); and Maggie Gale, *West End Women: Women and the London Stage 1918–1962* (London: Routledge, 1996).
9. Clifford Siskin, *The Work of Writing: Literature and Social Change in Britain, 1700–1830* (Baltimore: Johns Hopkins University Press, 1998), 6.
10. Ibid.
11. Donald Mullin, *Victorian Plays: a Record of Significant Productions on the London Stage, 1837–1901* (Westport, CT: Greenwood Press, 1987).
12. Kelly, *Modern Drama by Women*, 2.
13. Lawrence Besserman, ed., *The Challenge of Periodization: Old Paradigms and New Perspectives* (New York: Garland Publishing, 1996), xii, xxiii.
14. Margaret J. M. Ezell, *Writing Women's Literary History* (Baltimore: Johns Hopkins University Press, 1993), 64.
15. Ibid.
16. I have also discussed the genre/gender axis in another essay, "Theatre History, Historiography and Women's Dramatic Writing," in Maggie B. Gale and Viv Gardner, eds, *Women, Theatre and Performance: New Histories, New Historiographies* (Manchester: Manchester University Press, 2000), 46–59; see especially 56–7.
17. Linda Kintz, *The Subject's Tragedy* (Ann Arbor: University of Michigan Press, 1992), 6.
18. Davis and Joyce, *Drama by Women to 1900*, xv.
19. Anne Shaver, ed., *The Convent of Pleasure and Other Plays* (Baltimore: Johns Hopkins University Press, 1999), 7.
20. Susan Carlson, *Women & Comedy* (Ann Arbor: University of Michigan Press, 1991), 161.
21. For a full discussion of the misapplication of "closet" dramatist to Joanna Baillie, see my "Outing Joanna Baillie," in Catherine Burroughs, ed., *Women in British Romantic Theatre* (Cambridge: Cambridge University Press, 2000), 161–77.

22. Adrienne Scullion, *Female Playwrights of the Nineteenth Century* (London: J. M. Dent, 1996), lix.
23. Joanna Baillie, *Plays on the Passions* (London, 1798), 16.
24. Joanna Baillie, *Miscellaneous Plays* (London, 1804), iii.
25. Quoted in Catherine Burroughs, *Closet Stages* (Philadelphia: University of Pennsylvania Press, 1997), 89.
26. Marvin Carlson, "Theatre Audiences and the Reading of Performance," in Thomas Postlewait and Bruce McConachie, eds, *Interpreting the Theatrical Past* (Iowa City: University of Iowa Press, 1989), 88.
27. Ellen Donkin, *Getting into the Act*. Donkin opens her book with the observation, "In 1660, Charles II issued permission for actresses to join the legitimate theater. It has been a common error in theater history to assume by extrapolation that women were thereby also welcomed into other areas of theatre practice, particularly play-writing. They were not" (1).
28. Quoted in Davis and Joyce, *Plays by Women to 1900*, xvii.
29. Ibid.
30. Donkin, *Getting into the Act*, 41.
31. Brooke's clever title for her periodical's heroine predates Bridget Jones's nomenclature for the unmarried by about 250 years.
32. "The Old Maid", No. XVIII, 13 March 1756: 103 (in microform *Early English Newspapers*).
33. "The Old Maid," No. XVIII, 13 March 1756: 105.
34. Donkin covers Garrick's rage at Brooke in some detail. See her *Getting into the Act*, 44–56.
35. "The Old Maid," No. XXVI, 154. Brooke continues: "If it were not for exceeding too much the limits of my Paper, I could point out many abuses of the like nature, which have encreased upon us so much of late, that 'tis almost impossible to attend the Theatres, with the expectation of receive pleasure from some parts of the performance, without the certainty of suffering equal disgust from others" (154).
36. Ibid., 155.
37. Ibid., 156.
38. It took Brooke more than ten years to get *Rosina* onto the stage. She finally achieved a production by going into partnership with a woman friend to manage the King's Opera House and staging *Rosina* there. Once produced, *Rosina* was a great success and within three years of first production, there were eleven editions in print; see Donkin, *Getting into the Act*, 50–2. Further information about Frances Brooke and her opera *Rosina* can be found in the *Dictionary of National Biography*, 1328–9.
39. Donkin, *Getting into the Act*, 114.
40. Ibid., 120.
41. See Cecelia Macheski's introduction to the collection of Elizabeth Inchbald's *Remarks for the British Theatre* (New York: Scholars Facsimiles, 1990), 7, for further discussion of the playwright's financial achievements.
42. Elizabeth Inchbald, *Remarks for the British Theatre*, page 5 of the remarks on *King Lear*.
43. Ibid., page 3 of the remarks on *As You Like It*.
44. Ibid., page 3 of the remarks on *Such Things Are*.
45. Ibid., page 4 of the remarks on *Such Things Are*.
46. For an insightful comparison of the Brooke/Garrick and Inchbald/Colman relationships, see Donkin, *Getting into the Act*, 120.
47. Inchbald, *Remarks for the British Theatre*, page 3 of the remarks on *A Jealous Wife*.
48. See Donkin, *Getting into the Act*, 66–7.

49. Both letters are cited in Donkin, *Getting into the Act*, 128–9.
50. Bonnie G. Smith, *The Gender of History: Men, Women, and Historical Practice* (Cambridge, MA: Harvard University Press, 1998), 13.
51. Siskin, *The Work of Writing*, 195.
52. Ibid., 225 for an important connection to scholarly responsibilities in light of the new technologies which are, of course, changing how we archive work in radical and unpredictable ways.

5

Photography, Theater, Mnemonics; or, Thirteen Ways of Looking at a Still

Barbara Hodgdon

Speaking of how an image or structured complex of images initiates his theatrical work, Athol Fugard locates the starting point for *Sizwe Bansi is Dead* (1972) in his fascination with a studio photograph of a black man with a cigarette in one hand and a pipe in the other.[1] Fugard's play opens in a photography studio – a "strongroom of dreams" situated, not incidentally, next to a funeral parlor – where Styles, the aptly named photographer, explains his trade in "Reference Books, Passports, Weddings, Engagements, Birthday Parties and Parties" as "put[ting] down . . . on paper the dreams and hopes of my people – people who would be forgotten, if it weren't for Styles – so that even their children's children will remember a man. . . . 'This was our Grandfather' . . . and say his name."[2] As a photographer, Styles is also director, set designer and prop man. When a new patron, Robert Zwelinzima, who is actually Sizwe Bansi, arrives for a card, he casts the man as the future director of the Ford factory where Styles once worked as a laborer and poses him, first, as in the photograph remembered by Fugard; then, in a "movie" which shows him walking, as in Eadweard Muybridge's stop-motion studies, against a backdrop of the "City of the Future" – a snap destined for his wife, whom Styles imagines saying to their children, "Look, your Daddy's coming!" Prefaced by an explanatory letter to Bansi's wife, the play then dramatizes how Bansi's photograph, pasted into the actual dead Robert's passbook, gives him an identity that not only saves him from being jailed and deported back to the homeland but gives him access to a job. In staging the scene of the photograph – its indexical relation to its subject, its similarity to the relic's peculiarly erotic and metonymic attachment to the dead or dying body it represents, its mnemonic function, its schizophrenic nature, its flexible meanings, depending on the context in which it is found, the language which accompanies it, and the changing significance it accrues, its ability to lie like truth[3] – Fugard's play provides an allegory of the evidentiary politics and problematics surrounding the theater still, and offers a map for the history I want to tell.

Whether focused on the artistic ambitions of the medium, including only those genres which complement a formalist art-historical narrative, on its phenomenological characteristics, or on the institutional and historical practices and circumstances that invest photographs with specific relations of power, nearly all histories of photography open by attempting to define, or redefine, the photograph. Despite its existence for nearly 200 years, the photograph has a liminal status, and that is especially true of the theatrical photograph. Largely excluded from the critical gaze, the theatrical still constitutes a kind of abject entity: a vernacular of interest primarily, perhaps exclusively, to theater historians, it suffers a form of split consciousness which parallels the split in pictorial representation between fine and commercial art; ambiguous, composite, it disturbs identity, does not respect borders.[4] Yet, as in Fugard's play, the point on which all critical histories agree is that a photograph plays with death.[5] Associating photography with theater, Roland Barthes marks both as economies of death whose subject is disappearance; indeed, an early Kodak slogan – "Secure the shadow ere the substance fade" – might well serve as the theatrical photographer's mantra.[6] Although Peggy Phelan writes that performance leaves no left-overs,[7] the theatrical still is just such a left-over, the visible remains of what is no longer visible, a fragment that steals theater, stills it – and dis-tills it. Considered as performance in pieces, the theater photograph undertakes a visual conversation with performance: silent, impoverished, partial, it seizes appearances, violently severs them from their original context; inseparable from and traversed by the lived experience of theater, it requires anecdote, narrative, to supplement it.[8] Moreover, the theatrical still has a double history. Before and during the run of a performance, it takes life as a commodity, teaser or provocation; only when the performance is no longer "up" does the photograph reach the archive, where, signifying the death of the theatrical event, its materiality is less factural than textual, closer to written imagery than to painting. In the archive, too, one holds photographs in one's hands like pages,[9] links them to Shakespeare's text and to writing, to other pages, imagines a connection between a still and its "origin," searches for an edge between photograph and performance that will "push" the aura of theater into re-being, into consciousness.

My project here, which focuses primarily but not exclusively on stills from Royal Shakespeare Company (RSC) and English Shakespeare Company (ESC) productions,[10] is also double – in several ways. As in Barthes's *Camera Lucida* – written, significantly, on the ruins of structural linguistics – I want to oscillate between close looking and close reading, between a perhaps arbitrary, affective reading (Barthes's *punctum* – "what I add to the photograph and *what is nonetheless already there*") and one which, passing through knowledge and culture (Barthes's *studium*),[11] involves specific institutional currencies, sanctions and politics of literacy. And since I have seen most of the performances these stills "document" – itself an unstable, untheorized, dubious term – such a local history inevitably draws in my own memories. After all, not only do pictures constitute the stuff of memory – the way in which the brain internally displays thoughts to itself – but thinking itself involves scenography, the staging of perceptions into the spectacle of ideas. "Memory," writes Walter Benjamin, "is not an instrument for exploring the past but its theatre."[12] Writing at a moment when the physicality of the archive is fast being superceded by virtual domains, I will be looking backward as well as characterizing changes now taking place, producing a sort of time capsule that maps the DNA of the theatrical still and the kinds of ideological work it performs. Setting the evidentiary nature of the photograph into several different modes of production, I want to explore its status in relation to documentary practices as well as its use-value for promoting, advertising and commodifying performers, performances and, in particular, the work of the RSC. Although I will be raising other questions along the way, several are crucial to keep in mind: What constitutes "good looking"? How do theatrical stills constitute a "usable past" for doing theater history?[13] And what impact will recent shifts in RSC photographic practices have on historians' ability to reconstruct a performance past?

I want to begin outside the theater, with a photograph of Salvador Dali and Olivier's Richard III showing two fakes, two poses: "artist-at-work" and "actor-as-character" – a metapicture that stages "theater," or a trace of it, in the process of becoming something else (Fig. 1). A kind of *Las Meninas* of the theatrical still in which the relations of painter, actor-in-role and beholder gesture towards the interplay between painting, theater and photography, the photograph also models the doubleness which reappears in Dali's painting: the mirror image and the image of Olivier, straight on, that Dali sees but that the photograph does not reveal – the one evoking Renaissance portraiture (Dali imitating Titian or Bronzino), the other a more romantic, slightly diabolical half-face joined to Richard's at the lip, which itself appears double, so that the idea of voice ("Shakespeare" speaking through Olivier) appears as a sign of Richard which, repeated in the battling warriors and horses on the plain below, incorporates one of his most famous lines as image.

From here, it is an easy leap to Angus McBean's photo-paintings, many of which, belying his career as a mask-maker, offer metacriticisms of performance. Consider, for instance, the (in)famous "dirty still" of *Othello*, showing Olivier's black make-up smudged on Maggie Smith's cheek, betraying "theater" even as it freeze-frames its most revealing perspective (Fig. 2). A swanky studio image, its controlled illumination, sharp contrasts, subtle gradations of black-and-white values, exploitation of highlights and shadows give both performers an incandescent glamor, turning them into near-religious icons.[14] Looking at this or at any of McBean's images, does it matter that he himself has blocked the action to serve the photograph? Or, as in this still of *Troilus and Cressida*'s spying scene (Fig. 3), with its velvety blacks, eloquent varieties of depth, and painterly *chiaroscuro*,

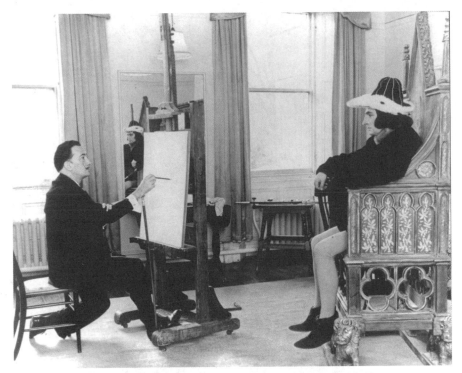

Fig. 1   Salvador Dali and Laurence Olivier, costumed as Richard III, c.1950–4.

that it results from combining two separate images?[15] Here, the photograph not only calls attention to the erotics of looking but, by suturing in the viewer as Thersites, the figure absent from representation, participates in a theater of its own[16] in which the idea of *taking* a picture – in itself an idiom of exploitation – erases the abyss between theater and its audience, puts the viewer inside the proscenium arch, capable of *making*, or re-making, the scene of looking.

If what appears in McBean's stills is the desire to reincarnate theater as high art,[17] theater haunted by the ghost of painting, as the boundary between the photograph and other performative media has become increasingly porous, the one absorbing the other, it is the still that is doing the haunting. As in any one of a number of Cindy Sherman's *Untitled Film Stills*, where the woman's posture and expression – wary, waiting – imply an "other" just offstage, Joe Cocks's photograph of Sinead Cusack as Portia arrests a moment of performance that, by vacating the space between viewer and subject, locks them together, overcoming boundaries between person and person (Fig. 4). Simultaneously photograph and performance – or, like Sherman's stills, performance art – the image distills and intensifies, elicits inner speech even as it speaks for its odd or interesting self. Writing of how a photograph is most subversive "when it is

Fig. 2 Laurence Oliver as Othello, Maggie Smith as Desdemona. *Othello*, John Dexter (dir.), National Theatre 1964.

pensive, when it thinks," Barthes speaks of unsought-for details outside the photographer's "intention" or the viewer's expectation as "pricks" or "bruises" akin to memory's tendency to overwhelm us occasionally with its "unauthorized" images.[18] Cusack's portrait of Portia is just such a "thinking still," capturing an instant of performance just beyond the Shakespearean logos – what the text intuits but does not say *directly*, in which the meanings of the still make an inchoate connection to the text but also perform alongside it.

So far, I have been indulging in "deeply layered" looking, a practice not unlike that of Clifford Geertz, who famously turned events, ceremonies and gestures into "thick descriptions."[19] The ideal lying behind such an ethnography is to bring an event or ritual *to* the viewer, to position her where it occurred and, if possible, to generate the sense of a "purified" reality. Yet the ethnographer also pays attention to how a particular image is produced and mediated, to its reflexive turn. With that in mind, consider these stills – historical traces with an uncertain status but nonetheless akin to the "thinking still" in having an edge at which "good look-

Fig. 3 Laurence Harvey as Troilus, Muriel Pavlov as Cressida. *Troilus and Cressida*, Glen Byam Shaw (dir.), Shakespeare Memorial Theatre 1954.

ing" is engaged but also frustrated. The first, of F. R. Benson's 1910 *Taming of the Shrew*, was once thought to reflect a Stratford performance; recently, however, Russell Jackson has argued, citing its framing, that it represents a still from a never-released film (Fig. 5).[20] Or take Laurence Burns's somewhat apocryphal photograph of Michael Bogdanov's 1978 *Shrew*, shot not at a dress rehearsal, Burns's usual and preferred practice, but during a set-up photo call where key moves were staged for retakes (Fig. 6). Until Paola Dionisotti remembered it, Burns failed to notice that Kate should not have been wearing her white cap; intriguingly, he imagined that perhaps Bogdanov (as he had done elsewhere) had written in a line for Jonathan Pryce's Petruchio commanding her to replace the cap. Even though other photographs of the moment exist without the cap problem, this is the "best" frame among them – that rare image in which, according to Burns, "the energy of the stage work continues glowing in a supposedly 'still' image."[21] Similarly, a photograph of the Battle of Agincourt from Matthew Warchus's 1994 *Henry V*, taken at a general photo call where only selected scenes were staged, shows scribes seated at either side of the stage platform, recording the battle for history; yet shortly after previews, the scribes were no longer there.[22]

Despite their (relative) distance from the "truth" of performance, I am especially drawn to the spontaneity of such theatrical accidents: I liken them to the

Fig. 4 Sinead Cusack as Portia. *The Merchant of Venice*, John Barton (dir.), Royal Shakespeare Company 1981.

drawing or cartoon which, because it bears evidence of work-in-progress, is equally or even more intriguing than the finished painting. Given that *any* theatrical still is suspected of being "subtle, false and treacherous" – a version of the Platonic rhetoric of visual corruption that longs for mythical purity and is obsessed with absolute indexical value – how might we theorize such images as part of a "usable past" for theater history? "Look here upon this picture, and on this," says Hamlet, the expert on counterfeits, who also claims, "There is nothing either good or bad, but thinking makes it so." As with the notion of "good" or "bad" texts, each representing variant readings, judgement rests on the arbitrary designations by which we locate value. What do theater historians want? To put the point in blunt Freudian terms, is it a penis or a phallus we're after? *Only* to capture the "look of the play" *as performed*? Yet if what we seek is performative, or "Shakespearean," force, why not also document its labor, the processes through which it comes into being? Rather than thinking

Fig. 5 Constance Benson as Katherina, F. R. Benson as Petruchio. *The Taming of the Shrew*, F. R. Benson (dir.), Shakespeare Memorial Theatre 1910.

Fig. 6 Paola Dionisotti as Katherina, Jonathan Pryce as Petruchio. *The Taming of the Shrew*, Michael Bogdanov (dir.), Royal Shakespeare Company 1978.

of the theatrical still as an epistemological problem, I want to argue for including such "stol'n and surreptitious copies" of performance – copy texts rather than "true originalls" – within the realm of evidence. For, as Walter Benjamin writes, "To articulate the past historically does not mean to recognize it . . . It means to seize hold of memory as it flashes up at a moment of danger."[23]

Suppose that we accept that risk. What difference might it make to reconceptualizing theater history? And what might such a shift mean for choosing theatrical stills and for their status within the book, the essay? Presently, it is the rare book, the even rarer (as yet unwritten?) essay which documents *both* performance "drafts" and images of "the real thing" (keeping in mind, of course, that it's *theater* we're talking about). Instead, what is most frequently reproduced as a stand-in for performance is an iconic image: used in a unilinear way to illustrate an argument, to which it bears a tautological relation, such a photograph becomes merely a visual footnote to narrative.[24] Take this still of Jack Cade's rebellion from the ESC's *Wars of the Roses* (Fig. 7). Showing off the eclectic style, hip one-offs, and breezy energy which, collapsing "chronicle

Fig. 7   Jack Cade's Rebellion. Michael Pennington as Cade, Jack Carr as Dick the Butcher. *Henry VI House of York, The Wars of the Roses*, Michael Bogdanov and Michael Pennington (dirs.), English Shakespeare Company 1988.

play" into collage and pastiche, brought the histories screaming and shouting into postmodernist stage history, it marks the ESC's project *as* rebellion – that is, the choice of still speaks an (admittedly ideological) performance within another ideological frame. Moreover, this particular image appears so regularly, has become so famously familiar, that one doesn't *see* it: it's just "there," like the wedding photo or casual portrait that sits on the dresser or piano. Equally familiar, equally unnoticed, is this image of Brook's *Dream*, which, given that performance's seminal position, has taken on the characteristics of a near-religious relic of mid-twentieth-century modernist theatrical practice (Fig. 8). Although it would be difficult to imagine an edition or stage history that did *not* include a still of Brook's production, this, or one similar to it, effectively blots out any others.

Consider, now, this less familiar image of the aristocrats and workingmen-actors, facing each other just after the *Pyramus and Thisbe* play (Fig. 9). Just as museum shops rarely have a postcard of *the* painting I want to bring home, when examining contacts, I always seem to desire a shot that's not been "taken" and wind up settling for another. This image, occurring close to the ending, serves as a mnemonic trace that triggers a "flashbulb memory" – that mixture of personal circumstance and public event held in memory, termed by cognitive theory the "Now Print" mechanism[25] – which radiates out from the photograph to bring back the sensory and intellectual joy I experienced when, bounding from the stage, the players joined the audience in celebration of their

Fig. 8 Alan Howard as Oberon/Theseus, Sarah Kestelman as Titania/Hippolyta, John Kane as Puck/Philostrate. *A Midsummer Night's Dream*, Peter Brook (dir.), Royal Shakespeare Company 1970.

Fig. 9   Workingmen and aristocrats. *A Midsummer Night's Dream*, Peter Brook (dir.), Royal Shakespeare Company 1970.

work. Or take this stunningly abstract still from the ESC's *Wars*, also tied to anecdotal memory (Fig. 10). The photographer, Laurence Burns, who was also one of the players, recalls a battle cue where, in full knitted chain mail and tabard, he started a sound tape, fired several gun blanks, shouted, let off an explosion, doused the stage with smoke guns, fought and killed somebody, dragged off the body and, changing his tabard, re-entered to re-set the stage, getting back to the tape machine in time to make sure the metal strip had stopped the cue and to re-cue it.[26] Reminiscent of New Historicism's famous (or infamous) privileging of the anecdote – the marginal made symbolically central – both instances point to how narrative, whether memory, anecdote or gossip, not only plays a prominent part in theatrical recall but always already invades the still – is swallowed into and interiorized within it, indivisible from it.[27]

Such issues, of course, point to how theatrical photographs, attesting to what at one time spoke for itself, are spoken, through historical and ideological frames as well as through personal and institutional agendas, open as well as covert. No image is ever neutral or transparent but is locked within domains of speaking and writing: detached from the space of the theater as a social site, the still carries its own (textual) politics on its back. As William Saroyan remarked, "One picture is worth a thousand words, but only if you look at the picture and say or think the thousand words."[28] In the case of the Shakespearean still, the proof of the picture lies not in itself as much as in how it conforms to the

Fig. 10 Battle. *The Wars of the Roses*, Michael Bogdanov and Michael Pennington (dirs.), English Shakespeare Company 1988.

(Shakespearean) discourse that engendered it. Among several captioning regimes, perhaps the most common – resembling ethnographic protocols such as the women of X tribe perform the ritual of the New Moon at Y place, Z time – identifies play, production date, director, set designer, actors-as-characters and, occasionally, photographer and archive. But when, as for this image of *2 Henry IV*'s crown scene (Fig. 11), the caption – "My due from thee is this imperial crown" – gives the still a Shakespearean alibi, citation references – and ventriloquizes – the photograph, and only qualified (textual) experts read its lips.[29] Representing a rhetoric of mourning for absent text, such captions not only "innocent" the still of its theatrical labor but underscore a deep mistrust of the image as image, perhaps an even deeper mistrust of theater itself. What captioning protocols might we devise that, while acknowledging how image, caption and text are embedded in a tripod of meaning,[30] would accord the image a more privileged status? What I am advocating, of course, involves shifting away from a critical practice in which textuality dominates performance and where the still has value only as it re-members Shakespeare. For such a practice marks the theatrical still as "a memory in the framework of forgetting,"[31] where its "real" subject – performance, and performance-in-process – becomes effaced. One way out of that bind is to ask not what a still expresses or records but what it *does*, not how an image authenticates "Shakespeare" but how it was

Fig. 11   Richard Burton as Prince Hal, Harry Andrews as Henry IV. *2 Henry IV*, Michael Redgrave (dir.), Shakespeare Memorial Theatre 1951.

articulated (and by whom), how it articulates an argument – whose argument? – and under what conditions.[32]

I will return to these issues in a moment, particularly in relation to how stills circulate theater history and are (textually) re-figured to address various constituencies. But I want to arrive there by way of a kind of photo album of performance photography which maps a "then to now" history-in-miniature of image-types. First, an image of the set for Bill Alexander's 1992 *Shrew*, the stage as memory space, exhibiting the designer's work (Fig. 12).[33] Second, a far from "perfect" still, again from Bogdanov's *Shrew*, of the set in the process of being demolished, it tropes a production which, at the outset, put an end to Italianate romantic realism, (literally) clearing a space in which to deconstruct the play (Fig. 13). Next, two full-stage photographs of the ending of the ESC's *Henry V* (Figs. 14, 15): taken from slightly different angles, they show two Henrys, Michael Pennington and John Dougall, and two Choruses, John Woodvine and Barry Stanton, in different costumes, marking the changing look of performance as it travels, over time, from 1986 to 1989, as well as suggesting how the still functions as a scene of encounter and interpretation. For a slightly different

Fig. 12 Set design by Tim Goodchild for *The Taming of the Shrew*, Bill Alexander (dir.), Royal Shakespeare Company 1992.

Fig. 13 Destruction of Chris Dyer's set for *The Taming of the Shrew*, Michael Bogdanov (dir.), Royal Shakespeare Company 1978.

perspective, consider this shot of a light cue from Adrian Noble's *Edward IV*, part of *The Plantagenets* (1989) – one of 160 images taken by a lighting engineer with non-professional equipment from the glassed-in director's booth at the back of the RST's dress circle (Fig. 16). When seen collectively, these capture theater as a temporal experience, providing insight not only into lighting design but also into the spatial poetics of performance, especially as seen from a "God's-eye" perspective other than that recorded by the full-stage photograph, usually taken from the stalls.[34] So, too, looking at a sequence of stills taken by Joe Cocks of the penultimate moments of Terry Hands's 1975 *2 Henry IV* enables a viewer to reconstruct the evolution in space of a narrative turning point as well as to register the actors' work – the physical attitudes and movement of their bodies, the shifts of emotion crossing their faces.[35] Here, as with a series of some twenty stills of Ben Kingsley and David Suchet during *Othello*'s temptation scene, viewing generates an illusion of proximity to performance: shifting from one image to another transforms acting into looking, and the shape and movement of the text into the conditions of the photograph.[36]

Fig. 14 Michael Pennington as Henry V, John Woodvine as Chorus, Francesca Ryan as Princess Katherine. *Henry V, The Wars of the Roses*, Michael Bogdanov and Michael Pennington (dirs.), English Shakespeare Company 1986.

Although the lighting-cue image is primarily a curiosity, this journey from uninhabited set to iconic image to performance work charts a range of graphic representation that is fast disappearing from view in the RSC archives – at least since the late 1990s. Moreover, where once one could examine ten or twelve contact sheets, now only three to five exist. Now, too, the RSC is on the way to eliminating the open photo call, hiring one "official" photographer and (since 1998) retaining copyright over all stills.[37] As a corollary, not only the number of stills but also the kinds of images taken has undergone a see-ing change. Instead of "landscapes" – RSC publicity's term for stills which record *mise-en-scène* – the focus is on shots of actors "in" character that cut out a single (or more than one) presence, a kind of photographic characterology married to star presence. In this not entirely new scene of theater photography, what is of primary interest is the photogeneity of subjectivity, interiority and internal temporality. Concentrating on being and the body (or parts of it) and all but eliminating action, this still – from Steven Pimlott's 2001 *Hamlet* (Fig. 17) – defines character not (as in the full-stage photo) as a narrative event but as a sort of somatically based emanation, a humanist necromancy.[38] Here, the close-up, photography's access to essence, dispossesses full bodily presence or any surrounding contextual detail; emphasizing eyes, faces and absorptive

Fig. 15 John Dougall as Henry V, Barry Stanton as Chorus, Francesca Ryan as Princess Katherine. *Henry V, The Wars of the Roses,* Michael Bogdanov and Michael Pennington (dirs.), English Shakespeare Company 1989.

emotional energy, it searches to make visible the invisible. Speaking a physical, concrete visual language seemingly independent of speech, the silent image nonetheless instantiates it, re-*sounds* text: in these examples, it is not difficult to discern what just has been or is about to be said; no caption is necessary to stabilize or fix appearance or meaning. And, in a curious throwback to early twentieth-century *carte-de-visite* images – cheap, quick, multiply produced, part of a burgeoning portrait industry, as in this postcard of Dorothy Green's 1912 Cleopatra (Fig. 18) – the spell of actor as character reappears in this recent card of Sam West as Hamlet (Fig. 19), "blasted with ecstasy," ready to travel as commodity, a collectible relic of theatrical culture.[39]

If the postcard image circulates as a teaser of actor-in-role, one of the major ways in which photographic images connect see-ers and seeing within a sensory web of cultural signification is the souvenir programme. Here, the still becomes part of a "Shakespearean state apparatus" which, by recycling past productions as well as representing the present performance, not only sells cul-

Fig. 16 Light cue. *Edward IV, The Plantagenets*, Adrian Noble (dir.), Royal Shakespeare Company 1988.

tural heritage but also manipulates desire and the play of imagination, sets the "new" in relation to a canonical master-narrative of the play's performance history. This double-page spread from the programme for Michael Boyd's 1996 *Much Ado About Nothing*, for instance, includes eleven stills symptomatic of the "look of the play" spanning forty years – Shakespearean memory work conveyed through images of performing bodies (Fig. 20). Kathy Elgin, who for years has composed programmes, views such images as underlining the RSC's variety and enhancing Company identity and as a means of showing off the often considerable progress of actors from relative Shakespearean obscurity to TV stardom. Over the past five to six years, however, fewer programmes have included stills of past productions, partly because of a general sense that the RSC, desiring to escape the "aura" of heritage, should be reflecting its present rather than fetishizing its past, partly because many (generally younger) directors wish their productions to stand alone without the preconceptions generated by the sight of performance past.[40] Indeed, Elgin conjectures that Michael Boyd might prefer to have no programme at all, so if you have this *Much Ado* programme, hang on to it, for it represents both a protocol that is currently being dismantled and an instance of policy – and political economy – in the making. Previously, rehearsal shots usually were replaced with production stills

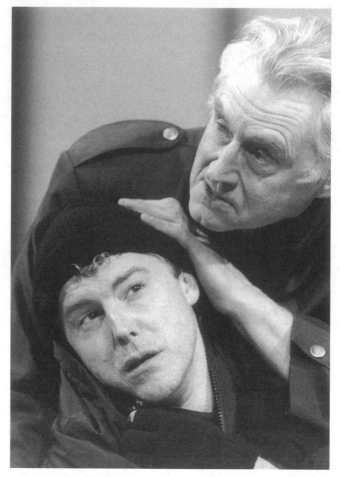

Fig. 17   Sam West as Hamlet, Christopher Good as Ghost. *Hamlet*, Steven Pimlott (dir.), Royal Shakespeare Company 2001.

after a programme's initial printing, but this one is comprised primarily of rehearsal stills – a move that, by deliberately creating both an inadequate descriptive system and an inadequate mnemonics, seems designed to ensure that *performance itself* is unique, un-representable: its presence occurs *only* in the theater.[41]

Whereas the rehearsal shots for Boyd's *Much Ado*, each captioned with a quotation, focus attention only on actors in the process of *making* characters, the programme for Steven Pimlott's *Hamlet*, incorporating *both* rehearsal and production stills, marks a different sort of visual encounter with performance

Fig. 18 Dorothy Green as Cleopatra. *Antony and Cleopatra*, F. R. Benson (dir.), Shakespeare Memorial Theatre 1912.

by setting rehearsal shots beside plot synopses, source materials or scholarly essays – Germaine Greer on "Hamlet and Heroic Doubt" and Frank Kermode's "New Words for a New Theatre" – and positioning production stills on a dou-ble-page spread, accompanied by three brief quotations. Both instances set up

Fig. 19 Sam West as Hamlet. Postcard promoting *Hamlet*, Steven Pimlott (dir.), Royal Shakespeare Company 2001.

a visual–verbal dialectic, suturing image and discourse, seeable and sayable, which serves not merely as a structuring of knowledge and power but as a key to the relation of theory and history – in this case, a relation between Pimlott's reading and the performance in history.[42] Although any programme, according to Elgin, is an attempt to get as much of "the truth" about a play and its performance into as brief a space as possible, and although her position as programme compositor allows her to re-dream the performance, re-envisioning it much as she chooses, usually in consultation with the director, this one, almost entirely choreographed and captioned by Pimlott, represents an unusual case of directorial control over charting both spatial dynamics and the exchange and resistance between still and language (Fig. 21). For one thing, he wanted the programme to have a space-y, airy look that would reflect and show off the newly reshaped RST stage – formal, white-walled, bare of scenery, focusing attention on actors and the spaces between them. Choosing stills, he and Elgin looked for images representing key moments or emblematic tropes – intriguingly enough, precisely the strategy of silent Shakespeare films[43] – as well as for those such as the one of Hamlet and the skull which, recognizable but not clichéd – would serve to redefine the play through performance. Here, the semiotics of the page, with blocks of white space between individual stills, tells

Fig. 20 Souvenir Programme for *Much Ado About Nothing*, Michael Boyd (dir.), Royal Shakespeare Company 1996.

Fig. 21 Souvenir programme for *Hamlet*, Steven Pimlott (dir.), Royal Shakespeare Company 2001.

the story of the remodeled stage; even more intriguing, however, is that, although the selected shots chart moments of heightened revelation, they are not arranged in narrative sequence. Here, a viewer must become her own Scheherazade,[44] make her own connections and speculations, piece together her own *Hamlet*. Here, too, although the citations – "What should such fellows as I do crawling between earth and heaven?"; "You would pluck out the heart of my mystery"; "Like sweet bells jangled . . . Blasted with ecstasy" – give the photo collage a (directorial-authorial) voice, they do not operate according to usual captioning protocols, over-reading the image *as* text, directing a viewer to a particular or preferred meaning. Instead, they function as threads on which the stills themselves are strung, floating among the images as touchstones, mantras, Brechtian banners.

Such a programmatic display marks an unusual opportunity for "good looking" in which photograph takes precedence over text. But once the still becomes caught up in publicity processes, performance, emancipated from its time-based ritual, gets appropriated "as itself" for the politics of advertising. Consonant with the shift away from the full-stage images I described earlier, emphasis falls on commodifying "the new" and capitulates to the (re)newed fashion for character and for privileging star actors. Here, two major strategies come into play. First and foremost is the shot publicity calls "The Image": a marketing-point still circulated on a leaflet that is made as soon as, if not before, the play goes into rehearsal, "The Image" also appears on hoardings outside the theater or, as for Pimlott's *Hamlet*, on a poster (Fig. 22). Featuring Sam West as theatrical property,[45] this photo represents quintessential Hamlet, his direct look at the viewer mapping a connection through the optical image between see-er and seen, his gaze locking the two together, emblematic of how the spell of this particular character generates an immediate desire for self-identification. A stunning image – in which, incidentally, the pose, with upright dagger, cites the poster for Zeffirelli's 1990 film – it mis-represents the performance, where a pistol, not a dagger, was Hamlet's weapon of choice. After West himself called attention to its inaccuracy, the image was replaced, for the production's London run, with another, equally emblematic, of Hamlet and his alter ego, Yorick's skull – which was displayed on the Underground, complete with laudatory blurbs (Fig. 23). A second strategy also aims at widespread coverage. This "showcase" of images for the 2001–2 season, chosen by the publicity director in consultation with the productions' directors, shows those stills made available on-line for press use (Fig. 24). Although "landscape" images do appear (primarily for *Alice in Wonderland*, though with intimations of *mise-en-scène* elsewhere), much preferred are close, tight shots that generate the most possible information – portraits of key actors in poses revealing "telling expressions and telling attitudes"; "artistic" images that tell the story, illustrate themes. *Twelfth Night*, for instance, features two images of Sir Toby and com-

Fig. 22   Sam West as Hamlet. Poster for *Hamlet*, Steven Pimlott (dir.), Royal Shakespeare Company 2001.

pany, one with Fabian, one with Sir Andrew, and others of Viola and Orsino, Feste, and Guy Henry's Malvolio: clearly, the tropes for sale are comedy and romance. In this pastiche, performance gets condensed into an easy-to-read format, a theatrical *USA Today*. Much like the jacket cover on a bodice-ripper, these images function as pictorial inducements, means of arousing enough prurient curiosity to justify spending money on a ticket.

Are such stills "false" to the visual truth of performance? Perhaps so; perhaps not. Yet since they do work to create a sustainable desire for theater, performance and Shakespeare, to see in them only a commercial diminishment is to desire to live in aesthetic exile, seeking sanctuary in a realm where theater – and theater history – might exist outside a highly competitive entertainment marketplace. Such an attempt to avoid attaching a merchandising stigma to theatrical stills indulges in a form of tacit cultural criticism tied to Fredric

Fig. 23 Sam West as Hamlet. Poster for *Hamlet*, Steven Pimlott (dir.), Royal Shakespeare Company 2001.

Jameson's desire to annihilate capitalist production, shot through as it is by an irrational commodity system generating worthless and superfluous goods.[46] Yet, given the increased emphasis on advertising which repositions the still according to publicity use-value rather than as a means of documenting either performance or its "final product," and given current practices in which the RSC empowers itself to define which images of theatrical culture will circulate, to make such nice distinctions is to close off access to what is an already shrinking storehouse of performance memory.

Clearly, we are at a moment when the paradigms that have governed the kinds of stills taken and the ways in which they are archived and manipulated

Fig. 24 2001–2 Season Press Publicity Image Showcase, Royal Shakespeare Company.

are undergoing rapid change: indeed, the "fate" of the theatrical still repli-
cates, in little, other institutional changes currently underway at the RSC. In
representing its work to the press, the Company is already transmitting
theatrical stills electronically; like Bill Gates, who in 1995 bought the sixteen
million images constituting the Bettmann archives and now sells electronic
reproduction rights, the RSC plans to digitize thousands of performance
images and is seeking grants and alliances with American universities to do
so.[47] Since photographs themselves eventually will still be archived and
on view, however, there probably is no danger of being reduced to someone
like *Blade Runner's* Deckard, whose unexpected, out-of-place piano is covered
with sepia and black-and-white photographs of unknown women, signs of
an unspoken nostalgia for a "lost" original. If, however, we accept the premise that the forms themselves encode the history of their production, then
transferring them to another medium contradicts the assumption that the
photograph is "the product of a distinctive complex of materials, labor, and
mentality." Even the photographs as reproduced in this book, for example,
constitute surrogate versions, varying (among other qualities and features)
in size, selective detail, texture, and color. Implicit here is not only the accuracy and value of the photograph as historical evidence, but the question of
authority in terms of changes made to a putative "original" – an issue which,
not incidentally, is analogous to the relations between dramatic texts and their
performances, diverse "imprints" taken from a "master" model. Still, T.S.
Eliot's concept of the objective correlative hints at how we may come to traf-
fic less in specific manifestations of a theatrical still than in the *formulae* for
their realization, a change in which *hard* evidence – the print, the negative, or
both – metamorphoses into *soft*ware.[48] Moreover, questions remain about
how, to whom, and at what if any cost the RSC's proposed digital
Wunderkammer of Shakespearean data will be made available: in all probability, what a consumer eventually will lease may well be something like the performance rights to a digitized score.[49] As Benjamin might have it, capital has
here reached the limits of its own logic in a move which erases all aura of
authenticity, replacing it, once and for all, with the glitter of reproducibility.
Digitized, the theatrical still becomes a quotation – no longer in possession of
its author, it has only the authority of use. Like Baudrillard's simulacrum, it is
a sign of a sign, a kind of replicant or clone that, arguably, puts theatrical presence under erasure through a process of genetic engineering, further troubling
the problem of deciphering whatever "truth" values burr onto the theatrical
still.[50] Yet however overtly fictional, because the digital image has the capa-
bility of returning authorial production to the whim of the hand, it perhaps
(again, arguably) approaches, at least in spirit, the creative processes of art. Just
as Deckard, in another scene, by electronically enhancing a photographic
image, moves across the terrain of externalized memory to transform its visual

field from two-dimensional photographic space to the present-tense modality of cinema,[51] the next step might be a video game played with theatrical stills, incorporating interactive re-performance[52] – or even something like an *RSC Classic* – a video or DVD preserving highlights from theater history.

At this potentially post-photography moment which is not yet beyond photography, it is certainly the case that such new imaging processes will result in a dramatic transformation of the meaning and value of the photographic image. But just as Sizwe Bansi's image, transplanted into Robert Zwelinzima's passbook, enabled him to survive and to find work, so too with the theatrical still. As theater historians, we will need to revisualize our ideas of what constitutes a "virtuous" image, of what display practices constitute "good looking,"[53] of how to rethink the consequences of this digital revolution to construct a newly "usable past" for theater history. Imagining a "poem of the act of the mind" which will replace a set scene that "repeated what / Was in the script," Wallace Stevens writes, "Then the theatre was changed / To something else. Its past was a souvenir . . . It has / To construct a new stage."[54] If photography, the medium which cheats death, is indeed passing, it will cease to be dominant only when the arrangement of knowledges and investments it represents is refigured as another cultural formation.[55] And that will necessarily entail inscribing another way of seeing and another "take" – or shot – at mapping the performance present as well as its future.

Notes

1. Athol Fugard, "Introduction," *Statements* (New York: Theatre Communications Group, Inc, 1986), n.p. Loren Kruger reports that similar images were common in South Africa.
2. Athol Fugard, *Sizwe Bansi is Dead* (1974), in *Statements*, 12–13.
3. I draw here from Roland Barthes, *Camera Lucida: Reflections on Photography*, trans. Richard Howard (New York: Hill and Wang, 1981), 92, 96; Victor Burgin, *In/Different Spaces: Place and Memory in Visual Culture* (Berkeley: University of California Press, 1996), 85; and Geoffrey Batchen, *Each Wild Idea: Writing, Photography, History* (Cambridge, Mass: MIT Press, 2001), 106.
4. See Julia Kristeva, *Powers of Horror: an Essay on Abjection*, trans. Leon S. Roudiez (New York: Columbia University Press, 1982), 4.
5. In the earliest days of photography, exposure time was so slow that if a subject wished to appear lifelike, she first had to act as if dead; decades later, Jean Cocteau remarked that the silent-film camera "filmed death at work." See Batchen, *Each Wild Idea*, 130; and Burgin, *In/Different Spaces*, 85.
6. Barthes, *Camera Lucida*, 90. For the Kódak slogan, see Nancy Martha West, *Kodak and the Lens of Nostalgia* (Charlottesville: University Press of Virginia, 2001), 161.
7. Peggy Phelan, "Introduction," in Tim Etchells, *Certain Fragments: Contemporary Performance and Forced Entertainment* (London: Routledge, 1999), 14.
8. On narrative supplementing image, see Abigail Solomon-Godeau, *Photography at the Dock: Essays on Photographic History, Institutions, and Practices* (Minneapolis:

University of Minnesota Press, 1991), xxix; see also John Berger, *About Looking* (New York: Pantheon Books, 1980), 52.

9. See Carol Armstrong, *Scenes in a Library: Reading the Photograph in the Book, 1843–1875* (Cambridge, Mass: MIT Press, 1999), 4–5.

10. Although some intriguing work exists on nineteenth-century theater photographs as well as on illustrations, engravings and paintings from that and earlier periods, the history of the twentieth-century theatrical still remains largely unexplored. See, for instance, Christopher B. Balme, "Interpreting the Pictorial Record: Theatre Iconography and the Referential Dilemma," *Theatre Research International*, 22,3 (1997), 190–201; Laurence Senelick, "Early Photographic Attempts to Record Performance Sequence," *Theatre Research International*, 22,3 (1997), 255–64; Shearer West, "Thomas Lawrence's 'Half-History' Portraits and the Politics of Theatre," *Art History*, 14,2 (1991), 225–49; and Geoffrey Ashton, "The Boydell Shakespeare Gallery: Before and After," in *The Painted Word, British History Painting 1750–1830*, ed. Peter Cannon-Brookes (London: Heim, 1991), 37–43. See also, and in particular, David Mayer, "'. . .quote the words to prompt the attitudes': the Victorian Performer, the Photographer, and the Photograph," forthcoming; my thanks to Mayer for sending me his article in typescript.

11. See Armstrong, *Scenes in a Library*, 3; Barthes, *Camera Lucida*, 25–7, 55.

12. Barbara Maria Stafford, *Good Looking*, 204; for the Benjamin quote, see Stafford, *Visual Analogy: Consciousness as the Art of Connecting* (Cambridge, Mass: MIT Press, 1999), 73.

13. Van Wyck Brooks, "On Creating a Usable Past," *The Dial* (11 April 1918), 337–41.

14. See Arthur C. Danto, "Photography and Performance: Cindy Sherman's Stills," in *Cindy Sherman: Untitled Film Stills* (New York: Rizzoli, 1990), 5–14.

15. On McBean and his restagings of performance, see Snowdon's introduction to Adrian Woodhouse, *Angus McBean* (London: Quartet Books Ltd, 1982), 14–15. See also Alison Light, "The Photography of Angus McBean: Masks and Faces," *Sight and Sound* (November 1994), 28–31.

16. See Stephen Heath, "On Suture," *Questions of Cinema* (Bloomington: Indiana University Press, 1981), 76–112.

17. As indeed they are. In the 1970s, Harvard bought four and half tons of McBean's glass negatives for a reported £40 000 and created a named archive. There is, however, some confusion over who owns what, for the Shakespeare Centre Library in Stratford claims ownership of some images, even though its archive holds no glass negatives.

18. Barthes, *Camera Lucida*, 27, 38, 47.

19. Clifford Geertz, "Thick Description: Toward an Interpretive Theory of Culture," *The Interpretation of Cultures* (New York: Basic Books, 1973), 3–32.

20. See Russell Jackson, "Stage and Storytelling, Theatre and Film: *Richard III* at Stratford, 1910," *New Theatre Quarterly*, 16,2 (May 2000), 107–21; esp. 116–17.

21. Laurence Burns, personal communication.

22. Or, in an image from the 2001 *1 Henry VI*, part of *This England*, the RSC's recent histories cycle, taken in the rebuilt Swan Theatre, again at a set-up call. Here, Clive Wood's York stands before a massive iron fortress, the *Henries*'s only set piece, as Aidan McArdle's Richard waves aloft Somerset's severed arm; visible here also are a technician and a gaggle of wires and equipment. Shakespeare's text, however, suggests that Richard displays Somerset's head ("Speak thou for me, and tell them what I did"), and of course, neither technician nor sound deck were visible during a performance. Not incidentally, the change from head to arm set up echoes with *Part 1*,

where Joan, with McArdle's Dauphin beside her, flaunted Bedford's severed arm at the English troops.

23. Walter Benjamin, "Theses on History," *Illuminations*, ed. Hannah Arendt, trans. Harry Zohn (New York: Schocken Books, 1968), 255.

24. See, for example, Dennis Kennedy, *Looking at Shakespeare: a Visual History of Twentieth-century Performance* (Cambridge: Cambridge University Press, 1993); Jonathan Bate and Russell Jackson, eds, *Shakespeare: an Illustrated Stage History* (Oxford: Oxford University Press, 1996); Sally Beauman, ed., *Henry V for the Centenary Season at the Royal Shakespeare Theatre* (Oxford: Pergamon Press, 1976); and Jonathan Croall, *Hamlet Observed: the National Theatre at Work* (London: NT Publications, 2001). See, for instance, Woodhouse, *Angus McBean*; *Theatre Year: a Selection of Photographs by Donald Cooper of Productions in London and Stratford*, introd. Michael Coveney (London: In (Parenthesis) Ltd, 1980); and *Snowdon on Stage*, with a personal view by Simon Callow (London: Pavilion Books Ltd, 1996). When theater photographs appear in coffee-table books, often accompanied by "puff" introductions, they invite a different kind of looking and serve different visual regimes, situating theater photography within art history protocols.

25. See Roger Brown and James Kulik, "Flashbulb Memories," *Cognition*, 5 (1978), 73–9.

26. Laurence Burns, personal communication.

27. See, for instance, Armstrong, *Scenes in a Library*, 1.

28. Saroyan is quoted in W. J. T. Mitchell, *Picture Theory* (Chicago: University of Chicago Press, 1994), 4.

29. On this and other captioning protocols, see my " 'Here Apparent': Photography, History, and the Theatrical Unconscious," in *Textual and Theatrical Shakespeare: Questions of Evidence*, ed. Edward Pechter (Iowa City: University of Iowa Press, 1996), 181–209; esp. 183–4.

30. See Solomon-Godeau, *Photography at the Dock*, 182–3.

31. See Carol J. Clover, "Dancin' in the Rain," *Critical Inquiry*, 21 (Summer 1995). 722–47. Clover argues that Stanley Donen's *Singin' in the Rain* is not about white women's voices but black men's bodies; I use her notion of a memory in the framework of forgetting (737) in a slightly different sense.

32. For these questions, see John Tagg, *Grounds of Dispute: Art History, Cultural Politics, and the Discursive Field* (Minneapolis: University of Minnesota Press, 1992), 103.

33. Echoing ideas that go back to memory devices used by classical rhetoricians, Freud conjectured that memories are like objects placed in the rooms of a house. For a discussion, see Daniel L. Schacter, *Searching for Memory* (New York: Basic Books, Inc, 1996), 40; see also Frances A. Yates, *The Art of Memory* (Chicago: University of Chicago Press, 1966).

34. Images of lighting cues exist for eight productions, including the three comprising Noble's *Plantagenets* and Mendes's *Tempest*: *Measure for Measure* (1987), *Love's Labour's Lost* (1990), *Antony and Cleopatra* (1992) and *Twelfth Night* (1994). For an analogue, see David Hockney's *Cameraworks* (1980). All are archived at the Shakespeare Centre Library. See also Batchen, *Each Wild Idea*, 111.

35. For a related discussion of these stills, see my " 'Here Apparent,' " 201–6.

36. See Armstrong, *Scenes in a Library*, 421.

37. Dean Asker, Head of RSC Publicity, personal communication. Many photographers, among them Donald Cooper, Ivan Kyncl and Laurence Burns, refuse to work under conditions in which their artistic authority is subsumed by the RSC and any potential future revenue cut off. A brief history: from the late 1960s to 1998, one photographer took official photographs, assigning copyright to the RSC for their use but

retaining negatives and publication rights elsewhere for book use. In 1998, however, the RSC instituted a complete buy-out in which an official photographer is permitted to shoot a full performance (usually a dress rehearsal, although sometimes only at an hour-long set-up call, where only selected scenes are staged); the RSC owns negatives and all publication rights. At this writing there is still an open photo call – the equivalent of the political photo op, where only a few scenes are performed – which any photographer who wishes to may attend, retaining all rights to their stills. Probably as soon as 2002–3, the RSC plans to stop the open call. By comparison with an earlier era when Joe Cocks (a former newspaperman) and Tom Holte documented, without cost, all the RSC work the Company could not afford to pay for, these policies represent considerable change. Not only are fewer images being taken (and archived) but, according to the staff at the Shakespeare Centre Library as well as individual photographers, the RSC's desire to control what images of their productions are seen, circulated and sold in order to create additional revenue seems misguided. My thanks to Sylvia Morris for providing this information.

38. On the emanation and elimination of action, see Armstrong, *Scenes in a Library*, 361, 374, 378, 383. For the link between photography and necromancy, see Sarah Boxer, "When Strindberg Found his Truth Machine," *New York Times*, 25 January 2002: B40. Strindberg's fascination with photography took form as a search for psychological portraits that would, through the camera's magic, give him true "telepathic contact" with the sitter's character.

39. The theatrical postcard has a long history, which has only recently begun to be explored in relation to Shakespeare. In 1906, approximately one-tenth of the 734 500 500 cards mailed featured Shakespearean "scenes" or actors; these were collected primarily by young women. See Anthony Byatt, *Picture Postcards and their Publishers: an Illustrated Account Identifying Britain's Major Postcard Publishers 1894 to 1939 and the Great Variety of Cards they Issued* (Malvern: Golden Age Postcard Books, 1978), n.p.; and Richard Bonynge, *A Collector's Guide to Theatrical Postcards* (London: Batsford, 1988). Edwardian postcards are on display at an internet site prepared by Harry Rusche: http://shakespeare.cc.emory.edu/index.cfm.

40. According to Kathy Elgin, some audience members (admittedly somewhat conservative patrons who subscribe to the mailing list) lament the absence of stills from past productions; she herself is also ambivalent about the changed policy. Personal communication.

41. Because they are expensive, rehearsal photographs are no longer taken on a regular basis; they are commissioned only if needed for early publicity, not as a record of the rehearsal process. Kathy Elgin, personal communication.

42. See Michel Foucault, *Heterologies: Discourse on the Other*, trans. Brian Massumi (Minneapolis: University of Minnesota Press, 1986), 196.

43. On the key scene, key phrase technique, see, for example, William Uricchio and Roberta E. Pearson, *Reframing Culture: the Case of the Vitagraph Quality Films* (Princeton: Princeton University Press, 1993), esp. 87–95.

44. For the idea of a visual Scheherazade, see Danto, "Photography and Performance," 9.

45. See Walter Benjamin, "The Work of Art in the Age of Mechanical Reproduction," *Illuminations*, 246.

46. Stafford suggests that such notions fuel Michel Foucault's trope of power relations as punitive and militaristic. See *Good Looking*, 58; see also Armstrong, *Scenes in a Library*, 364.

47. At this writing, the RSC is collaborating with MIT's Comparative Media Studies program to construct such a digital archive.

48. I draw here on D. F. McKenzie, " 'What's Past Is Prologue': the Bibliographical Society and the History of the Book," in D. F. McKenzie, *Making Meaning: "Printers of the Mind" and Other Essays*, ed. Peter D. McDonald and Michael F. Suarez, S. J. (Amherst and Boston: University of Massachusetts Press, 2002), 259–75; esp. 271–5.

49. For more on Gates's project and also on the Corbis Corporation, which since 1996 has offered electronic reproduction rights to 700 000 digital images representing, so they claim, "the entire human experience through history," see Batchen, *Each Wild Idea*, 133–4, 150–1. Stafford mentions the fear that images will become porous, thinned out by cyberspace in *Good Looking*, 68.

50. See Batchen, *Each Wild Idea*, 143–4, 154.

51. See Scott Bukatman, *Blade Runner* (London: BFI, 1997), 59.

52. At this writing, MIT's Comparative Media Studies program is preparing a video game based on Michael Boyd's *The Tempest* (2002).

53. See Stafford, *Good Looking*, 204.

54. Wallace Stevens, "Of Modern Poetry" (1942), in *The Collected Poems of Wallace Stevens* (New York: Alfred A. Knopf, 1970).

55. See Batchen, *Each Wild Idea*, 143. Batchen draws on Foucauldian formulations.

6

Vicarious: Theater and the Rise of Synthetic Experience

Joseph Roach

> "The Theater is your Poets Royal Exchange, upon which, their Muses (that are now turnd to Merchants) meeting, barter away that light commodity of words."
>
> Thomas Dekker, *The Gull's Hornbook* (1609)[1]

Historians of the "consumer revolution," the origins of which have been variously traced to periods ranging from the Elizabethan age to the eighteenth century, tend to think of commodities as things.[2] Theater historians need to complicate that definition because they know performance is not a thing; it is a service of a very dynamic and labile kind. Professional playwrights and performers manufacture and sell experiences. Over time, these experiences have largely replaced others that were once available for free, when amateurs amused one another by performing Mysteries or Carnivals in the demotic swirl of the public street. Once entertainment began to emerge as commercialized leisure – a development coinciding with many other London-centered, capitalist ventures – playhouses, controlling admission with gates and marked by signs like inns, multiplied: at The Theatre, The Rose, The Swan, The Globe, and their competitors, poets and the companies they served retailed a "commodity of words," which Thomas Dekker, himself a popular playwright, ruefully called "light."[3]

Theaters also offered spectacle, which is neither more nor less transitory than the spoken word in the actor's mouth, though it does tend to cost more to produce. By 1631, Ben Jonson, caught between the for-profit public theater and the lavishly subsidized spectacle of the Stuart court masques designed by Inigo Jones, found his role as an experience-merchant apocalyptically demeaning:

> Pack with your pedling poetry to the stage,
> This is the money-got, mechanic age.[4]

120

The complaints of Dekker and Jonson illuminate a major (and relatively neglected)[5] perspective on English theatrical history: popular or patrician, the seventeenth-century stage became central to the capitalization and commodification of leisure as synthetic experience. Synthetic experience is that which is fabricated to imitate or replace more mundane realities, and its success as a substitute for whatever passes for real life renders it a highly marketable but volatile commodity.

In other words, substitution pays. The authorities conduct public executions with great theatricality and wide popular interest, but they do not customarily charge admission; in the theater, feigned mayhem typically sells: "the die is cast," as Bert States once said of the fifth acts of English tragedies, "the cast must die." That people will part with good money to experience experience (by living through someone else's performance of it) is a discovery as exciting to some as fire. To them, performance, like fire, releases energy from matter that is utterly consumed in the process, disappearing as a condition of its emergence, leaving behind little but the desire for more. The traditional comparison of theatrical performances with dream states marks both the intense allure and the instability of the experience that they both impart. Like the desire for heated living space and warm food, however, the continuous consumption of synthetic experience turns luxury into habit, which soon enough becomes necessity. The only certain escape from the tyranny of habit is either deprivation or novelty. These forces and their consequences are well known to historians of the commercial theater, but they have sparked little analysis and less explanation.[6] What I am proposing to explore here is the deeper motivation that I believe stands behind them. That is the theater's answer to the human need, regulated by both curiosity and fear, to experience the world vicariously as well as directly.

Vicariousness suggests the derivative nature of experience from some prior authenticity. That is why the word is most often used as an adjective. *Vicarious* is cognate to *vicar*, in the sense of one who serves as substitute, agent or administrative deputy (as in "Vicar of God" for the King of England). It means that which has been delegated, as in *vicarious authority*; also: that which is performed or suffered by one person as a substitute for another or to the advantage or benefit of another, as in *vicarious sacrifice* or *vicarious pilgrimage*; most familiarly, it means that which is realized through the imaginative or sympathetic consciousness of another, as in *vicarious experience* and *vicarious thrills*; or, tangentially but provocatively, that which occurs in an unexpected or abnormal part of the body – bleeding from the gums sometimes occurs in the absence of a normal discharge from the uterus, as in *vicarious menstruation* (*OED*). In each case, the adjective modestly defers to the noun it modifies. Taken together, these aggregated usages describe a particular way of seeing the world, one in which signs are quite plausibly taken for wonders.

There is a religious, even specifically eucharistic aura to the word *vicarious*, even as it necessarily recedes from the proximity of its validating source. Over the long term, vicariousness tends to secularize or at least Protestantize experience: wherever symbolic enactments substitute for real presence, the celebrants must to some extent defer the authoritativeness of the event to an absentee. Thus, in William Davenant and John Dryden's Prologue to their adaptation of *The Tempest* as *The Enchanted Island*, God's authority is invoked indirectly by tracing its passage through His earthly vicar (the King) to the honored poet, for whom the actor speaking the Prologue substitutes in turn, much as divine inspiration was circuited through the poet to the Rhapsode and ultimately to the audience in Plato's *Ion*: "Shakespear's Pow'r is sacred as a King's."[7]

Actors playing a role as a link in such a chain of substitutions appear vicariously as a condition of their employment, but even innocent civilians occasionally practice the art of living through the actions and experiences of others. In fact, the steady market for such services is what creates employment not only for actors, but also for other professionally appointed deputies, such as royals, diplomats, priests, celebrities and their burgeoning kin. These body doubles are not there *for* other people – they are there *instead* of them.

Despite the transhistorical proliferation of instances of vicariousness – all imaginative representations and performances depend in some way on its insinuating appeal – the English theater of the seventeenth century is an especially promising place to explore its peculiar operations in the setting of more or less well-documented commercial performances. The historic contingencies of living vicariously through the theater in this period include the aforementioned rise of consumerism and the commercialization of leisure, the growing but still incomplete secularization of cultural and social life, and the emerging phenomenon of colonial contact with remote and unfamiliar peoples, who were known to most metropolitans vicariously or not at all. The balance of this chapter is devoted to these contingencies – commercialization, secularization and colonization – as they stimulate markets for synthetic experiences that the stage can readily supply. In the first section, a brief account of "china scenes" in dramatic works by Ben Jonson and William Wycherley illustrates one way in which synthetic experience can be imparted to an audience by the satirical representation of a synthetic behavior onstage: in this case, shopping as vicarious sex. In the second section, the most intimate confessions in Samuel Pepys's *Diary* disclose how synthetic experience emerges from the uneasy play of private desires and the public performance of them – secular rituals for which the theater offered the models that infiltrated and eventually displaced those provided by the church. The final section offers a speculative consideration of tourism as one of the most successful of vicarious experiences to have been conceptually pioneered by the English theater; here the playhouse itself, renamed "The Enchanted Island," stood in for the dream destinations on a colonizing itinerary of global trade. The free-standing playhouse with its "light commodity of words" eventually competed with the newspaper and the novel as media of synthetic experience, but for a time it nearly cornered the market for sources of living vicariously. What follows attempts to characterize the salient features of that time.

China scenes: the theatrical origins of the shopping class

Scholars have recently drawn attention to the nearly simultaneous innovation of two kinds of public building in Elizabethan and Jacobean London: first, the playhouses, newly constructed in the "Liberties" adjacent to the walled City or installed in older buildings on similarly privileged ground within it, and second, the shopping-mall-like "exchanges," namely Sir Thomas Gresham's Royal Exchange (1566–8), followed by Sir Robert Cecil's New Exchange (1609). Of this conjuncture of art and commerce, Peter Thompson has written: "It is a historical coincidence that makes its own meanings."[8] Janette Dillon has argued more specifically that the theaters and exchanges worked together to produce revolutionary commercial spaces between the mercantile City of London and the Court in Westminster, which was increasingly both a physical site (in Whitehall and the emerging "Town") and a set of attitudes and practices available for appropriation.[9] These behaviors featured conspicuous consumption of fashionable commodities and commodified experiences: clothing, furnishings, imported goods, food and beverages, exotic pets and servants, dancing lessons, sexual services, and performances. Standing between City and Court, reflecting and provoking them both as in Janus-faced hyperbolic mirrors, magnifying the aspirations and opportunities of their patrons to consume and to be seen consuming, were the professional theaters and the commercial exchanges – public gathering places rivaled in capacity only by churches.

This was most conspicuously true of the strategic positioning of the New Exchange in the London cityscape. Seeking to build on the success and attraction of the Royal Exchange located within the old City walls and correctly forecasting the westward movement of fashionable residential life towards Westminster, Sir Robert Cecil located the New Exchange just off the Strand. His intent was clearly to establish a shopping destination, physically closer to the most desirable consumers and marketed to stimulate and fulfill their aspiration for what historians of consumption call "social emulation."[10] The connection of this enterprise to the most fashionable contemporary theatrical performances was explicit. Cecil employed Ben Jonson to write and Inigo Jones to design a masquelike entertainment, *Britain's Burse*, which welcomed King James I as the celebrity ribbon cutter at the grand opening in 1609. This was prescient indeed. In the same year as the opening, Dekker had advised his Poet: "Your Gallant, your Courtier, and your Capten, had wont to be the soundest paymaisters, and I think are still the surest chapmen."[11] In 1638, Inigo Jones laid out the Covent Garden Piazza as a speculative development of high-end residences and shops not far from the New Exchange, and by the second half of the seventeenth century, this location had become the center of a combined theater-market district that flourished in the eighteenth century and still operates today as a nodal point of entertainment and tourism.

Prophetically, *Britain's Burse* boasted a "china scene," in which the most successful luxury import of the age took center stage as a promotional prop. In entertaining a fashionable audience by representing one of its most desirable acquisitive experiences at the site of future transactions, Jonson echoed a line from his *Epicoene, or The Silent Woman*, which was also performed in 1609. In Act 4, scene 2, Lady Haughty invites the "Ladies Collegiate" to "go to the china-houses, and to the Exchange."[12] By using the china trade as a marker of female consumption, Jonson anticipated the satirical terms of William Wycherley's *The Country Wife* (1675). In the notorious "china scene" of this popular play, the rake Horner conceals his fornication with other men's wives by the fiction that he is selling them china from a closet in his lodgings. The word *china* is thus coarsely mobilized in the service of an on-going dirty joke, but it also represents the synthetic experience of shopping as a vicarious extension of sex. China stands in for what women want.[13] In a homewares-department tug of war, a tour de force of social emulation recycled as mimetic desire, Lady Fidget contends for the choicest goods with Mrs Squeamish, who is affronted to learn that supplies are limited:

> *Re-enter Lady Fidget with a piece of china in her hand, and Horner following.*
> *Lady Fidget.* And I have been toiling and moiling for the prettiest piece of china, my dear.
> *Horner.* Nay, she has been too hard for me, do what I could.
> *Mrs Squeamish.* Oh, Lord, I'll have some china too. Good, Mr Horner, don't think to give other people china, and me none; come in with me too.
> *Horner.* Upon my honour, I have none left now.
> *Mrs Squeamish.* Nay, nay, I have known you deny your china before now, but you shan't put me off so. Come.
> *Horner.* This lady had the last here.
> *Lady Fidget.* Yes, indeed, madam, to my certain knowledge, he has no more left.

Wycherley's dialogue imitates the plangent cadences of a frustrated shopper who will not accept disappointment, baited by a more successful rival who gloats. Neither Mrs Squeamish nor the playwright will easily let the matter rest:

> *Mrs Squeamish.* O, but it may be he may have some you could not find.
> *Lady Fidget.* What, d'ye think if he had any left, I would not have had it too? for we women of quality never think we have china enough.
>
> (*The Country Wife*, IV, iii)[14]

The china scene, perhaps the most famous scene in Restoration comedy, is carefully prepared for by an earlier shopping scene, the longest one in *The Country Wife* and one of the longest in the canon of Restoration comedy (III. ii). Significantly for my purposes, Wycherley sets this scene in "The New Exchange," Sir Robert Cecil's Jacobean mall, which continued in use after the Restoration. He depicts a vertiginous whirl of rapidly entering and exiting characters intent on their business. Here Margery Pinchwife, the country wife of the title, learns how to shop in the city. She does so vicariously, disguised as a man. Her anxious husband vetoes her impulse to purchase some racy books – "*Covent-Garden Drollery*, and a play or two" – but other impulses prove less tractable, and she allows herself to be spirited away by the predatory Horner, who plies her (offstage) with kisses and treats. The stage direction for their re-entrance plants a vivid image that will be recapitulated later by Lady Fidget and Horner's post-coital entrance into the "china scene":

> *Enter Mrs Pinchwife in man's clothes, running, with her hat under her arm, full of oranges and dried fruit; Horner following.*

To reinforce the connection between the two scenes – and to represent vicariously the importance of goods and services by symbolically highlighting the use of hand props in each – Margery identifies the forbidden fruit to her enraged husband as "China oranges." A quickly educable modern consumer, she shops 'til he drops.

Wycherley's china scene and the scene in the New Exchange dramatize a tenet of the commercialization of leisure that the theater since the seventeenth century has continued to advance, not only on the stage, but in the box office as well: to create a market, stimulate desire; to stimulate desire, promote vicarious sex.

Chapels of Satan

Taking the long view, Matthew Arnold envisioned the slow but steady usurpation of the forms of religion by "poetry" in modern societies. If the reader substitutes "performance" for "poetry" and "synthetic experience" for "idea" in the key passage from Arnold's "The Study of Poetry" (1880), the amended text evocatively describes the process of secularization that opened an ever-widening cultural space for the stage:

> The future of poetry is immense . . . There is not a creed which is not shaken, not an accredited dogma which is not shown to be questionable, not a received tradition which does not threaten to dissolve . . . But for poetry the idea is everything; the rest is a world of illusion, of divine illusion. Poetry attaches its emotion to the idea; the idea *is* the fact. The strongest part of our religion today is its unconscious poetry.[15]

Crucially, poetry does not simply replace religion; it insinuates itself unconsciously into its functions, meeting the growing need for more supple and accessible rituals, public and private.[16] The inception and spread of "Bardolatry," the veneration and canonization of Shakespeare, who represented the meeting point of poetry and performance, might be cited as the best evidence in support of this view of secularization. That is not to say that the relationship between religion and culture could ever be wholly sundered. The anti-theatrical London City Fathers, steeped in Tertullian, foresaw the continuing threat of the historic relationship between theater and religion – a competition for the attention of the public between rival performances – when they repeatedly called for the demolition of the playhouses as "Chapels of Satan" and then acted vigorously on their proposal in 1642. When the theaters reappeared in 1660, they did so as semi-autonomous commercial operations under the aegis of the Crown. Secularization took on a particularly poignant meaning during that strange twilight of sacral monarchy when the precariously restored Stuarts became the titular heads of the theater as well as the Church of England. Abetting the rise of synthetic experience by the transmission of celebrity to his theatrical surrogates, Charles loaned his coronation robes to the playhouse to costume the player kings, whom the biographer of the greatest actor of the age characterized as monarchs of a "Mimic State."[17]

The vexed interactions between the king's body politic and his body natural were never more explicitly imagined than they were during the reign of Charles II.[18] The great theater-loving diarist (and ambitious consumer of luxury goods) Samuel Pepys testifies both as a troubled witness to the King's two bodies and as a vicarious emulator of their contradictory desires. Pepys found the King's sexuality troubling. Along with his fellow diarist John Evelyn, he feared the cheapening of the King's sacred person by his lascivious acts. At the same time, Pepys struggled unsuccessfully to contain the urgency of his own vicarious identification with Charles as a sexual celebrity. It was not long after he noted his worries about the King's excessive indulgences that Pepys began to confide to his *Diary* about his own habit of masturbating in church.

Pepys's onanistic acts, which he records in frank (albeit coded) detail, were discreet, but they were also clearly performances. Like shopping in *The Country Wife*, attending church in the *Diary* might erupt at any moment into concupiscible riot. Even if the audience ultimately included only himself and his God (if Pepys was discovered by others, he never remarks on it), the performer, who was no atheist, rehearsed and staged his self-pleasuring with a stylishness that mimics theatrical convention, not excluding the ironic incorporation of established ritual by indulging himself during services, such as High Mass on Christmas Eve (once) and sermons (at least twice). In recording these intimate moments for posterity (whether he intended them to be read or not), the diarist discloses his voracious appetite for synthetic experience.

Pepys's diary has become a long-running hit among theater historians researching Restoration performances, but they are more likely to report on assignations with pretty actresses than on his public enactments of private vice. Luckily for them, Pepys made a habit of theater-going too. Between 1 January and 31 August 1668, for instance, he went to the theater no fewer than seventy-three times. In fact, he expressed guilt over his over-indulgence of this form of self-gratification in terms similar to those he used to reproach himself for the other. Ashamed by the way he has neglected business on account of his excessive theater-going, he repeatedly vows not to darken the playhouse door again, only to record his attendance a few days later. Similarly, on 29 June 1663, he vows never again "to make bad use of my fancy with whatever woman I have a mind to."[19] Within a fortnight, however, he records two episodes of onanistic fantasy – one in honor of a court lady, the other featuring the Queen herself (*Diary*, 2: 230, 232).

Recent critical discussion of Pepys's guilty pleasures corrects Francis Barker's emphasis (in *The Tremulous Private Body*) on the centrality of bourgeois shame as the motive for their expression and asserts the interpenetration of public and private acts in the *Diary*.[20] To explain the importance of this unique source in documenting the rise of synthetic experience, I want to go a step beyond that discussion by raising two issues concerning Pepys's personal performances in relationship to stage performances in the 1660s: the first is their vicariousness; the second is their commodification of leisure. For Pepys, synthetic experience requires the production of a mental image – very often that of a woman marked by glamor, fashion and celebrity (or at least notoriety) – which instigates the process that Elaine Scarry, in *Dreaming by the Book*, describes in this way: "Imagination produces a mimesis of sensation by miming the deep structure that brings sensation about."[21] Like the theater, imagination is a parade of substitutes, surrogates, stand-ins and stunt doubles. Performance, in other words, stands in – imaginatively, vicariously – for an elusive entity that it is not but that it must vainly aspire both to embody and to replace. Vicariousness, like performance (or like "Restoration" for that matter), suggests the derivation of experience from some prior authenticity. That is one way to understand the process of Shakespearean adaptation at any time, but particularly in the 1660s, when poets, pondering their belatedness, (re)constructing a repertoire, looked back to the "Giant Race before the Flood." But they invoked that authority only to manufacture and market a different kind of synthetic experience in its name, one in which painted women competed with the painted scenery as eye-filling spectacles.

Pepys seems not to have masturbated at the theater, however. That would have been redundant. Judging from the doubly coded language of the diary entries recording his auto-eroticism, masturbating during religious services made him feel more guilty but also more excited. Pepys's keyword is "mi cosa" ("my thing"). Thus, the entry for 11 November 1666 reads: "Here at church (God forgive me), my mind did courir upon Betty Michel, so that I do hazer con mi cosa in la eglisa meme" (*Diary*, 7: 365). Betty was the teenage daughter of one of Pepys's friends. Next month, riding beside her in a coach just before Christmas, Pepys celebrated the season by persuading her to "poner mi cosa en su mano nudo" ("to take my thing in her gloveless hand" [*Diary*, 7: 419]). Next Christmas Eve, 24 December 1667, he masturbated himself during High Mass in the Queen's Chapel, Whitehall. Though he considered himself a staunch anti-papist, the elaborated liturgy and the presence of her most Catholic majesty with her attendants seem to have inspired him to virtuosic efforts: "The Queen was there and some ladies . . . But here I did make myself to do la cosa by mere imagination, mirando a jolie mosa and with eyes open, which I never did before – and God forgive me for it, it being in the chapel" (*Diary*, 8: 588). On 3 May of the next year, he tried it with eyes wide shut, so to speak: "After dinner to church again where I did please myself con mes ojos shut in futar in conceit the hook-nosed young lady, a merchant's daughter, in the upper pew in the church under the pulpit" (*Diary*, 9: 184). Having thus performed with and without his eyes, Pepys challenges himself to masturbate without his hands, but this time not in church, but alfresco, on his way to work in his boat on the Thames: "Lying down close in my boat, and there, without any use of my hand, had great pleasure, and the first time I did make trial of my strength of fancy of that kind without my hand, and had it complete avec la fille que I did see aujour-dhuy in Westminster Hall. So to my office and wrote my letters" (*Diary*, 6: 331).

The obligatory element, in expectation and execution, was the mental image of a woman – sometimes one who was physically present (as with the Queen in her chapel and the hook-nosed merchant's daughter); more often one who was absent (as with Betty Michel in the first church episode or an unnamed girl whom Pepys had spied briefly in Westminster Hall). That the real power of such events resided in the summoned mental image – hence in memory, in performance, in synthetic experience – is suggested by the fact that Pepys closed his eyes to fantasize about the merchant's daughter, even though she was then present to his sight in her pew beneath the pulpit. To complete his performance, he turned her into a "conceit," to use his word. The efficacy of this practice he confirmed empirically by the water-born "trial of [his] strength of fancy," exciting himself to ejaculation, hands-off, by restoring the image of the randomly encountered but vividly memorable "fille" (*Diary*, 6: 331).

Pepys's diurnal encounters and vistas in and around London and Westminster provide him with a panoply of erotic images and potential "conceits" for later use. Their staging can be highly theatrical, replete with dramatic conflict, sets, costumes and props. The intensity of these images grows in proportion to Pepys's proximity to King Charles and his women, the stimuli for his synthetic experience, the model and the objects of his synthetic behavior. On 13 July 1663, for instance, Pepys sees the King, the Queen and the King's mistress, Lady Castlemaine, taking the air. The King is paying attention to his wife. Castlemaine is in a royal pout. Pepys is captivated not only by the glamor of the Queen, but also by the flirtatious play of the court ladies, especially Mrs Steward, who staged an impromptu fashion show, featuring their feathered hats. (They may have been trying to divert attention from the little public drama of adultery and jealous pique, yet another erotic triangle among many in which the lovely and long-suffering Queen Catherine played the hypotenuse.) Pepys records: "All the ladies walked, talking and fiddling with their hats and feathers, and changing and trying one another's, but on another's head, and laughing. But it was the finest sight to me, considering their great beautys and dress, that ever I did see in all my life. But above all, Mrs Steward in this dresse, with her hat, cocked and a red plume, with her sweet eye, little Roman nose and excellent *Taille*, is now the greatest beauty I ever saw I think in my life" (*Diary*, 2: 230). Resisting the temptation to linger over the red plume as a multi-purpose fetish object, equally available to Marxian or Freudian interpretation, I want to draw attention to the efficacy of the image of Mrs Steward and secondarily the Queen in the private climax of Pepys's fantasy and subsequent auto-performance: "to bed – before I sleep, fancying myself to sport with Mrs Steward with great pleasure" (*Diary*, 2: 230). Then, two nights later: "to bed, sporting in my fancy with the Queen" (*Diary*, 2: 232).

The glamour of the image of these women, like fashion itself, resides in two contradictory and competing values. The first of these is patina, the traditionally established qualities of fabric, flesh and accessories that allow the court women to perform their cultural authority as established worthies. The second is novelty, the power to replace at will those very signifiers of tradition by discretionary spending. Thus Pepys's *Diary* records that he "in the privy Garden saw the finest smocks and linen petticoats of my Lady Castlemaynes, laced with rich lace at the bottomes, that ever I saw; and did me good to look upon them." Pepys's images also derive most intensely from women – Lady Castlemaine, Mrs Steward, the Queen herself (not to mention the actresses Nell Gwyn and Moll Davis) – erotically associated with the King, serial adulterer, and God's anointed Vicar on Earth.

Appositely for my purposes, Pepys's vicarious behavior also derived from the authority of Shakespeare, whose power, according to Dryden, was "sacred as a King's." In the Restoration theater, Shakespearean adaptations, with actresses taking over the boys' parts, offered the charms of layered patina and novelty similar to those that Pepys encountered in the royal mistress's undergarments. Shakespeare, more than any other playwright, insinuated his imagery into Pepys's consciousness of his own sensations. He did so, for instance, in a key passage in which the diarist's imagination fixes again on the favorite object of his fantasies, Lady Castlemaine, who came to him in a mid-August night's wet dream in the plague-year of 1665. Hamlet's "To be or not to be" soliloquy, which Pepys had already heard the great actor Thomas Betterton deliver a number of times, frames the recovery of his erotic dream as a waking fantasy:

> Up by 4 a-clock, and walked to Greenwich, where called at Captain Cockes and to his chamber, he being in bed – where something put my last night's dream into my head, which I think is the best that ever was dreamed – which was, that I had my Lady Castlemayne in my armes and was admitted to use all the dalliance I desired with her, and then dreamed that this could not be awake but that it was only a dream. But that since it was a dream and that I took so much real pleasure in it, what a happy thing it would be, if when we are in our graves (as Shakespeare resembles it), we could dream, and dream but such dreams as this – that then we should not need to be so fearful of death as we are in this plague-time. (*Diary*, 6: 191)

In a way that recalls the controlling metaphor of Calderon's *La vida es sueño* – that even dreams themselves are dreams, nesting dolls of consciousness – Pepys enjoys even his own experiences vicariously. Castlemaine, standing in for an actress, exists for him as a voyeuristic image to be acquired, savored and refleshed at intervals, most often at the theater, where he noted her presence in the company of the King, and at Court, where that glimpse of a lacy hem sent him into an ecstasy. A celebrity before the age of mass culture, Castlemaine's image circulated widely in the absence of her person. Among many portrait commissions, she had herself painted as religious icons, not only as Mary Magdalen, but also as the Virgin Mary, posing with her bastard son by Charles II on her knee as the Christ Child, blasphemously flattering the King.[22] Pepys associated her explicitly with the graphic postures of Aretino, the notorious pornographic manual of positions and technique that he believed she had mastered in order to beguile the King. Pepys vowed to obtain a copy of her famous portrait by Sir Peter Lely, and he did so as soon as it was engraved in 1666. Castlemaine not only made Pepys want to masturbate, she also made him want to shop.

Performance is the perfect commodity in the age of the commercialization because it seems to disappear completely at the moment of its iteration, leaving behind only a hunger for more. The poignancy of Pepys's fantasy about taking his dreams of Castlemaine with him to the grave is in the evanescence of the vicarious experience it discloses. It is the midsummer night's marketer's dream, a sentiment from a play that Pepys detested but emulated:

> If we shadows have offended,
> Think but this, and all is mended,

That you have but slumb'red here
While these visions did appear. (*A Midsummer Night's Dream*, V. i. 423–6)

Pepys's guilt about play-going and masturbation is intensified by their expense as luxury experiences that vanish apparently without a trace. But that disappearance is only apparent. Performance leaves a residue behind in the form of the market demand it has produced. Again, the marketing genius of selling people leisure time in the guise of their own experience is that it turns luxury into habit on the way to making it a necessity. The ultimate product in the rise of synthetic experience is, therefore, not the commodity but the consumer. Samuel Pepys's account of its role in the performance of his daily life is early but prescient testimony to its fabulous success.

Four corners of the world, calculated for the meridian of London

In his pioneering critique of modern tourism, Dean MacCannell writes: "Increasingly, pure experience, which leaves no material trace, is manufactured and sold like a commodity."[23] His insight reminds theater historians to look not so much for the present in the past as the past in the present – in this case, synthetic experience as an enduring legacy of the early modern stage. In the history of popular performance, tourism emerged as vicarious experience long before the safety and affordability of travel made actual tours possible for large numbers of people. Vicarious tourism occurs when the commodified experience of a local event substitutes for the direct experience of a remote destination. In the seventeenth century, the key development was the elaboration of the stage into a medium that is both a means of imaginary conveyance to exotic locales and an exotic locale in itself, at once discovering and masking the vast ambition of Britain's contemporaneous colonial projects.[24]

The Restoration theater was certainly well suited to offer this kind of synthetic experience.[25] "The Play-House is an Inchanted Island," as contemporary commentator Tom Brown put it, touting the theater itself as an exotic destination in his tour-guide of London, playing on the sub-title of the Davenant–Dryden *Tempest*.[26] The full title of Brown's *Amusements Serious and Comical, Calculated for the Meridian of London* is significant in the history of vicarious tourism as performance. The word *meridian* means a representation of a great circle or half circle of the celestial sphere, numbered for longitude (as on a map or globe), passing through the poles at its zenith. A meridian can mark the longitudinal coordinate of a place, and it can show one aspect of the relationship of that place to an entire world. The imagery of navigation indicates that Brown's text is a travel narrative. It fixes the coordinates of a voyage across town, as if that town were the globe, charting a course through "The Court," "The Walks," "Bedlam" and "Westminster-Hall," bound for the

archipelago of the theater district and its insular playhouse. The professed purpose of the entire voyage is touristic and ethnographic:

> London is a World by it self. We daily discover in it more New Countries,
> and surprising Singularities, than in all the Universe besides. There are
> among the *Londoners* so many Nations differing in Manners, Customs, and
> Religions, that the Inhabitants themselves don't know a quarter of them.

But on this grand multicultural tour, Brown finds his definitive ethnographical
object in his encounter with the actors, as he describes the performance of their
bizarre rituals of staged authenticity. He calls them "Natives":

> Let us now speak a Word or so, of the Natives of this Country [the play-
> house], and the Stock of Wit and Manners by which they Maintain them-
> selves, and Ridicule the whole World besides. The people are all somewhat
> Whimsical and Giddy-Brained: When they Speak, they Sing, when they
> Walk, they Dance, and very often do both when they have no mind to it.[27]

The introduction of moveable scenery allowed these "Natives" to depict globe-
spanning locales on painted canvas vistas shimmering under candle-powered
suns and moons. Now, in the twinkling of an eye, machines could move the
wings and change the scene, potentially to any of one of the four corners of the
world and back again. Though the expense of new scenes limited the number
of times a theater could provide such novelty, stock settings could nevertheless
instill regular habits of visualizing world geographies, however schematized.
A few synecdochical properties – a scimitar, a parasol, a palm tree – could evoke
exotic realms. The repertoire, which covered the four corners of the globe,
demanded no less: here the violent Surinam of Aphra Behn's account, as dramatized by Thomas Southerne in *Oroonoko* (1695), or the eroticized Africa of
Settle's *Empress of Morocco* (1673); there the sun-drenched, blood-drenched
Mexico of Dryden and Howard's *The Indian Queen* (1664) and Dryden's sequel
The Indian Emperour (1665), or the ritualized and intrigue-ridden India of
Dryden's *Aureng-Zebe* (1675), from which the eponymous character's scimitar
ended up as a famous prop,[28] and Orrery's *Mustapha* (1665), which dramatized
some of the same material as the key transitional text of the period, Davenant's
Siege of Rhodes (1656). Other, less frequently revived plays in this genre of vic-
arious tourism include Dryden's *Amboyna* (1673), Settle's *The Conquest of China*
(1676) and *Ibrahim the Illustrious Bassa* (1676), Behn's *Abdelazer* (1676) and *The
Widow Ranter* (1689), Henry Purcell's operatic setting for *The Indian Queen* (1695),
Mary Pix's *Ibrahim* (1696) and Delarivier Manley's *The Royal Mischief* (1696).

   Not every tourist vista was conceived for a play that seemed to require it. The
most ambitious scenic extravaganza of the period was Henry Purcell's operatic

adaptation of *A Midsummer Night's Dream* as *The Fairy Queen* (1692). If the stage directions can be credited, the most spectacular scene in the performance was the one interpolated into the final scene at Oberon's command. At a historical moment alive with *chinoiserie* in imported luxuries, *The Fairy Queen* offered theater-goers a vicarious tour of a setting that was appositely dream-like: "The Scene is suddainly Illuminated, and discovers a transparent Prospect of a Chinese Garden, the Architecture, the Trees, the Plants, the Fruit, the Birds, the Beasts, quite different from what we have in this part of the World." A Chinese man and woman sing of the Edenic beauty of creation. A dance of six monkeys animates their vision. Then, magically unbidden, "six pedestals of China-work rise from under the Stage; they support Vases of Porcelain, in which there are six China-Orange Trees."[29] Here is another "China scene," but this time the consumers are vicariously transported to the exoticized point of origin to inspect the goods in their putatively authentic, native setting. The Chinese-garden scene thus contains an early version of what Hollywood calls a "product placement," a shot that includes a consumer item displayed in the background or used by the characters. "Porcelain" is such a product, and the designer placed it prominently at the visual climax of the most eye-popping spectacle of the age. Oberon's masque in *The Fairy Queen* invites the audience to live vicariously as dream-state visitors to an unthinkably remote place from which expensive souvenirs just happen to be available in local speciality shops. It offers a fitting summation of the sheer ambition of the synthetic experiences offered up by the seventeenth-century stage.

In order to succeed, commercial theater must give people what they want; but it also tells them what they ought to want. That includes not only re-organizing their imaginations to match what can be reliably purchased, but also (and more fundamentally) manipulating the boundaries between public and private expressions of desire, stimulating the anxious need for social emulation where it seems to lag, harnessing and directing it where it already flows abundantly. Cultural critics occasionally cite the shopping mall as the successor and heir to the great cathedral, but they should not forget the theater as a link in that architectural genealogy. "One of the primary advantages offered by praying in the presence of others," Ramie Targoff notes about the obligatory performance of common prayer in seventeenth-century England, "was the possibility it provided for imitation."[30] Prayer exemplifies the voice of private expression that merges publicly with a chorus of communicants, who in the fullness of time will consist of specialized congregations of shoppers, celebrity-groupies or tourists. That is why the example of Pepys's *Diary*, admittedly a sample of one, remains crucial: from an unusually candid interior perspective, it documents the ways in which the theater annexes mundane life by inventing new rituals that secularize the old. When Arnold spoke of "unconscious poetry" as the unorthodox but efficacious form of modern worship, he also described the rise of synthetic experience to a place of prominence that it has never relinquished. Like the word *notorious*, which appears alone as the title of a celebrated film, *vicarious* is an adjective that justly aspires to the condition of a noun.

Notes

1. Thomas Dekker, *The Gull's Hornbook* (1609), quoted in A. M. Nagler, *A Sourcebook in Theatrical History* (New York: Dover, 1952), 133.
2. The generative work is Neil McKendrick, John Brewer and J. H. Plumb, *The Birth of a Consumer Society: the Commercialization of Eighteenth-Century England* (Bloomington: Indiana University Press, 1982). See also Ann Bermingham, "The Consumption of Culture: Image, Object, Text," in Ann Bermingham and John Brewer, eds, *The Consumption of Culture 1600–1800* (London: Routledge, 1995), 1–20.
3. Dekker, *The Gull's Hornbook*, 133.
4. Ben Jonson, *Expostulation with Inigo Jones* (1631), quoted in Nagler, *Sourcebook*, 155.
5. A very important exception is Jean-Christophe Agnew, *Worlds Apart: the Market and the Theater in Anglo-American Thought, 1550–1750* (New York: Cambridge University Press, 1986); see especially Chapter 3, "Artificial Persons," 101–48; see also Nancy Klein Maguire, *Regicide and Restoration: English Tragicomedy, 1660–1671* (Cambridge: Cambridge University Press, 1992), especially Chapter 4, "The Commercial Market: Genre as Commodity," 132–7.
6. The scholar most interested in the business of theater in the seventeenth and eighteenth centuries, Robert D. Hume, marshals detailed evidence to prove that people in the commercial theater were in it for the money; see, for example, *Henry Fielding and the London Theatre, 1728–1737* (Oxford: Clarendon Press, 1988).
7. *The Tempest, or the Enchanted Island* (London: Printed by T. N. for Henry Herringman, 1674), Prologue.
8. Peter Thompson, "English Renaissance and Restoration Theatre," in John Russell Brown, ed., *The Oxford Illustrated History of Theatre* (New York: Oxford University Press, 1995), 177.
9. Janette Dillon, *Theatre, Court, and City, 1595–1610: Drama and Social Space in London* (Cambridge: Cambridge University Press, 2000), passim. See my "Space Wars," *Theater*, 30, 3 (2000): 128–31.
10. For a review of the literature on this concept, see John Storey, *Cultural Consumption and Everyday Life* (New York: Oxford University Press, 1999), 4–10.
11. Dekker, *Gull's Hornbook*, 133.
12. Ben Jonson, *Ben Jonson's Plays* (New York: Dutton, 1967), 1: 531.
13. Elizabeth Kowaleski-Wallace, *Consuming Subjects: Women, Shopping, and Business in the Eighteenth Century* (New York: Columbia University Press, 1997), 52–69.
14. William Wycherley, *The Country Wife*, ed. Thomas H. Fujimura (1675; Lincoln: University of Nebraska Press, 1965).
15. "The Study of Poetry," in Dwight Culler, ed., *Poetry and Criticism of Matthew Arnold* (Boston: Houghton Mifflin, 1961), 306.
16. For the relationship of poetry and prayer in the seventeenth century, see Ramie Targoff, *Common Prayer: the Language of Public Devotion in Early Modern England* (Chicago: University of Chicago Press, 2001) and Richard Rambuss, *Closet Devotions* (Durham: Duke University Press, 1998).
17. Charles Gildon, *The Life of Mr. Thomas Betterton, the Late Eminent Tragedian* (London: Printed for Robert Gosling, 1710), 10.

18. Harold Weber, "Carolinean Sexuality and the Restoration Stage: Reconstructing the Royal Phallus in *Sodom*," in J. Douglas Canfield and Deborah C. Payne, *Cultural Readings of Restoration and Eighteenth-Century Theater* (Athens: University of Georgia Press, 1995), 67–88.

19. *The Diary of Samuel Pepys*, ed. Robert Latham and William Matthews (Berkeley: University of California Press, 1976), 2: 204. Subsequent references parenthetical.

20. James Grantham Turner, "Pepys and the Private Parts of Monarchy," in *Culture and Society in the Stuart Restoration: Literature, Drama, History*, ed. Gerald MacLean (Cambridge: Cambridge University Press, 1995), 95–110.

21. Elaine Scarry, *Dreaming by the Book* (New York: Farrar, Stauss, Giroux, 1999), 256, note 6.

22. Catherine MacLeod and Julia Marciari Alexander, *Painted Ladies: Women at the Court of Charles II* (London: National Portrait Gallery and the Yale Center for British Art, 2001), 116–35.

23. Dean MacCannell, *The Tourist: a New Theory of the Leisure Class* (1976; New York: Schocken Books, 1989), 21.

24. This subject has received much welcome critical attention of late; see, for instance: Mita Choudhury, *Interculturalism and Resistance in the London Theater, 1660–1800: Identity Performance, Empire* (London: Associated University Presses, 2000); Bridget Orr, *Empire on the English Stage 1660–1714* (Cambridge: Cambridge University Press, 2001); and Laura Brown, *Fables of Modernity: Literature and Culture in the English Eighteenth Century* (Ithaca: Cornell University Press, 2001).

25. See Joseph Roach, "The Enchanted Island: Vicarious Tourism in Restoration Adaptations of *The Tempest*," in Peter Hulme and William H. Sherman, eds, "*The Tempest*" and Its Travels (London: Reaktion Books, 2000), 60–70 and "The Global Parasol: Accessorizing the Four Corners of the World," in Felicity Nussbaum, ed., *The Global Eighteenth Century* (Johns Hopkins University Press, forthcoming).

26. Tom Brown, *Amusements Serious and Comical, Calculated for the Meridian of London* (1700; 2nd edn: Booksellers of London and Westminster), 48.

27. Brown, *Amusements*, 22, 56–7.

28. *The Tatler*, No. 42, 16 July 1709.

29. *The Fairy Queen: an Opera* (London: Printed for Jacob Tonson, 1692), 49, 51. See Gary Jay Williams, *Our Moonlight Revels: A Midsummer Night's Dream in the Theatre* (Iowa City: University of Iowa Press, 1997), 38–60.

30. Targoff, *Common Prayer*, 11.

7
Zoo Stories: "Boundary Work" in Theater History

Una Chaudhuri

> "Zoos ultimately tell us stories about boundary-making activities on the part of humans . . . Western metropolitan zoos are spaces where humans engage in cultural self-definition against a variably constructed and opposed nature. With animals as the medium, they inscribe a cultural sense of distance from that loosely defined realm that has come to be called 'nature.' "
>
> Kay Anderson[1]

> "You don't go to a zoo to see a lion or a tiger, but rather to see a *mise en promiscuité* of African lions, polar bears, Bengal tigers, Australian kangaroos."
>
> Alain Fleischer[2]

My point of departure is an improbable one for a project in theater ecology: a formulation by F. T. Marinetti, founder of the modernist theatrical movement that was arguably the least interested in, if not most hostile to, the claims of the natural world. The Futurists' unabashed technophilia was the cutting edge of that programmatic suppression of the non-human upon which modernity's ideal of progress increasingly depended. That suppression returned, as often happens, in metaphor, and among the many metaphors with which Marinetti, like other modernists, theorized the emerging theater are two that interest me especially: the zoo and the circus. Marinetti compared the zoo to the conventional psychological theater, which he despised, and the circus to his Futuristic ideal of a theater of action and energy:

> The conventional theater exalts the inner life, professorial meditation, libraries, museums, zoos, monotonous crises of conscience, stupid analyses of feelings, in other words, psychology, whereas on the other hand the circus and variety theater exalt action, heroism, life in the open air.[3]

Like other theatrical modernists, notably Frank Wedekind[4] and Max Reinhardt,[5] Marinetti was drawn to what he saw as the freedom, dynamism, danger and passion of the circus. With its (apparently) novel configurations of animal and human behavior, the circus represented transformation and transcendence, principles that the modernists valued so highly. The circus offered the spectacle of nature overcome, set aside, or remade by the imagination and ingenuity of humankind. From this perspective, the zoo appeared, by contrast, as a space of rationalistic analysis and static observation.

Though he did not know it, Marinetti's formulation mirrored a new animal discourse that was arduously installed in Western culture from the eighteenth century onward, within which the zoo eventually emerged as an exemplary site of serious, even scientific public knowledge about the natural world. The main themes of this evolving discourse were observation and education; its main ideological purpose was to justify the cruelty involved in the age-old practice of removing animals from their natural habitats and forcing them to endure lifetimes of loneliness and captivity for the entertainment of human beings. In the rhetoric of this discourse, the circus was often invoked, as were other animal acts and animal sports, as examples of an opposite relation to animals – a barbaric and unethical relation – utterly different from the enlightened one supposedly represented by the zoo. The contrast conveniently masked the fact that the origins of the zoo lay in impulses and practices that were virtually indistinguishable from those underlying the use of animals in circuses: namely, acquisitiveness, exoticism, sensationalism and cruelty. Marinetti's contrast, then, was as bogus as it was common.

But it is not my purpose here to contest Marinetti's formulations, nor to test the value of his metaphors as descriptors of modernist theater. Rather, I want to propose that his models be understood not as metaphors at all, but instead as cultural and institutional *contexts* within an expanded scene of theater history. It is not only metaphorically that the zoo and the circus can illuminate theater history: their relation to theater is not only the *paradigmatic* one that Marinetti intended; it is also a syntagmatic one, a relation of contiguity and continuity, of cultural co-presence. Like all those other metaphors with which the modernist theater attempted to theorize itself – the theater as laboratory, as temple, as fairground booth, lecture hall, street accident, court of law, sports arena – the circus and the zoo were not only cultural institutions *like* theater; they were also cultural institutions existing *alongside* theater. As such they deployed contemporaneous ideological discourses in ways that paralleled but also significantly differed from their use in theater. To explore the relationships – formal, taxonomic and material – between the theater and these institutions is to link the projects of theater history and cultural studies. In what follows, I initiate one such linkage: by enquiring into the relationship between theater and animals, I propose to relate theater history to that branch of cultural studies that, in the last decade of the twentieth century, began "to bring 'nature' 'back into' social theory by contesting its abstraction from society."[6]

Cultural studies turns to the animal as it has previously turned to other marginalized groups (like the insane, the disabled, the "primitive"), with a recognition of the constituent power of the margin. It turns to the animal with the recognition that it is often the most active ideological categories that are hardest to see, since ideology works by naturalizing its terms and veiling its taxonomies. As the editors of an important recent collection on animals put it: "animals have been so indispensable to the structure of human affairs and so tied up with our visions of progress and the good life that we have been unable to (even try to) fully see them. Their very centrality prompted us to simply look away and ignore their fates."[7] In recent decades, however, many disciplines have begun to "take animals seriously,"[8] looking at them through disciplinary lenses that include the geographical, the literary, the philosophical, the art-historical, the psychoanalytical[9] and the performative (the latter being represented so far mainly by a special issue of the journal *Performance Research*).[10] What might it mean to turn a specifically theatrical lens on animals? What light might be shed on cultural constructions of animality by framing them in terms of dramatic movements, genres and structures, or in terms of theatrical protocols, conventions and aesthetics?

Conversely, what might be revealed by turning an animal lens on theater, or – to use Alain Bleakely's suggestive phrase – by "animalizing" performance? Two possibilities immediately present themselves. First, the ambiguous politics of animal studies might help to illuminate the equally ambiguous politics of theater. Like theater, animals have never secured a clear and strong position on either the right or the left in the ideology of progress. Even today, decades after that ideology has been under attack from the left, only a few branches of feminism and postmodernism have embraced the animal. Most progressive movements tend to associate animal movements with premodern or New Age stances, and accordingly to dismiss them politically. Thus the animal, like the theater, is a politically ambiguous site, with a potential for generating perspectives and practices beyond the hardened binaries of the past. This politically deconstructive potential of the animal has, in recent years, drawn postmodern artists and philosophers[11] to it as to "a reminder of the limits of human understanding, and also of the value of working *at those limits*."[12]

Second: theater history might also find in the animal a useful site for understanding the historical role of performance in what social scientists call "boundary work": the drawing and blurring of lines of demarcation between and within groups, by means of which social relationships are configured and reconfigured over time. The boundary work that goes on around animals involves the configuration of the human itself, and animal acts are a principal site of this configuration. As the editors of a recent book on the subject write:

"The animal act configures the human in the company, in the obscure language and thought, of the animal. Animal vitality and consciousness are vicariously restored to the human being, allowing for conceptual breakthroughs and flights of fancy."[13] Animal performance, then – especially animal performance alongside or within contexts of human performance – is ideologically fraught. That old piece of advice to actors to avoid being on stage with a live animal may be more than the phenomenological common sense it is usually taken to be; it may be, as the same writers say, that "the spectacle of animals and humans performing together calls the spectator to other self-recognitions than that of the responsible citizen of the polis or the autonomous subject of philosophy and ethics."[14] The performing animal, in short, is the exemplary actor on that conceptual stage that one recent book memorably calls "the nature–culture borderlands."[15]

The history of theater offers many points of entry for an enquiry into the theatrical animal. Long before the modernist romanticization of circus, theatrical activity unfolded in the vicinity of spectacular and usually violent animal acts, most famously in ancient Rome and Elizabethan England. In both theater cultures, the syntagmatic relationship between animal acts and theatrical presentation was rendered literal by geographical proximity, as is so graphically seen, for example, in the maps of the South Bank, reproduced in many a theater history textbook, which shows the bear- and bull-baiting rings right next to the Globe. The syntagmatic relationship might also have been actualized in a certain amount of performative overlap, as for example in the possibility that the bear called for in *The Winter's Tale* may not have been an actor in an animal suit but rather an actual bear borrowed from the neighboring Bear Gardens, owned and operated by Philip Henslowe.[16] As for the paradigmatic relation between animal and human entertainment, it is perhaps reflected in the agonistic form of Greek tragedy, and certainly has appeared throughout theater history in imagery and action, ranging from Macbeth's remark about being "tied to a stake" and having "bear-like" to "fight the course,"[17] to Lucky's animal act in *Godot*: "Think, pig!" The paradigmatic use of another and extremely popular form of animal entertainment is the subject of a fascinating recent study entitled *Shakespeare and the Hunt*.[18]

The sharing of architectural forms between animal spectacles and theatrical representation also has a long history, and a strangely inverted moment in that history gives me a point of entry into the theatrical "zoo story" I want to tell here. In 1960, the Bronx Zoo became the first zoo in history to have an in-house multidisciplinary design team. Appointed to the head of the team was Jerry Johnson, a theater designer. His mandate was to infuse the exhibits with visual drama. By "contriving zoo exhibits as stage sets, like gigantic dioramas," Johnson set a new aesthetic standard in zoo design, making exhibits that were "beautifully convincing and almost mystical in their visual appeal." [19]

The Bronx Zoo is at the center of my zoo story, but, as another famous zoo story puts it: "sometimes a person has to go a very long distance out of his way to come back a short distance correctly."[20] The quotation, of course, is from the most famous zoo story in modern theater, Edward Albee's, which premièred in 1961 in New York's Provincetown Playhouse. Ironically, there is no zoo in *The Zoo Story*, at least no zoo is *seen* in it, and in fact there is no zoo story either. Although Jerry keeps promising a zoo story, he never actually gets to it. His zoo story is first displaced by another animal story – "the story of Jerry and the dog" – and later by his murder-suicide, in which his death cry (according to the stage direction) is the "sound of an infuriated and fatally wounded animal." In his book *Reading Zoos*, Randy Malamud characterizes this displacement as typical, saying that most zoo stories situate themselves "*against* the zoo – resisting it, subverting it, deconstructing it . . . The zoo alleges that it can tell a story, its own story, roughly along the lines of 'Here is a zebra.' The zoo story instead more routinely tells something like 'Here is a voyeur'; 'Here is a victim'; 'Here is a sadist'; 'Here is a corpse.' " [21]

Approximately four decades before Albee's play opened, another zoo story had premièred at the same historic New York theater: Eugene O'Neill's *The Hairy Ape*. This zoo story did not displace the zoo: on the contrary, it made the zoo the scene of its climactic and tragic final act, in which the protagonist, Yank, engineers something resembling Jerry's murder-suicide, but this time at the hands of an animal rather than a fellow human. Yank's encounter with the gorilla in the play's final scene is a rare instance (outside children's theater) of human and wild animal sharing the stage, a rare *live* performance of interspecies interaction, which is the stock in trade of so much popular cinema and television, from *Dr Doolittle* to *The Silence of the Lambs*.[22] It is, in fact, a classic piece of "boundary work," the use of animality to configure human subjectivity in performance. The explicit target of O'Neill's reconfiguration is the injustice of the class system, but his use of this particular animal, a gorilla, in this particular venue, complicates and obfuscates his class analysis by unconsciously linking it to *racial* difference.

Both Albee's zoo and O'Neill's are, explicitly, New York zoos, the former quite specifically the Central Park Zoo. In both plays, as the critical literature has amply explicated, zoos are troped as exemplars of the alienation and brutality of modern metropolitan civilization, the caged animal standing in for the disempowered and mystified subject of industrial capitalism. In both plays, too, zoos function as ambiguous sites for the fantasy of erasing or overcoming the class differences that American ideology programmatically obscures.[23] Albee's play is set in that paradigm of the carefully constructed public space, Central Park, within which different classes are supposed to be able to safely engage in certain performances of democracy. The class encounter here – between the upper-class Peter and the *lumpen* Jerry – goes horribly wrong. The territorial battle over the park bench turns lethal, turning this zone of supposedly safe civic interaction into a dangerous wilderness where brutish members of society can prey on their social superiors. Three decades after Albee's play, the word "wilding" was used to describe an actual crime in the same park, this time with race added to class in the encounter of difference.[24]

Both the Central Park and its zoo have, of course, played significant roles in the city's geography of class and race. Class was a consideration in the decision to put the new New York zoo, when it opened in 1899, up in the Bronx. The Central Park Menagerie was by then attracting increasingly large numbers of visitors, most of them coming up from the ghettoes of the lower East Side. The rowdy presence of these fervent animal-watchers had begun to represent a threat to Fifth Avenue real-estate prices; if many of them could be deflected north, it was suggested in the fund-raising process, that threat would be reduced. Just as Central Park itself had originally been conceived partly as a buffer between classes masquerading as a place of communion between them, the Bronx Zoo was part of an effort to redeploy the principle of distance in the service of a new, more proxemous notion of animals. The history of this new notion provides interesting parallels with the history of modern theater, with which it shared the pursuit of verisimilitude and authenticity.

The appointment of Jerry Johnson and the Bronx Zoo design team institutionalized a practice that had been launched with much fanfare in the early years of the twentieth century by one of the greatest zoo innovators of all time, Carl Hagenbeck, whose own peculiar history and interests made him particularly receptive to and reflective of the characteristic ambivalences of the modern zoo. Hagenbeck's project encapsulates many of the very agendas, problematics and tensions that make the zoo an illuminating context for theater history. Like the second generation of theatrical modernists, Hagenbeck was a passionate innovator who found himself challenging the hard-fought victories of a recent and equally passionate revolution, that of nineteenth-century empirical science. His innovation, like that of all the anti-naturalist modernisms, occupied the slippery ground that greets rationalists who venture beyond positivism. In theater, that ground was claimed mainly by theatricalism and expressionism, and certain fundamental precepts of both those movements can be discerned in Hagenbeck's project.

Hagenbeck's Tierpark opened in Hamburg, Germany, in 1907. It was the first zoo to move its captives into the open air and place them in naturalistic landscapes that sought to mimic their natural environments. Hagenbeck's professed goal was twofold, mixing in equal parts concern for the animals' well-being, and concern with the enjoyment of their human spectators. The radical incommensurability of these two goals conveniently escaped Hagenbeck, as it has many of his successors in "zoo culture."

Like all progressive zoo thinkers after him, Hagenbeck wanted animals to enjoy more freedom than was allowed by the sanitized interior enclosures of nineteenth-century zoos. These zoos, self-proclaimed models of scientific empiricism and taxonomic inquiry, took elaborate pains to present their captives as objects of study: singled out, set apart, abstracted from reality, labeled, explained. A host of design elements helped to concretize the scientific frame: animals were grouped according to scientific classification rather than geographical origin, cages were harshly lit and coldly tiled to resemble laboratories, extreme cleanliness and odorlessness were sought by extreme means (cages were designed so they could be flushed like toilets), and animals were scrupulously "protected" from what were considered unhealthy draughts of fresh air and disease-carrying exposure to natural soil.

The scientific zoo was a self-conscious alternative to the genre of animal display that Hagenbeck himself had been most closely linked to by his personal history. Having started out with six performing seals at a local fairground, Hagenbeck had rapidly built one of the world's largest animal dealerships. His first Tierpark, which attracted huge paying crowds, was in fact a modern exemplar of that ancient ancestor of the zoo: the menagerie. Dating back thousands of years before the Christian era and spread around the world, the practice of collecting and displaying exotic animals either in cages or in enclosed parks was originally affordable only to a tiny elite. In the early modern period, however, colonial expansion and commercialization gradually increased both the supply and demand for exotic animals. The private menageries that had been status symbols for European royalty since the sixteenth century, were slowly transformed into more "democratic" institutions, relocated from palace gardens like Versailles and Windsor Castle to public parks like Paris's Jardin des Plantes and the Zoological Gardens of London.[25] Here, in keeping with the Baconian idea that not only words but also *things* were viable instruments of knowledge and instruction, and with the help of the growing terminology of scientific classification, the spectacle of the caged animal could delight the masses under cover of instructing them. Like its contemporaneous theatrical form, naturalist melodrama, the scientific zoo supplied sensation dressed as sober truth.

The kind of zoo that Hagenbeck envisioned in the early years of the twentieth century had a markedly different ideal. "I desired, above all things," Hagenbeck writes in his autobiography, "to give the animals the maximum of liberty." His very next lines show, however, that this desire was party construed in theatrical rather than actual terms: "I wished to exhibit them not as captives, confined within narrow spaces, and looked at between iron bars, but as free to wander from place to place within as large a limit as possible, and with no bars to obstruct the view and serve as a reminder of captivity."[26] The supposed natural freedom of animals could not simply be asserted; it had to be *shown*, translated into visual terms for spectators. The animals had to be seen to *be* free, "as they really were," going about their natural lives in natural ways. This meant that spectators had to be helped to disregard the reality of the animals' captive state, to forget the vast distance they had been moved from their natural habitats to this site of display. In short, the bars of the cage had to be replaced by an invisible fourth wall. The familiar paradox of realist theater came into play: the more authenticity sought, the more illusion required. Hagenbeck embarked upon an elaborate design project, experimenting with terraces, platforms, panoramas and vistas to create the illusion of natural habitats.

But the emphasis on freedom was not merely aesthetic. It was, in fact, a key element of a certain (prevalent though not dominant) view of animality, one that is also embedded in Marinetti's contrast between circuses and zoos. This view, of which the extreme and most elaborated philosophical statement came from Nietzsche, equates animality with vitality, health, freedom, even sanity. It stands in partial opposition both to the mechanistic view of animals inherited from Cartesian rationalism (and coded in the protocols of the scientific zoo) as well as to the religious view of animals coded in medieval and early modern schemas like the Great Chain of Being. While both those views inferiorized animals in relation to human beings – the Cartesian with regard to consciousness and feeling, the Christian with regard to morality – the romantic, Nietzchean view idealized them, especially in relation to modern Western humanity. This account of animality, then, proved particularly attractive to counter-traditional artists seeking metaphors for a critique of repressive modern civilization. The romantic, vitalist, view of animality persists throughout the century, appearing in dramatic works like Peter Shaffer's *Equus*, and, very recently, Mabou Mines's *Ecco Porco*.

O'Neill's *The Hairy Ape* is a complicated and self-contradictory version of this view of animality, reflecting the clash of romantic and populist discourses within American ideology. The inspiration for the play was the story of a sailor whom O'Neill had briefly known in his seafaring days, and who committed suicide by throwing himself overboard in mid-ocean. O'Neill wondered, why this man, "*so proud* (as he put it) *of his animal superiority and in complete harmony* with his limited conception of the universe, should kill himself."[27]

The driving force of O'Neill's play is the question of what it means to be "in harmony" with the universe; or, in Yank's favorite word, to "belong." That the zoo should be Yank's last resort in his quest for identity and belonging is, of course, deeply and intentionally ironic, although the irony intended is tragic rather than, as I read it, discursive and ideological. In the remainder of this paper I want to read O'Neill's final scene through its setting, which encapsulates many of the material and ideological contradictions by which the modern zoo assists in the boundary-work necessary for framing modernist forms, including modernism's tragedies of self-consciousness.

The zoo that is explicitly called for in O'Neill's play, the New York Zoo, had a few years before been the venue of an extraordinary piece of "boundary-work." In 1906, the New York Zoo had for a period of time displayed in its Monkey House an African man, a pygmy named Ota Benga. Ota Benga had been brought to the United States from the Belgian Congo in 1904 by African explorer Samuel Verner and displayed along with other pygmies at the 1906 World's Fair in St Louis. He was then transferred to the Bronx Zoo, where he was housed with many monkeys, several chimpanzees, a famous gorilla and an orangutan. The accounts of Ota Benga's experience are chilling: "There were 40,000 visitors to the park on Sunday. Nearly every man, woman and child of this crowd made for the monkey house to see the star attraction in the park – the wild man from Africa. They chased him about the grounds all day, howling, jeering, and yelling. Some of them poked him in the ribs, others tripped him up, all laughed at him."[28] Under threat of legal action from local Black clergy, the director of the zoo compromised to this extent: during the day, Ota Benga was allowed to leave his cage. He had to circulate around the zoo in a white suit, and he returned to the monkey house every night to sleep. After repeated protests by Black clergy, Ota Benga was eventually released, soon after which he committed suicide.

The practice of exhibiting "exotic" humans alongside animals dates back to antiquity, and was a regular feature even of Carl Hagenbeck's first Tierpark, where a group of Lapps were displayed in full Arctic regalia, including skis and reindeer, and Eskimos paddled around in kayaks, supposedly hunting seals.[29] This kind of boundary-blurring was, of course, also a kind of boundary-making, part of the metropolitan zoo's project of defining Western civilization and its inhabitants as superior not only to nature but to nature-identified, "primitive" populations who would not be entirely out of place in the inferiorizing space of the zoo.

The final scene of O'Neill's play, in which a man exchanges places with a zoo animal, encapsulates the role of the zoo in the kind of boundary-work that then serves human culture's ideological programs. It shows clearly how the zoo is a site of boundary-blurring and identity crises, which facilitate the demeaning classifications and oppressive identifications by means of which cultural power is wielded. In O'Neill's scene, the gorilla is set apart from other animals, but they are not far away. The presence of a horde of monkeys, unseen but chattering loudly, confirms his animality. At the same time, and crucially for Yank's tragic pusposes, he is also humanized, explicitly and specifically, as follows: "*The gigantic animal himself is seen squatting on his haunches on a bench in much the same attitude as Rodin's 'Thinker.'* "[30]

O'Neill's zoo exemplifies several other versions of the permanent identity crises that characterize zoo animals. The first of these is what might be called the "crisis of individuality." The stage direction reads: "In the monkey house at the Zoo. One spot of clear gray light falls on the front of one cage so that the interior can be seen. The other cages are vague, shrouded in shadow from which chattering can be heard. On the one cage a sign from which the word 'gorilla' stands out." By convention and necessity, zoos usually have only one or two animals standing in for the entire species. Their representational status is often (as is the case in O'Neill's play) signaled by the signage on their enclosure: they are labeled generically: "Gorilla," "Chimpanzee," etc., rather than "A gorilla." This abstraction is dictated by the educational mission of the zoo. But the embodiedness of animals, their seductive "flesh and blood" reality, militates against the official generalizing impulse. Visitors mostly prefer to relate to the animal as a unique individual rather than a representative type, a preference which has led to the interesting and now highly controversial phenomenon of "zoo pets," animals who are singled out for special attention and various anthropomorphizing treatments, including naming, costuming, even performances, by both zoo keepers and zoo visitors. (The orangutan with whom Ota Benga was exhibited in the Bronx Zoo was name Dohung and was trained to ride a bicycle. The sign on Ota Benga's cage combined both conventions: it gave his name, but it also identified him as "The African Pygmy.") The zoo pet inconveniently disrupts the scientific boundary work of zoos, but it usefully mediates between the divergent agendas of exhibitors and spectators, a mediation that pays off economically.

Another identity dilemma for the zoo comes from the fact that not all animals are equally fascinating or adorable to human beings. Visitors' preference for the more striking-looking animals – "charismatic mega-fauna," as they are sometimes called, or, as one writer dubs them, "National Geographic animals" – conflicts with the modern zoo's commitment to context, accuracy and completeness in its account of animal life. O'Neill's gorilla – as well as his real-life counterpart in the Bronx Zoo at that time – falls into this category. The gorilla's "high-exhibition value," as it is called, was reflected in a pamphlet published by the New York Zoo around the same time as O'Neill's play. It contains the following chilling information and advice:

[The Gorilla] is very rarely seen in captivity. The only specimen which up to 1911 had ever reached America alive lived but five days after its arrival. Despite the fact that these creatures seldom live in captivity longer than a few months, they are always being sought by zoological gardens. The agents of the New York Zoological Society are constantly on the watch for an opportunity to procure and send hither a good specimen of that wonderful creature; and whenever one arrives, all persons interested are advised to see it *immediately* – before it dies of sullenness, lack of exercise, and indigestion.[31]

Amazingly enough, the author of this pamphlet is William T. Hornaday, the first director of the Bronx Zoo, and the man who had overseen and defended

the exhibition of Ota Benga in the Monkey House. A visionary animal advo-
cate and a leader of the movement to enlist zoos in the cause of wildlife preservation, Hornaday's attitudes furnish some of the most vivid examples of the
ideological complexity and internal contradictions of human discourse on
animals. His love and admiration of animals was balanced by contempt for certain human beings, some of them visitors to his zoo, whom he described as
"low-lived beasts who appreciate nothing and love filth and disorder."

The rhetorical use of animals in the articulation of racial and class prejudice
has been amply documented by cultural historians.[32] Hornaday's example
alerts us to the sobering and politically confusing fact that the source of discourses of bestialization can sometimes be animal lovers and advocates. A well-
known and sensational example is the following story about Adolph Hitler
watching an animal film: "During the scenes showing men savagely torn to
pieces by animals, he remained calm and alert. When the film showed animals
being hunted, he would cover his eyes with his hands and asked to be told
when it was over. Whenever he saw a wounded animal, he wept."[33] A more
complicated and perhaps more disturbing example is that of primatologist
Dian Fossey, whose defense of endangered gorillas often involved serious disregard and disrespect for the rights and needs of native Rwandans.[34] Her racial
prejudice is apparent in the binary formulation she offered for the species'
endangered status: it was, she said, because of "the encroachment of native
man upon its habitat – and neglect by civilized man."[35]

The native–civilized dichotomy is of course pervasive in O'Neill as in other
early modernists. But in *The Hairy Ape* the mediating role played by animals in
that dichotomy emerges most clearly. Yank's moment of tragic self-consciousness
crucially involves a construction of the animal as fundamentally and blessedly
territorial, unalienable, beyond the reach of the debilitating geopathologies
of modern human beings. Yank concludes that the gorilla "belongs" but he
doesn't:

> Youse can sit and dope dream in de past, green woods, de jungle and de rest
> of it. Den yuh belong and dey don't. Den yuh kin laugh at 'em, see? Yuh're
> de champ of de woild. But me – I ain't got no past to tink in, nor nothin'
> dat's coming', on'y what's now – and dat don't belong. Sure, you're de best
> off! . . . You belong! Sure! Yuh're de on'y one in de woild dat does, yuh lucky
> stiff! (230)

Yank's construction of animality as essentially territorial is implicitly contested
by its setting. The zoo is the place where the modern world stages its account
of the "place" of animals. The semiotics of the zoo, however, make that
account profoundly paradoxical and self-contradictory: the zoo is the place of
animals who have been displaced from their "real" places, animals whose real

places are too distant from urban centers to allow easy access. Indeed, it is the most distant, most "exotic" animals who were and remain the zoo's *raison d'être*, and zoo visitors' desire for proximity to these animals has challenged zoo designers from Carl Hagenbeck and his famous bar-less enclosures to the designers of Disney's Animal Kingdom and their notion of "environmental immersion" for both animals and spectators. To overcome the physical and conceptual distance that separates modern city-dwellers from wild animals requires presentational techniques consonant not only with changing views of particular animals and of animals in general, but also with the ever-changing conventions of dominant visual media. These conventions are often in stark conflict with the zoo's more ecological agendas. For example, when plate glass windows replaced iron bars as the means of containment, the intended gain in freedom was entirely the spectator's, who could now escape from the unpleasant and symbolically powerful materiality of cages and iron bars. For the animal, however, it was just one more sensory deprivation, one more concretization of the geopathology that began with its capture in the wild.

The zoo animal leads a remarkable bifurcated ideological existence, inscribed on the one hand within the modern zoo's increasingly high-minded claims of education, ecological consciousness-raising, preservation of endangered species, and, on the other, the persisting low-brow voyeurism of zoo-goers, which even the most serious zoos still cater to, with practices like public feeding-times and even public mating.[36] The zoo inherits and extends the culture's double-coding of animals as objects of knowledge and objects of fantasy. The very first elephant ever to be seen in America was first exhibited on Broadway (well, the corner of Broadway and Beaver Street!) and then at the first commencement of Harvard University![37] Conversely, the great touring menageries of the Ringling Brothers and Barnum and Bailey advertised themselves as "Traveling Universities of Natural History," and boasted thousands of animals "advantageously displayed in electric-lighted dens, where they may be studied at close range."[38]

The coexistence of knowledge and fantasy in human beings' dealings with animals unsettles and disproves Marinetti's contrast between zoo and circus with which I began. *The Hairy Ape*, however, suggests why this contrast, tenuous as it is, is ideologically useful. In the film version of the play, made in 1944, the scene with the gorilla was moved from its climactic position, and placed several scenes before the end. Rather than concluding a tragedy of self-consciousness, the meeting with the caged animal initiated a comedy of social conformism. Instead of killing himself, Yank saves various people, including his former upper-class tormentors, and ends up cheerfully well-adjusted to his station in life! Interestingly enough, the encounter with the gorilla does not take place in the New York Zoo. It takes place in the tent of a traveling circus. Yank goes to the circus after seeing a poster featuring its chief attraction, a gorilla named Goliath. The poster shows Goliath holding a swooning young white-clad woman in his arms. The story's displacement from tragedy to comedy, zoo to circus, mirrors its ideological transformation from O'Neill's romantic socialism to Hollywood's pacifying fatalism. Whereas O'Neill's animal had emulated Rodin's heroic human thinker, Hollywood's working-class man is made iconographically to mirror that exemplary spectacular beast of the popular modern imagination King Kong.[39]

In modernism, Baudrillard has said, "Animals must be made to say that they are not animals."[40] The modern zoo is a principal site of this paradoxical program of loud silencing. But the zoo stories of the modern theater are actively involved in it as well. A final and current example: Steven Berkoff, writing about his recent monologue "Dog," remarks: "Naturally the desire to be beast is overwhelming." Then he adds: "and what better beast than a fascistic, football-loving lager lout who owns a pit bull."[41] Playing both roles – man and dog – Berkoff reminds us that the modern theater, no less than the modern zoo, is an important site for the ceaseless boundary work that is the chief burden of the beasts.

Notes

1. Kay Anderson, "Animals, Science, and Spectacle in the City," in *Animal Geographies: Place, Politics and Identity in the Nature-Culture Borderlands*, ed. Jennifer Woloch and Jody Emel (London: Verso, 1998), 276.
2. Alain Fleischer, quoted in Chris Dercon, "Many Dreams of Many Gardens," trans Bruno Groeneveld, in *Theater Garden Bestarium: the Garden as Theatre as Museum* (Cambridge, Mass: MIT Press, 1990), 19.
3. F. T. Marinetti, *Marinetti: Selected Writings*, trans. R. W. Flint (New York: Farrar, Strauss and Giroux, 1972), 120.
4. See Jennifer Ham, "Taming the Beast: Animality in Wedekind and Nietzche," in *Animal Acts: Configuring the Human in Western History*, ed. Jennifer Ham and Matthew Senior (London: Routledge, 1997), 145–64.
5. Reinhardt's famous *Grosses Schauspielhaus* in Berlin was the refurbished Shuhmann Circus.
6. M. Fitzsimmons and D. Goodman, "Incorporating Nature: Environmental Narratives and the Reproduction of Food," in *Remaking Reality: Nature at the Millennium*, ed. B. Braun and N. Castree (London: Routledge 1998), 194.
7. Jennifer Wolloch and Jody Edel, "Preface," in *Animal Geographies*, xi
8. David Degrazia, *Taking Animals Seriously: Mental Life and Moral Status* (Cambridge: Cambridge University Press, 1996).
9. Some important recent works are: Arnold Arluke and Clinton R. Sanders, *Regarding Animals* (Philadelphia: Temple University Press, 1996); Alan Bleakley, *The Animalizing Imagination* (London and New York: Macmillan Press and St. Martin's Press, 2000); Susan Davis, *Spectacular Nature: Corporate Culture and Sea World* (Berkeley: University of California Press, 1997); Aubrey Manning and James Serpel, *Animals and Human Society: Changing Perspectives* (London: Routledge, 1994); Bob Mullan and Garry Marvin, *Zoo Culture* (Urbana: University of Illinois Press, 1987, 1999); Chris Philo and Chris Wilbert, *Animal Spaces, Beastly Places: New Geographies*

of Human–Animal Relations (London: Routledge, 2000); Paul Shepard, *How Animals Made Us Human* (Washington, DC: Island Press, 1996); Roy Willis, ed., *Signifying Animals* (London: Unwin Hyman, 1990).

10. *Performance Research*, 5, 2 (Summer 2000).

11. See, for example, Jean Baudrillard, *Simulacra and Simulation* (Ann Arbor: University of Michigan Press, 1994); Gilles Deleuze and Felix Guattari, *A Thousand Plateaus: Capitalism and Schizophrenia*, trans. Brian Massumi (Minneapolis: University of Minnesota Press, 1988); and Jacques Derrida, "The Animal That Therefore I Am (More to Follow)," *Critical Inquiry*, 28, 2 (Winter 2002): 369–418.

12. Steve Baker, *The Postmodern Animal* (London: Reaktion Books, 2000), 16.

13. Ham and Senior, *Animal Acts*, 1.

14. Ibid.

15. Jennifer Woloch and Jody Emel, eds, *Animal Geographies: Politics and Identities in the Nature–Culture Borderlands* (London: Verso, 1998).

16. Matthew Bliss "Property or Performer?: Animals on the Elizabethan Stage," *Theatre Studies*, 39 (1994): 45–59.

17. The recent film *Scotland, PA* offers a hilarious and provocative rumination on the relationship between power and animality in *Macbeth*. The transformation of the Macbeths into pioneers of the fast food hamburger chain reads like a gloss on the title of Carol Adams's famous book, *The Sexual Politics of Meat: a Feminist-Vegetarian Critical Theory*, revised edn (New York: Continuum, 2000).

18. Edward Berry, *Shakespeare and the Hunt: a Cultural and Social Study* (Cambridge: Cambridge University Press, 2001).

19. Hancocks, *A Different Nature: the Paradoxical World of Zoos and their Uncertain Future* (Berkeley: University of California Press, 2001), 106.

20. Edward Albee, *The Zoo Story*, in *Two Plays by Edward Albee* (New York: Signet, 1959), 21. Further page references are to this edition.

21. Randy Malamud, *Reading Zoos: Representations of Animals in Captivity* (New York: New York University Press, 1998), 55.

22. See Cary Wolfe and Jonathan Elmer, "Subject to Sacrifice: Ideology, Psychoanalysis, and the Discourse of Species in Jonathan Demme's *Silence of the Lambs*," *Boundary 2: an International Journal of Literature and Culture* 2, 3 (Fall 1995): 141–70.

23. In *Zoo Story*, Jerry ironically asks: "Say, what's the dividing line between upper-middle-middle-class and lower-upper-middle-class?" (20).

24. Joan Didion, "New York: Sentimental Journeys," *The New York Times Review of Books*, 17 (1991); <http://www.nybooks.com/articles/article-preview?article_id=3377>.

25. The former in 1804, the latter 1847.

26. Carl Hagenbeck, *Beasts and Men*, trans. Hugh S. R. Elliot and A. G. Thacker (London: Longmans, Green, 1910).

27. Quoted in Doris Falk, *Eugene O'Neill and the Tragic Tension* (New York: Gordian Press, 1958, 1982), 136.

28. Phillip Verner Bradford and Harvey Blume, *Ota Benga: the Pygmy in the Zoo* (New York: St. Martins Press, 1992), 269.

29. Vicki Croke, *The Modern Ark: The Story of Zoos, Past, Present and Future* (New York: Scribner, 1997), 145.

30. Eugene O'Neill, *Anna Christie, The Emperor Jones, The Hairy Ape* (New York; Vintage Books, 1995), 195. Further page references to *The Hairy Ape* are to this edition.

31. William T. Hornaday, *Popular Official Guide of the New York Zoological Park*, 1921.

32. See especially, Steve Baker, *Picturing the Beast: Animals, Identity, and Representation* (Manchester: Manchester University Press, 1993).

33. Robert Payne, *The Life and Death of Adolf Hitler* (New York: Prager, 1960), 461.

34. Karal Armbruster, "'Surely, God, These Are My Kin': the Dynamics of Identity and Advocacy in the Life and Works Dian Fossey," in Ham and Senior, *Animal Acts*, 218.

35. Dian Fossey, "Making Friends with the Mountain Gorillas," *National Geographic*, 137 (January 1970): 574–85.

36. The San Diego Zoo offers a tour called "Night Moves" billed as "a unique dating experience" "focusing on the wild courtship and mating rituals of the facility's exotic – and erotic – residents." Quoted in Malamud, *Reading Zoos*, 236.

37. Hancocks, *A Different Nature*, 87.

38. Quoted in Hancocks, *A Different Nature*, 87.

39. "The original monstrosity of the beast, object of terror and fascination, but never negative, always ambivalent, object of exchange also and of metaphor, in sacrifice, in mythology, in the heraldic bestiary, and even in our dreams and our phantasms – this monstrosity . . . has been exchanged for a spectacular monstrosity: that of King Kong wrenched from his jungle and transformed into a music-hall star." Jean Baudrillard, "The Animals: Territory and Metamorphosis," in *Simulacra and Simulation*, 135.

40. Ibid., 129.

41. Steve Berkoff, "Dog," Director/Writer's Program Note, Playbill for *One Man*, The Culture Project @ 45 Bleecker Street, 23 January–10 March 2002.

8
History Plays (in) Britain: Dramas, Nations, and Inventing the Present

Loren Kruger

My title can be read literally as a reference to the history play and its perform-ance on British stages, but it also invokes the ambiguously linked metaphors: history as drama, an account of the past shaped by conflicts between individ-uals and society and by groups within society, and punctured by revelations, reversals and other climaxes; and history as play, as an unpredictable succes-sion of events that do not inherently lend themselves to orderly interpretation. If the first half of the title implies that "history plays Britain" like a role or game, the second half might redeem this whimsy for scholarship by proposing that the history play at its best provides a compelling interpretation of the past in the present, and illuminates the process of locating theater in history. Sweeping as it is, this proposition cannot but come up against the frontiers between the nation and its others, and the gulf between the present and the past. National boundaries – England/Britain; Britain/Empire/Commonwealth – are both hotly contested and thoroughly muddled. This intellectual paradox and its material consequences have received some attention from social and political historians as different as Linda Colley (*Britons: Forging the Nation*) and Tom Nairn (*The Break-up of Britain*) but not as much from English theater his-torians who habitually reduce Britain to England and, even further, to central London stages.[1] This geographical parochialism, the tendency of the London critic to see Britain from his privileged perch in the capital, is often matched by the temporal parochialism that masquerades as expansiveness, in the habit of treating theater events that shaped the sensibility of the influential critic as though it were eternally present. A British theater history of the present, how-ever broadly defined, can be compelling history and plausibly British only if it combats parochialism on both geographical and temporal fronts.

While the geographical parochialism of English commentators has been challenged on several fronts, the temporal parochialism manifest by the expan-sive "contemporary" is so habitual as to be practically invisible. The problem of the contemporary in the history of the present, in the sense not only of the *"othering of the past"*

current theater but of the past that remains present to those writing its history, is manifest in the persistence with which British historians, theatrical or otherwise, refuse to frame the present in history and the present *as* history. The last half-century is still, half a century after the fact, called "postwar," as in David Childs's 2000 edition of *Britain since 1945* or Dominic Shellard's 1999 *British Theatre since the War* or, even more loosely, "contemporary."[2] In the case of the "contemporary," the normally normative character of periodization, which Thomas Postlewait identifies as a key if not always reliable category of regulating meaning in (theater) history, appears to break down.[3] Like its companion term, "modern," which is used sometimes as a synonym for "contemporary" and sometimes as an antonym to it, "contemporary" serves less to mark the boundary of a historical period and more to signal the attachment of the author to the events so called. Its meaning thus moves from the relative term, "at the same time as" (as in: Jonson's career was partly contemporary with that of Shakespeare), to "in our time" or, simply, absolutely, "ours" (as in: Jan Kott's *Shakespeare our Contemporary*). The translation of the "contemporary theater" into the theater present-to-us expresses the pervasive assumption that mid-century theater in general and its recurring if contested emblem, John Osborne's *Look Back in Anger*, in particular, are still our contemporary, still an organic part of us, even if, as Aleks Sierz, chronicler of "British drama today" wrote at the turn of this century, this play and its era serve as a foil for the "in-yer-face" nihilism of the 1990s in a play like *Some Explicit Polaroids*, Mark Ravenhill's drama about the collision of people and principles associated with conflicting generations (the 1970s v. the 1990s).[4] Although Sierz claims that Ravenhill and *his* contemporaries offer a complete departure from the macho attitude of Angry Young Men in the Cold War (149) and the obsession with the "state of the nation" play they engendered, he reinserts Ravenhill's play into this category by comparing his "unparalleled feeling for the Zeitgeist" with Osborne's in his time and thus judging the later play by the criteria of contemporaneity and up-to-datedness established by the earlier one.

This assumption or what we might call the fallacy of the enduring present persisting in the ever-repeated iteration of the "contemporary," has several consequences for theater as for general history of Britain. The perception of an enduring present, which allows commentators to refer to a half-century *as* "contemporary," paradoxically depends on the iteration of states or moments each of which compel immediate attention before passing away. The power of the enduring present depends on an erasure of this iteration and thus also of the historicity of the contemporary. Most obviously, it obscures key questions of periodization: when does the "postwar" period of anger mixed with nostalgia begin? With the defeat of Nazism and the victory of Labour in 1945? With the independence of India and the advent of decolonization in 1947? Or with the much touted and now also much criticized "revolution" ushered in by *Look*

Back in Anger on 8 May 1956 (VE Day plus eleven years)? What is lost in the presumption that the postwar theater begins only in 1956? What might be gained by insisting that the postwar period be reformulated literally (to begin in 1945) and to constitute figuratively the long 1950s? When do these "long 1950s" end?[5] With the consolidation of Conservative power (and affluence) in 1959? With the return of Labour in 1964? What are the boundaries of the "long 1960s," beginning for our purposes with the expansion of Arts Council funds under the Wilson government for the "spreading" as well as the "raising" of culture in a democracy, and the subsidy of dissidence (in the form of socialist, anarchist and later feminist, gay and anti-racist theater), and ending with Thatcherism in 1979?[6] Or perhaps in 1984, with the Arts Council policy of pre-serving elite institutions in the "Glory of the Garden" and the Tories' first attempt to abolish the GLC, postponed but not prevented by regional resist-ance to centralized "haughty culture"?[7] What follows this period? The long fin-de-siècle? The end of national history (of theater or other institutions) in the era of globalization?[8]

The notion of the enduring present also reinforces assumptions of geo-graphical centrality, as it marks as present above all the theater in London. In particular, it has overemphasized the artistically if not socially transformative force of theaters such as the Royal Court, in 1956 a new but influential insti-tution whose reputation for revolution was celebrated by critics from John Russell Taylor to Richard Findlater, exposed as bourgeois renovation by John McGrath, and, more recently, put in its place on a continuum with the West End by Stephen Lacey and Dan Rebellato, while overlooking significant work in other acknowledged theater capitals or in places and institutions on the routes of itinerant theaters beyond the horizon of the capitals.[9]

More subtly, perhaps, the enduring present privileges the immediate urgency of the commonly called "state-of-the-nation play" over more reflective genres, such as the history play, which may dramatize events and characters of the past or seek to cast the present in a historical light. The history play is a more restricted category than the state-of-the-nation play, but the latter may be too broad to be useful (what publicly performed play has *nothing* to say about the state of the nation?) and too indiscriminately attached to the play of the moment. The former's reflective character punctures the fallacy of the endur-ing or recurring present encouraged by the unreflected enthusiasm for each new sensation. History plays, by which I mean not only drama that may rep-resent the present as the outcome of historical forces as well as recall historical conflicts in the present, but also texts and performance that make history not by creating a sensation but by illuminating their present moment as a legacy of dramatically conflicting pasts, can present a persuasive analysis of the his-toricity of the contemporary and the present inheritance of the past, as well as a compelling dramatic picture. From Terence Rattigan's melancholy look back on Empire in the postwar life of T. E. Lawrence in *Ross* (1960), to John Arden and Margaretta D'Arcy's critical counter-histories of Empire in Britain from *Armstrong's Last Goodnight* (1964) to *The Island of the Mighty* (1973) and *The Non-Stop Connolly Show* (1975), from John McGrath's chronicle play on Scottish dispossession from the Clearances to North Sea Oil in *The Cheviot, the Stag and the Black, Black Oil* (1973) to Caryl Churchill's dramatization of utopian aspirations in the English Revolution in *Light Shining in Buckinghamshire* (1976), from McGrath's satirical chronicle of English/Scottish relations in *Border Warfare* (1989) to James Kelman's bleak tableau of historical agency blocked in the so-called Age of Revolution, *Hardie and Baird* (1990), much of the most compelling drama has attempted not only to play and replay but also to re-form the history of Britain. The history play at its best draws attention to the key elements buried by appeals to the Zeitgeist of the enduring present: the periodization of the last half-century in the theater and without, the character of succeeding presents as history; the critical representation of the implications of that periodization, of the passing of social structures and structures of feeling and the persistence of others; and the dimensions of Britain on stage and off excluded by the habitual focus on the London sensation.

By refocusing attention on history plays rather than immediate states of the nation, on stages outside London, and on the long 1950s rather than the moment of 1956 mythologized by Taylor and Tynan and confirmed in its centrality by Shellard's overview and even by more probing accounts by Lacey and Rebellato, this chapter will attempt to reform and reformulate the history of British theater at the turn of the half-century, at the moment when, as it were, the "contemporary" theater had its day.[10] Before we can consider the specific conditions of the history of the present in that moment or the status of history plays as critical historiography, however, we should find appropriate theoretical tools to critique the epistemological claims that underlie assumptions about the enduring present and its catch-all cover, the Zeitgeist.

The persistence of monuments: the characters of history and the roles of the past

The power of the Zeitgeist as a persuasive measure of history testifies to the ongoing influence of its originator, G. W. F. Hegel, who used the notion of the "spirit of the age" to inaugurate an epochal and dialectical conception of history against the notion of historical movement by incremental steps, favored by Enlightenment thinkers like Immanuel Kant.[11] Hegel's conception is dialectical in that he sees history made in the "collisions between existing, known duties, laws and rights, and the contingencies that are averse to this fixed system" (*Philosophie der Geschichte*, 44–5/ *Philosophy of History*, 29) and between these contingencies and the "world historical figures" or "historical men" who shape them (45/29–30); it is epochal, in that the moment of collision is formed by the clash of competing spirits and ages (40/25). Arguing against absolute adherence to either the divine law of Providence or the Enlightenment law of reason above men, he asserts that reason in history is realized only in human agency, in the "passions, genius, active powers" (25/13) of (mostly) men whose "deeds produce a state of things and world-historical relations [*Weltverhältnisse*] that appear exclusively to be their affair and their creation" (46/30).

In this view of history, which Hegel reiterates in the account of dramatic action in the *Aesthetics*, the essential spirit of the *longue durée* of the epoch is concentrated in the dramatic collision between the world-historical protagonist and the existing order. His definition of dramatic action is in turn deeply anchored in history; he defines dramatic action as *"collision* of circumstances, passions, and characters" in which individual "passion" collides with "the concrete spheres of family, state, church," and other aspects of an "organized national life."[12] This dialectical engagement of drama and history has given Hegel's theory the unacknowledged power of common sense in current notions of drama, even when the lines of influence are not explicitly traced. Mid-twentieth-century British playwrights may not cite Hegel, but his impact is registered through the inheritance of Shakespeare as reinterpreted by English Germanophiles from Samuel Coleridge through Thomas Carlyle to A. C. Bradley, and the early twentieth-century history play, especially in John Drinkwater's imitations of Friedrich Schiller, Hegel's model modern dramatist. This influence is especially noteworthy in the not-quite post-imperial 1950s, especially in playwrights such as Rattigan whose work reflects the persistent appeal, if not Hegel's formulation thereof, of the world-historical individual as the most legitimate representative of historical forces, even as devolution demotes that individual to the rank of private person.[13]

Hegel's dramatic conception of historical change might encourage the investment of a single dramatic moment with the force of epochal change, at the expense of a broader understanding of the *longue durée*, but he anticipates this problem at the outset of *The Philosophy of History*; he distinguishes scholarly, mediated or "reflective" [*reflektierte*] history from the naïve, unmediated history that treats events as a succession of nows, each apparently unique and urgently compelling, rather than as present moments coalescing the dialectical collision of conflicting pasts (*Philosophie der Geschichte*, 11/ *Philosophy of History*, 1). In this critique of unreflective or "originary" history, Hegel thus anticipates the problem of the contemporary. The assumption that the past is still our contemporary is problematic above all because it rewrites what should be critical history as though it were "history from the source," the immediate recollection of events by those experiencing them. As Hegel defines it, "history from the source" [*ursprüngliche Geschichte*], "originary" rather than "original" history, is history written by contemporary participants, about "deeds, events, and social conditions [*Zustände*], which they had before their eyes and to whose spirit they belonged. [*zugehört haben*]" (*Philosophie der Geschichte*, 11/ *Philosophy of History*, 1, trans. modified). Hegel's claim that this kind of history "simply transfer[s] what was passing in the world around them to the realm of the intellectual notion [*geistliche Vorstellung*]" (11/1, trans. modified) may overstate the point, but it does draw due attention to the problem that plagues even astute historians of the theater, as an event, an institution, or an aesthetic object: the privilege granted eye-witnesses, who record their immediate attachment to the events that pass before their eyes as though they were the evidence of enduring transformations. This is the mode of the hyperbolic theater review that claims to make history; Kenneth Tynan's punchline dubs *"Look Back in Anger* . . . the best young play of its decade" before the decade was out and reiterates this claim in the "End of a Twelvemonth" in which he hails the play as an "oasis of reality in a 'theatre hermetically sealed off from life,' " speaking "from the source" as if to posterity.[14]

If Tynan's review confirms in part the naivete of "history from the source" as an immediate transfer of "events" to the realm of "the intellectual notion," it also suggests the engaged *interest* of the critic concerned at the moment of the contemporary theater event to make of that event a lasting monument to the new. As such it suggests that even the most immediate account of the contemporary event is already mediated by concerns that go beyond it. Tynan's contemporary account (the review of the première) thus paves the way for the use and abuse of this historical event in the service of concerns contemporary with later moments. The two editions and multiple printings of John Russell Taylor's *Anger and After* have established *Look Back in Anger* as the emblem of the enduring present, in the cover image of Kenneth Haigh as the original Jimmy Porter and the characterization of the play as "the event that marks 'then' decisively from 'now.' "[15] The present tense, persisting even in reprints in the second decade after the event, marks this account as "history in the service of [present] life" but it also masks the ideological charge of the "use and abuse of history" beneath this apparently neutral term. As Stephen Lacey demonstrates, the London critics' emphasis on the vitality, youth and contemporaneity of the central character and his drama, masked the continuity in form and content between *Look Back in Anger* and the sexual and political status quo it allegedly attacked.[16]

By reiterating the revolutionary ardor of *Anger* over the evidence of reactionary sentiments in the play and its author, Taylor's account constitutes what Friedrich Nietzsche, in his essay *On the Advantage and Disadvantage of History for Life*, calls "monumental history."[17] Nietzsche argues against Hegel that there is no naïve unmediated history "from the source," only a dichotomy between "antiquarian history" that suffocates the present under the weight of the past in the name of "preserving and revering" ("Vom Nutz und Nachteil," 114/ *On the Advantage and Disadvantage*, 19), and "monumental history," which represents the "effect" as "exemplary and worthy of imitation" at the expense of the understanding of "causes" of historical change ("Vom Nutz und Nachteil," 110–11/ *On the Advantage and Disadvantage*, 17). Nietzsche's title, weighing the advantage and disadvantage of each method "in the service of life," may preserve a certain ironic detachment from both history and life, but his argument that the "past itself suffers *damage*" (17) [*leidet selbst Schaden*] (111) under monumental history is registered more strongly in the usual English translation, "on the use and abuse of history." In the context of theater history, it illuminates the way in which the monumentalization of *Anger* obscures the causes of the youth rebellion in 1950s Britain and of the limitations of a rebellion in a society with an entrenched class hierarchy and a stunted legacy of resistance. At the same time, Nietzsche's characterization of monumental history as the representation of the "effect in itself" without the cause, alerts us to the power of the monument and its guardians to erase causes under the appearance of self-evidence, as though the revolutionary power of *Look Back in Anger* were at once unique and disconnected from its temporal and social contexts. We can see this in the proliferation of apparently neutral accounts and collections of documents, which persist, well into the 1990s, in starting "postwar" British theater in 1956.[18]

If, as the reiteration of 1956 as the self-evident origin of "contemporary theater" suggests, the monument seemed firm up until the half-century mark of 1996, the years since this date have marked a shift away from the fixity of the enduring present to a revisionist view of this once decisive caesura between "then" and "now." Lacey's *British Realist Theatre: the New Wave in its Context 1956–65* (1995) retains the conventional marker of 1956, but his critical juxtaposition of Osborne's play with the more focused social critique and activism of the New Left performs a critical archeology of the monument, not so much to obliterate but, in Michel Foucault's reformulation of Nietzsche, to excavate the "conditions of its emergence [*apparition*]" and thus to prepare the way for critical archival work that might produce an account of the conditions of suppression of other moments of theater historical significance and prepare the way for a revised genealogy.[19] Rebellato's polemically titled *1956 and All That: the Making of Modern British Drama* (1999) claims, as the blurb has it, to "look back beyond anger," but succeeds better at deconstructing the monument itself, demonstrating that the Royal Court was closer to the West End than the mythology of dissidence allows, and that the Court's promotion of a theater of youth and vitality went hand-in-hand with the association of revolution with heterosexual virility and the consequent emasculation of homosexual dissidence; it stops short, however, of replotting the genealogy of theatrical revolt itself with landmarks as yet unearthed.[20] Shellard's *British Theatre Since the War*, published the same year, makes the dubious assumption that "the war" is an unambiguous referent for all readers, but his account does provide causes for the "effect" of 1956, first by opening with a chapter covering 1945–54 and, second, by inserting 1956 into a broader trajectory, which begins with the Arts Theatre Club, which brought Beckett's *Waiting for Godot* to London in 1955, and concludes with the establishment of a National Theatre Company in 1962. This trajectory, extended in a collection of essays on *British Theatre in the 1950s*, puts the Royal Court and its signature production in their place, as it were, by revaluating theaters other than the Royal Court with claims to innovation, and reaffirming the vitality of those institutions, such as the West End Group, and authors, conventionally dismissed as conventional or, to recall the phrase that Tynan attributed to Arthur Miller, "hermetically sealed off from life."[21] Nonetheless, this revaluation is more reaffirmation than revision, since it does little to undo London's indifference to the rest of Britain, and thus misses a key opportunity not merely to *add* new names to a British theater history whose pantheon remains essentially the same but rather to rewrite the general history itself as a post-imperial, if not post-British history, rather than a blandly "contemporary" theater.

Provincializing England: a post-imperial lens on the long 1950s

Looking at theater, history, and Britain in the 1950s under a post-imperial lens not only reveals hitherto hidden trends in the theater history of Britain but also compels a revision, even, as Nairn argues, a "break-up," of *Britain* itself. Thanks in part to Nairn, it is now relatively uncontroversial to speak of Britain after devolution as post-imperial if not quite "after Britain," but attachments to Empire and the imperial idea of Britain were still powerful in England in the 1950s. The post-imperial lens focuses attention not merely on imperial(ist) moments in British theater history, as Nandi Bhatia uncovers in *Look Back in Anger*, but on the thematic and institutional representation of England and English drama as though it spoke self-evidently for Britain, and for the invented but powerfully resonant entity called "the English-speaking world."[22] It also casts light on the structural rather than merely incidental marginalization of drama outside this charmed sphere, which is treated as a non-representative supplement to the general narrative of legitimate theater history, or apparently non-existent altogether. In speaking for the hidden impact of the margin on the core, not merely periphery, of this legitimate narrative, I am drawing on Foucault's outline, in his response to Nietzschean genealogy and to Hegelian universal history, of a critical genealogy that challenges monumental history by finding historical moment not only in the "singular event" but also in the recurrence, evolution, and disguised re-appearance on "different stages" and "different roles" played by apparently ahistorical events, and, crucially, in narratives and instances that mark the

"lacunae" or "the moments at which 'historical events did not take place'"
[*n'ont pas lieu*] ("Nietzsche, la généalogie," 136/ "Nietzsche, Genealogy," 140,
trans. modified).

While this critical genealogy may look modest against the imperious sweep
of universal history, in the sense that it begins by rendering visible previously
invisible dramas and minority voices in the theater, it acts more strongly than
its modest appearance might suggest, by compelling the reconceptualization
of the general narrative hitherto legitimated as (unqualified) theater history.
To paraphrase post-colonial historian Dipesh Chakrabarty's critique, in
Provincializating Europe, of European historicist thinking that relegated Indian
history to the category of the "also ran" or the "catcher-up" after a "universal
history" that is by (European) definition European, the object here is to
"provincialize England," to deconstruct English claims to universality or, in
this instance, to the full and exclusive *occupation* of Britain and the idea of
"Britain."[23] The remainder of this chapter will turn to a key instance of the
under-written theater history of post-imperial Britain. The dramatization of
Britain in Scotland is still in standard "British" theater histories, apparently
beyond the boundaries of Britain, even though, as Nairn reiterates, the Scots
have always taken "Britain" more seriously than the English.[24] The drama of
Britain in Scotland appeared on stages with demonstrable *national* standing,
from the Edinburgh Festival with David Lindsay's *Ane Satire of the Thrie Estaites*
revived after 400 years by the Edinburgh Festival in 1948 to John Arden's
response in *Armstrong's Last Goodnight*, written for and produced by the
Citizens' Theatre in Glasgow in 1964, and revived in a new production by the
English National Theatre at the Chichester Festival and then at the Old Vic in
1965. As Scottish historians have noted, the Scottish cultural revival is an
exemplary post-imperial phenomenon, insofar as it appears to have compen-
sated for the deficit left by the decline of the British Empire in which Scottish
intellectuals, politicians, merchants, and others played a significant role that
resists latter-day reduction to the position of (post-)colonial subaltern.[25] As a
response to the demise of the imperial project of "Greater Britain," in which
Scottish actors had played a shaping if subordinate role, the dramatization of
Britain in Scotland in the post-imperial period has a *trans-national* as well as a
provincial aspect. Drawing on Chakrabarty's caveat that "provincializing
Europe cannot be a nationalistic, nativist or atavistic project" (43), which
would merely mirror the imperial idea with the local response, I argue that the
dramatization of Britain in Scotland is not merely a supplement to or a simple
rebellion against English hegemony. My project here is not to reiterate what
has become the platitude of post-colonial heroic pathos nor to replace English
chauvinism (whether of the imperial or "little" variety) with its Scottish mir-
ror-image, but to show in the Scottish dramatization of Britain, including a
Scottish play by an English author, both the deconstruction of habitual English

↳ ? = What qualifies a "Scottish" play?

assumptions about exclusive occupation of the power of "Britain" and the construction of a theater history engaged with the contestation of this power.

Despite the promotional blurb that opens the *Twenty-First Anniversary Conspectus* celebrating the Citizens' Theatre's "significant contribution to the cultural life in Scotland" in 1964, the founders of the Glasgow theater shared with those of the Edinburgh Festival a belief in the potential of these institutions in two "cold, windy Northern" cities to rival other institutions both national and international.[26] From its first season in 1947, the Edinburgh Festival hosted companies from Europe such as those headed by Louis Jouvet and Jean-Louis Barrault in Paris, or Giorgio Strehler in Milan. Granted funding from CEMA, the wartime forerunner of the Arts Council, in 1943, shortly after the Shakespeare Company at the Old Vic, the Citizens' Theatre, unlike the Old Vic, does not appear in Shellard's "Table of Significant Events."[27] But the Citizens' had, in addition to noteworthy Scottish plays by Robert McLellan, Joe Corrie, and the theater's director, James Bridie, as well as a Scottish National spirit inherited from the ailing Scottish National Theatre Company, from the outset a more international repertoire than the Old Vic or the Royal Court, which, as Rebellato notes, became more emphatically English in its first decade.[28] What is remarkable about the repertoire at the Citizens' Theatre and at the Edinburgh Festival is not only the Scottish element but the predominance of history plays that dramatize the complexity of past and present English/Scottish relations in ways that challenged both the pieties of Union and the counter-clichés of romantic rebellion.

Robert McLellan is an exemplary contributor to this revisionist history through drama. His best known play, *Jamie the Saxt*, first produced by the Curtains Theatre Company in Glasgow in 1937 and revived at the Citizens' Theatre in 1947, is a sly "historical comedy" that begins by presenting James VI of Scotland as the comic object of court and church intrigues and ends by showing him out-intriguing others and preparing his entry to London as James I of England. However, his "comedy of the 18th century," *The Flouers of Edinburgh*, which was directed by James Gibson for Gateway Theatre at the Edinburgh Festival in 1957, the same year as *The Entertainer* appeared at the Royal Court, commands attention for its pointedly post-imperial satire of English–Scottish relations and, secondarily, of British imperialism generally.[29] Although it follows eighteenth-century conventions in weaving a comedy of rival suitors around Kate, the ingenue of the piece, the romance takes its cue from local rivalries with international resonances. Particularly compelling is the tension between the chief suitor, Charles, an Anglicized Scot keen to dismiss the "barbarities" of Scottish custom and language (until compelled by Kate to propose in Scots), and various antagonists, from the father who challenges his son's approval of sending "backward" Highlanders to Canada while claiming that Scottish and English are equal after Union – "the terms 'Scotch' and 'English' became obsolete with Union" – with the retort "I'll wager ye winna fin mony Englishmen caiin themselves British and stertin to talk and dress like Scotsmen" (175), to Sidney, an English army officer, who is romantically fond of the "natural splendor" of Scottish customs (188), to a Scottish Nabob recently returned from India, who astonishes Sidney by claiming knowledge of literature in Persian and Sanskrit, even "in ane wha hasna taen the bother to learn English"(211). Although the Nabob is in part a figure of fun and in part an ambiguous representative of British imperialism, McLellan creates in him a character whose very cosmopolitan ambiguity trumps the Celtic stereotypes of English comedy.

The value of *The Flouers of Edinburgh* for the theater history of Britain lies not merely in its satire of Scotland's absorption into the British Empire, or in its variation on the history play, although it does offer a more complicated picture of collective and individual historical agency than do the more heroic (and more Hegelian) depictions of singular "historical men" in patriotic history plays such as Bridie's *John Knox* (Citizens' Theatre, 1947) or Sydney Goodsir Smith's *The Wallace, A Triumph in Five Acts* (Edinburgh Festival, 1960), or the more ambiguous but no less Hegelian drama by Rattigan, *Adventure Story* (on Alexander the Great), which played at the Citizens' in 1949, after opening in London in 1947.[30] In weaving together the history play with the romantic rivalry between suitors from the eighteenth-century marriage plot and the linguistic rivalry between Scots and English and the uneven development of internal colonialism and the centralization of power and prestige in London, *The Flouers of Edinburgh* prompts a review not only of Scots and other British languages on the twentieth-century stage but also of English plays in the Restoration and eighteenth century, especially those that deal directly or indirectly with imperial relations, and, to complete the circle, of current black British revisions of this history, such as the work of Tara Arts (since 1979).[31] It also invites the investigation or perhaps the invention of an undiscussed generic category, which we might call the comedy of colonial manners, which would include the representation of cultures of internal as well as imperial colonization.[32] Since plays in this category, such as *The Flouers of Edinburgh* or *Love and the Hyphen* (1902–12), the long-running Anglo-Boer hit by South African actor-manager Stephen Black, use other languages in addition to the Queen's English to dramatize colonial relations as well as the comedy of grammatical errors, their illegitimate status outside the English canon is not surprising but this comedy offers a critical replay of enduring English prejudices against other forms of the language, which were much in evidence after Union, as historical research into performance and visual representations of "savage Scots" confirms.[33] The appearance of a play like *The Flouers of Edinburgh* at the Edinburgh International Festival, as well as the play's treatment of the construction and deconstruction of British identities, highlights the potential contribution to national theater history of this comedy of colonial manners.

While McLellan uses Scots comedy not only to probe the fault-lines in British identity formation but also to complicate any simple expression of Scottish or Scots nationalism, the Edinburgh Festival's first Scottish play, the revival of David Lindsay's pageant *Ane Satire of the Thrie Estaites* (1948), was presented as an expression of "national modesty" rather than the explicitly Scottish National aspirations favored by Bridie. The Festival directors allegedly accepted the idea only when suggested by Tyrone Guthrie, of Scottish descent but international acclaim, after they had failed to interest the London-based Old Vic to produce a play on Mary Queen of Scots to be written by Bridie. The production thus represents the phenomenon by which local elites recognize the national claims of local culture only after the display of international interest. This phenomenon, which commentators from Canada to the Antipodes have noted more often than those in the imperial center, suggests the translation of "national modesty" into "cultural cringe."[34]

Written by Scottish writer and diplomat David Lindsay (1486–1555) as a satire of conflicts among Scottish clergy, nobles and merchants at a time of tension between James V of Scotland and his uncle Henry VIII of England and among the churches of Rome, England and the Presbyterian insurgency in Scotland, the play was performed for James and his queen Marie de Lorraine in 1540, two years before the king's death would leave his daughter Mary (later Queen of Scots) at the mercy of these factions. The play was expanded for a nine-hour public pageant before the Queen Regent Marie in Edinburgh in 1554, but burnt by church elders in 1558.[35] Depending on one's point of view, *Ane Satire of the Thrie Estaites* testifies to Lindsay's diplomatic balance, criticizing spiritual and temporal corruption while refraining from wholesale allegiance to Reforming zealots, or to its author's equivocal manipulation of independence-minded Scottish militants for the sake of state stability. Although now acknowledged as a major text of the Scottish Renaissance, its historical location has been misrepresented in English theater history.[36] Under Guthrie's direction, a slightly Anglicized version of Scottish playwright Robert Kemp's adaptation opened in August 1948 under the auspices of the Scottish Theatre, whose cast was assembled from Scottish repertory companies.[37] Since the "best theatres" had been earmarked for opera (Glyndebourne), ballet (Sadler's Wells), and visiting theaters (the Barrault–Renaud Company), *The Satire of the Three Estates* was performed in the Assembly Hall of the Church of Scotland. Presided over by a "portrait of Guthrie's great-grandfather, a former Moderator of the Assembly" and guarded by the "statue of John Knox in the forecourt," the seat of this thoroughly anti-theatrical national church was usurped by theater, as the moderator's throne was covered over by an apron stage for the occasion.[38] In Guthrie's view, the theatricality invoked by the transformation of the Assembly Hall was anti-illusionist: "each member of the audience was being ceaselessly reminded that he [*sic*] was not lost in an illusion, was not at the Court of King Humanitie in Sixteenth Century Scotland but was . . . part of a large audience taking part, 'assisting' as the French very properly express it, in a performance, participants in a ritual."[39] It was also of international import, constituting in his view, a "bolder and more elaborate" experiment in non-naturalistic staging than any other to date in the English-speaking world (337). Moreover, as the Anglicized title of the play suggests, the prestige of this production derived less from its emblematic Scottish status than from its reputation as "the major dramatic offering at an international festival" and, inadvertently "the smash hit of the Festival," and a candidate to be "repeated every year, rather in the manner of *Jedermann* [Everyman] at the Salzburg Festival."[40] Revived seven times (in 1949, 1951, 1959, 1973, 1984, 1985, 1991) after its initial production at the Festival, *The Satire of the Three Estates* acquired the status of a national emblem legitimated by and for *international* consumption.

Premièring at the Citizens' Theatre in 1964, eight years after the revival of *Ane Satire of the Thrie Estaites* as *The Satire of the Three Estates*, John Arden's *Armstrong's Last Goodnight* should be understood not only as a response to the emblematic status of the *Satire* as an instance of international mediation and of its author as a diplomat of imperial sensibility if not imperial power, but also as an ironic look back, by a (Northern) English writer, on the history of history plays whose performance in Scotland went largely unnoticed in London but which nonetheless offers a critical revision of the history of Britain and its theater. Arden's preface pointedly argues for an intervention in both political and theater history, while reminding readers and audiences that his play "is founded upon history but does not attempt to present an accurate chronicle."[41] Drawing in part on a sixteenth-century ballad about the hanging of John Armstrong of Gilnockie, Border rebel, bandit and descendant of the heroes of Bannockburn, and in part on Lindsay's expressed disdain for this romantic image, captured in the portrait of a pardoner selling the hanging rope as a relic in his *Satire*, *Armstrong's Last Goodnight* depicts the conflict between Lindsay, James V's herald, diplomat, and subtle man of state, and Armstrong, the rough rebel who is ambushed by Lindsay's promotion of discord among the Border freebooters and false promises of royal favor. Although the historical Lindsay had nothing to do with the elimination of Armstrong, he took a keen interest in stabilizing English/Scottish relations; his disdain for rebels like Armstrong and those who would romanticize them is clear in the extract from the *Satire* quoted by Arden: "ane cord . . ./Quhilk hangit John the Armistrang/ . . . / Gude, halie pepil, I stand for'd/ Quha ever beis hangit with this cord/ Neidis never to be drownd."[42]

Writing his play in a modern, stageworthy Scots that could convey "twentieth century concepts" and "still suggest the sixteenth century" (*Plays: One,*

239), Arden invokes the Scots revival of Goodsir Smith and others, but implicitly criticizes the romantic but parochial portraits of Border heroes in plays like Smith's *The Wallace* by including Gaelic (used by Lindsay's Highland scribe, McGlass, as well as by Lindsay for secret negotiation with the king before Armstrong's hanging) and French (by Lindsay and his paramour). Arden's recollection of the Glasgow production, which was "in comparison with the Royal Court or Chichester – under-budgeted, unevenly cast, hastily prepared," as the "sharing of a lively experience with the audience – this was of course the experience of Scotland – of a discontented 'region' of the United Kingdom aware of its historical claim to its own unique identity . . . and aware of the theatrical reflection of that claim upon the stage" (*Plays: One* 6), suggests that the audience knew this tradition well. Reviewing this "world première" for the *Glasgow Herald*, Christopher Small praised Arden for using Scots "with a force and dexterity in both verse and prose that many Scottish writers must envy" and the Citizens' production for "rousing echoes that [would] be heard farther and longer than the applause."[43] Heralding the première with a detailed interview with the author and a discussion with the designer, Juanita Waterson, and publishing the review on the Parliament and court page rather than in the usual entertainment slot, the editors of the newspaper confirmed the reviewer's sense of the play's national impact.

Although the multilingual dimension of *Armstrong* would later qualify it as "the best 'Scottish play' ever written" in the ironic view of a critic favoring the later regime that transformed the Citizens' Theatre in the 1970s from the "decent gentility" of the Bridie era to a cosmopolitan "garden of sensual, artistic, intellectual and moral riot," it was in the first instance an obstacle for English (and Anglicized Scottish) critics who forgot the French and Gaelic and found the Scots simply alienating.[44] Writing from Glasgow, Small chastized London audiences by noting that "it is doubtful whether audiences in the Metropolis . . . [would] be able or willing to understand it."[45] Arden responded to this alienation by reversing the order of the opening scenes. Whereas the first act of the Scottish production opened with the complex negotiation between English and Scottish envoys mediated by Lindsay, followed by two scenes at Armstrong's castle, and concluded with Lindsay's visit to persuade Armstrong that his interests lie with the Scottish Crown, the English version began with Armstrong and the savage dispatch of his rival Wamprey, a scene which, as Arden had it, "more or less explains itself in visual terms" (*Plays: One*, 245). Although Arden clearly wanted the linguistic variation to highlight the different social roles of the characters, and rearranged the opening to "make the English audience familiar with the language before the complex exposition of the plot" (245), London reviewers responded to the opening scenes of violence, pageantry and the rough costume of Armstrong's clan in ways that reflected a long-standing English unease with the "savage Scot" as well as a fascination with the exotic tableau of Scotland; "image . . . rather than analysis" caught their attention.[46]

After being dismissed in London in 1965 as "a(nother Arden) failure," *Armstrong's Last Goodnight* has since been reclaimed for *English* theater history as a "bridge between Brechtian practice and the mainstream English stage" and a prototype for "large-scale epics" which opened more than a decade later in London, as diverse as "*Nicholas Nickleby, Maydays*, and *Pravda*."[47] While Arden's informed deployment of Brecht deserves due attention, especially since he read Brecht in German at a time when most English-speaking commentators treated Brecht as a source of formal tricks or as the exemplar of an allegedly insoluble contradiction between politics and art, Arden shared with Brecht an interest in indigenous popular forms as well as the international avant-garde.[48] Brecht drew inspiration at the outset of his career from the satirical cabaret and popular songs used by entertainers like Karl Valentin, as well as the political revisions of this tradition by communists and others in Weimar Germany, and his development of the theory and practice of epic (narrative, or story-telling, rather than grand or large-scale) theater and of *Verfremdung* (best translated as *dis-illusion*) was intended to be a critical intervention against, rather than an instance of "alienation," the usual and unfortunate English translation.[49] Arden reiterated, from *Serjeant Musgrave's Dance* (1958) on, that the ballad offered the most appropriate form for "translating the concrete life of today in terms of poetry that shall at the one time illustrate that life and set it within the historical and legendary tradition of our culture."[50] Arden's comments on the ballad share with those of Charles Parker and Ewan McColl, who produced a series of ballad documentaries on BBC Radio (1958–64), a keen interest in the formal and social diversity of the form, from the archaic and rural to the modern, urban and even militantly political, as well as its capacity for telling "true tales."[51] The critical deployment of ballads in *Armstrong*, from first – to celebrate Armstrong in the heroic manner – to last – in the verses he sings as the king's hangman strings him up, to strip away his braggadocio along with his motley finery as the veneer of the heroic Scot over the beaten bandit – is not only dramatically vivid; it also anticipates the more recent historian's critique of the romantic effusions of the "ballad" version of Scottish history.[52]

Arden's appeal to indigenous tradition in "Telling a True Tale" is thus the very opposite of a retreat to parochial nationalism. In the same essay, Arden notes the migration of the ballad form to the American popular song, and both *Musgrave* and *Armstrong* combine reworking of ballad sources with allusions, however indirect, to contemporary instances of (post-)imperial aggression: the British Army in Cyprus, in the first case, and Belgian, European and United Nations complicity in the death of Patrice Lumumba, briefly leader of a newly independent Congo, in the second.[53] This allusion highlights, in Arden's view, the "basic similarity in moral, rather than political, economic or racial problems" faced by his Lindsay and by twentieth-century diplomats such as the UN envoy to the Congo, Conor Cruise O'Brien (*Plays: One*, 239);[54] it also brings to the fore the difference between a common English tendency to see *Armstrong* as a representation of the "sheer *otherness* of the past" and the Scottish confirmation of Arden's intention to highlight the complexity of present claims on the past. Consonant with Brecht's conception of the "historical sense," which links "delight in distance" not with a picturesque remoteness but with "delight in what is close and proper to ourselves," the play of history in *Armstrong* highlights the drama (the conflict as well as the compelling interest) of present re-presentations of the past.[55]

The textual (and *inter*-textual) genealogy and performance history of *Armstrong's Last Goodnight* make it an exemplary site for a revision of British theater history that might provincialize the habitual assumption of metropolitan authority in London. The syncretic form and language not only of *Armstrong* but also of other plays that test the boundaries of post-imperial Britain pull readers, performers and even reluctant spectators away from attachments to clear-cut heroic battles between England and Scotland or other others, native and foreign, high art and low culture, without, however allowing them to forget the current political resonances of its central conflict. Enabling theater historians to see not merely Scotland or England but Britain as a whole and also in pieces, this genealogy offers a compelling case for plotting the evolution of a drama of national scope and of theatrical innovation, which provincializes London by spotlighting innovation elsewhere. It also highlights the international dimension of this innovation, from Guthrie's pointedly anti-illusionist, internationalist, but still *pre*-Brechtian staging of *The Satire of the Three Estates* and Robert McLellan's playful satire of the heroic mode of Scottish history and drama, to John McGrath's revision of British imperial history and its ideological replication in *Border Warfare* (1989) and *Ane Satyre of the Four Estaites* (1996), which uses a more thoroughly Scottish present-day dialect to challenge the authority of the Anglicized text of 1948, and current Scots translations of classics from ancient Greek to modern Canadian French.[56] It also highlights the national and international significance of institutional developments outside London, from the Theatre Workshop, which was acclaimed in Eastern and Western Europe in the 1940s, before London paid any mind, to the cosmopolitan Citizens' under the aegis of Giles Havergal, Philip Prowse and Robert MacDonald (1970 ff.), and the establishment, in the Glasgow dubbed European City of Culture (1990), of the Tramway as *the* British site (as opposed to London) for visiting international companies from the Wooster Group and Goat Island to Andrei Serban and the Romanian National Theatre.

This provincializing genealogy honed in the north can help us to probe the recesses of apparently completely documented institutions for instances of "historical moment," in Foucault's phrase, which target the metropolitan (London-based) view of British theater history from the south as well. For, while post-colonial writers in English from Africa, the Caribbean and South Asia have an undoubtedly different historical relation to the imperial capital than do the dramatists of post-imperial Scotland, they have argued that their intervention rewrites the script of English and British identities, or, in Simon Gikandi's phrase, "maps of Englishness," not merely those of the post-colony.[57] Looking again at the Royal Court in the long 1950s, we find not only the "repatriation of European drama," which Rebellato reads as a sign of an "English" resurgence in the mainstage repertoire, but also the work of playwrights whose Commonwealth affiliation raises questions about the boundaries of British theater history and drama in English. Sunday night programs "without decor" in 1959 included early and still unpublished work by Wolé Sóyínká, which predate the premières of his first published plays, *The Lion and the Jewel* (Ibadan, 1959) and *Dance in the Forests*, (Lagos, at the independence celebrations in 1960). These little-known plays, "Eight Men Dead at Hola Camp" (on British reprisals against the Mau Mau in Kenya) and "The Invention" (on apartheid in South Africa), are noteworthy for being anti- rather than post-colonial and, in the latter case, for focusing on South Africa rather than Nigeria. "The Invention" also invites comparison with the first performance in 1960 of a play by a South African at the Royal Court. This was not by Athol Fugard, who received no attention from the Court and left for Belgium after briefly working backstage for Joan Littlewood, but by the Afrikaans playwright Bartho Smit, whose sensationalist miscegenation melodrama *Die Verminktes*, appeared in English translation as *The Maimed*.[58] Now acknowledged as major playwrights in English, neither Fugard nor Sóyínká appears in standard collections or encyclopedias of British drama, although their dramatic use of multiple Englishes certainly deserves a place in an investigation of the spatial, temporal, and linguistic boundaries of Britain and the English canon. Phenomena at both extremes of visibility, from the growing stature of English-language playwrights outside of Britain, to the practically invisible activity of several of these outsiders in Britain at a formative time in their careers, and, as an odd supplement, the appearance of another South African writer, author of a *single* unproduced play, in *Contemporary British Dramatists*, draw attention to the blurred categories of British theater in the post-imperial period as well as the faintness of the archival record of theater in the margins of the metropolitan repertoire, and suggest that this investigation has barely begun.[59]

Notes

1. Linda Colley argues, in *Britons: Forging the Nation, 1707–1837* (New Haven: Yale University Press, 1992) that by 1837, Scotland was "comfortably contained within a bigger nation" (373) but that, by the 1990s, "a substantial rethinking of what it

means to be British" was necessary (375). Writing more combatively in the teeth of Margaret Thatcher's victory and the defeat of Scottish devolution in 1979, Tom Nairn launched an attack on the complacent assumption of English primacy in Britain in *The Break-up of Britain*, 2nd edn (London: Verso, 1981).

2. David Childs, *Britain since 1945: a Political History*, 5th edn. (London: Routledge, 2000). Dominic Shellard's overview, *British Theatre Since the War* (New Haven: Yale University Press, 1999), published well after renewed debates on Scottish and Welsh (to say nothing of Irish) devolution, invites the expectation of a broadly *British* theater, yet, apart from a five-page excursus on "drama away from London" (174–9), focuses exclusively on London. The problem with "contemporary" can be seen by comparing two publications in the 1990s: *Contemporary British Drama, 1970–90*, ed. Hersh Zeifman and Cynthia Zimmerman (Toronto: University of Toronto Press, 1993) covers the most recent generation, while the encyclopedia, *Contemporary British Dramatists*, ed. K. A. Berney (London: St. James Press, 1994), includes entries from the postwar period to the 1990s.

3. Thomas Postlewait, "The Criteria of Periodization in Theatre History," *Theatre Journal*, 40 (1988): 299–320.

4. Aleks Sierz, *In-Yer-Face Theatre: British Drama Today* (London: Faber, 2001). Subsequent citations in the text.

5. My sources here vary from Childs's conventional political history to the perceptive outsider's view of François Bédarida's *Social History of Britain, 1850–1990*, trans. A. S. Forster and Jeffrey Hodgkinson (London: Routledge, 1991), and the cultural histories of Robert Hewison, *In Anger: British Culture and the Cold War* (New York: Oxford University Press, 1981) and *Too Much: Art and Society in the Sixties* (New York: Oxford University Press, 1986). The phrase "the long 1950s" and its companions are my own.

6. I am drawing here on Nairn's argument about the limits of dissidence in *The Break-up of Britain*, as well as on his sources: Perry Anderson's critique of the late and limited (relative to European) development of a dissident intelligentsia in Britain after the 1944 Education Act, in "The Origins of the Present Crisis" (1964) and "Components of the National Culture" (1968), in *English Questions* (London: Verso, 1992), and Raymond Williams, in several books from *The Long Revolution* (London: Chatto and Windus, 1961) to *Resources of Hope* (London: Verso, 1989). "Raising" and "spreading" culture was the motto of Roy Shaw, Secretary General of the Arts Council in the 1960s and 1970s; see *Patronage and Responsibility* (34th Annual Report of the Arts Council of Great Britain, 1978–9) and Robert Hutchison, *The Politics of the Arts Council* (London: Sinclair Brown, 1982). For two of many accounts of the revolutionary claims of this subsidized dissidence, see Catherine Itzin, *Stages in the Revolution: Alternative Theatre in Britain: 1968–78* (London: Methuen, 1980) and Sandy Craig, ed., *Dreams and Deconstructions: Alternative Theatre in Britain* (Ambergate: Amber Lane Press, 1981).

7. See *The Glory of the Garden* (London: Arts Council, 1984), the response, *Haughty Culture* (Manchester: North West Arts, 1984), and commentary by Baz Kershaw, *The Politics of Performance: Radical Theatre as Cultural Intervention* (London: Routledge, 1992), esp. 170–84; also Robert Hewison, *Heritage Culture* (London: Methuen, 1989) and Patrick Wright, *On Living in an Old Country* (London: Verso, 1985).

8. As John Bull notes in *Stage Right: Crisis and Recovery in British Contemporary Mainstream Theatre* (New York: St. Martins Press, 1994), 17, by 1988, 17.5 percent of London audiences were apparently American, while the plethora of new British plays was replaced by revivals, especially musicals, targeting the tourist consumer.

On the consumerist turn in London theater in the age of globalization, see Kershaw, "Discouraging Democracy: British Theatres and Economics 1979–1999," *Theatre Journal*, 51 (1999): 267–83.

9. The role of the Royal Court as the renovator of the West End rather than the radical dissident it appears to be in contemporary accounts of Taylor, Kenneth Tynan and the contributors to *Encore* is by now well known. Although Tynan, in reviews reprinted in *A View of the English Stage* (London: Methuen, 1984), and Taylor, in his influential book, *Anger and After* (1962; revised edn, London: Methuen, 1969), set the tone of celebrating dissidence, which was reiterated into the 1980s by compilers like Richard Findlater (in *At the Royal Court: 25 Years of the English Stage Company* [New York: Grove, 1981]), skepticism about the success of dissidence appeared early, in John Whiting's satirical remarks in 1959, "At Ease in a Bright Red Tie" (rpt: *New Theatre Voices of the Fifties and Sixties: Selections from Encore Magazine 1956–1963*, ed. Charles Marowitz, Tom Milne and Owen Hale [London: Methuen, 1965], 105–10) long before John McGrath's critique of the Royal Court and its middle-class audiences in *A Good Night Out: Popular Theatre, Audience, Class and Form* (1981; 2nd edn, London: Nick Hern, 1996). As Dan Rebellato shows, the Court was linked to the West End and to key non-profit institutions such as the Old Vic and the Shakespeare Memorial Theatre by overlapping personnel, connections to cultural arbiters in the London press and government and, despite the myth of poverty, a relatively generous Arts Council subsidy (second only to the Old Vic from 1957); see Rebellato, *1956 and All That: the Making of Modern British Drama* (London: Routledge, 1999), 37–69.

10. Stephen Lacey, *British Realist Theatre: the New Wave in its Context: 1956–1965* (London: Routledge, 1995) and Rebellato, *1956 and All That*, take the prestige of *Look Back in Anger* as their critical object and succeed in their different ways in demystifying the myth, but, by virtue of their focus, confirm the priority of the play nonetheless.

11. Immanuel Kant, *On History*, ed. and trans. Lewis White Beck (New York: Macmillan, 1963), 22. G. W. F. Hegel, *Vorlesungen über die Philosophie der Geschichte*, in *Werke* (in twenty volumes), ed. Eva Moldenhauer and Klaus Markus Mickel (Frankfurt: Suhrkamp, 1970), 12: 11, hereafter cited as *Philosophie der Geschichte* in the text; *The Philosophy of History*, trans. J. Sibree (New York: Dover, 1956), 1, hereafter cited as *Philosophy of History*.

12. G. W. F. Hegel, *Vorlesungen über die Ästhetik* (Frankfurt a. M.: Suhrkamp, 1970), 3: 475–76; *Aesthetics*, trans. T. M. Knox (Oxford: Clarendon Press, 1998) 2: 1159. For the genesis of the commonsense understanding of drama out of Hegel's dialectic between subjectivity and social relations, see Loren Kruger, "Making Sense of Sensation: Enlightenment, Embodiment, and the End(s) of Modern Drama," *Modern Drama*, 43 (2000), 543–63.

13. Of the recent studies of history plays in twentieth-century Britain, Nilofer Harben's *Twentieth Century English History Plays* (London: Macmillan, 1989) focuses on plays and protagonists one might call Hegelian, but her emphatic distinction between the "distortion" of the past for dramatic purposes and an allegedly neutral documentation of history (225) is not grounded in the theory of history. R. Keith Peacock, *Radical Stages: Alternative History in Modern British Drama* (Westport, Conn: Greenwood, 1991) relies on a loose framework of "Marxism" to bind together diverse plays from the long 1960s, the heyday of alternative drama and historiography in Britain, without however investigating British inflections of the Marxist tradition. Richard Palmer, *The Contemporary British History Play* (Westport, Conn: Greenwood, 1998) refers to the theory of history, in the names of R. G. Collingwood

and Hayden White, but his brief introduction leaves no room for reflection on their sources or on the tangled epistemologies of history and theater, which I attempt to outline here.

14. Kenneth Tynan "Look Back in Anger" and "End of a Twelvemonth" (1956) in Tynan, *A View of the English Stage*, 178, 199. The internal quotation is attributed to Arthur Miller.

15. Taylor, *Anger and After*, 9.

16. Lacey, *British Realist Theatre*, 18–39, shows the links between Osborne's play and the contemporary discussion of youth rebellion but also the differences between the evident nostalgia in Osborne and his protagonist and the organized New Left's critique of the Empire. Sierz critiques the "deliberate parochialism" (in George Steiner's phrase) of the "myth of Anger" in England as against youth revolution elsewhere, in "John Osborne and the Myth of Anger," *New Theatre Quarterly*, 46 (1996): 136–46.

17. Friedrich Nietzsche, "Vom Nutz und Nachteil der Historie für das Leben," *Unzeitgemässe Betrachtungen* (Munich: Insel, 1981), 111, hereafter "Vom Nutz und Nachteil," in the text; *On the Advantage and Disadvantage of History for Life*, trans. Peter Preuss (Indianapolis: Hackett, 1980), 17, hereafter *On the Advantage and Disadvantage*.

18. *New Theatre Voices of the Fifties and Sixties* begins the 1950s in 1956. While this might be explained in terms of the magazine *Encore*'s investment in the "revolution" of 1956, that excuse cannot so simply apply to apparently neutral documentation such as *British Dramatists, 1956–95: a Research and Publication Sourcebook*, ed. William Demastes (Westport: Greenwood, 1996).

19. Michel Foucault, *L'Ordre du discours* (Paris: Gallimard, 1971), 58, trans. Rupert Sawyer as "The Discourse on Language", appendix to *The Archeology of Knowledge* (New York: Pantheon, 1972), 230, and, more broadly, "Nietzsche, la généalogie, l'histoire" (1971), in Foucault, *Dits et écrits 1954–1988* (Paris: Gallimard, 1994), 2: 136–56; "Nietzsche, Genealogy, History," trans. Donald Bouchard and Sherry Simon, in Foucault, *Language, Counter-Memory, Practice*, ed. Donald Bouchard (Ithaca: Cornell University Press, 1977), 138–64. Subsequent references in the text cited as "Nietzsche, la généalogie" and "Nietzsche, Genealogy."

20. Rebellato's account of the sexual politics of the Royal Court elaborates Alan Sinfield's argument, in *Literature, Politics and Culture in Post-war Britain* (Oxford: Blackwell, 1989), that the Angry Young Men defined their rebellion in terms that associated revolution with an allegedly virile working-class as against an allegedly inherently effete aristocracy.

21. The contributors to *British Theatre in the 1950s*, ed. Dominic Shellard (Sheffield: Sheffield Academic Press, 2000) continue this revaluation; see Christopher Innes, "Terence Rattigan: the Voice of the 1950s," 53–63; Steve Nicholson, "Foreign Drama and the Lord Chamberlain," 41–52, and John Bull, "Looking Back on *Godot*," 82–94.

22. Nandi Bhatia suggests that the attachment to Empire shows through not only in Jimmy's sympathy with his upper-class father-in-law but in the apparently unremarkable use of racial slurs; see her "Anger, Nostalgia, and the End of Empire: John Osborne's *Look Back in Anger*," *Modern Drama*, 42 (1999), 391–400.

23. See Dipesh Chakrabarty, *Provincializing Europe: Postcolonial Thought and Historical Difference* (Princeton: Princeton University Press, 2000), 7: "Historicism enabled European domination of the world in the nineteenth century . . . [it] is what made modernity or capitalism look not simply global but rather as something that became global *over time*, by originating in one place, Europe, and then spreading outside it. This 'first in Europe, then elsewhere' structure of global historical time is historicist;

different non-Western nationalisms would later produce local versions of the same narrative, replacing 'Europe' by some locally constructed center." Chakrabarty's conception in combination with Nairn's critique of the "enigma of Englishness" provides a compelling theoretical framework for the critical analysis of the boundlessness of English authority in the minds of the English (and their theater historians) and its historical and ideological limits that appear to escape them.

24. Tom Nairn, *After Britain: New Labour and the Return of Scotland* (London: Granta, 2000), 299.

25. For a lucid reiteration of this thesis, see Matthew G. H. Pittock, *Scottish Nationality* (Basingstoke: Palgrave, 2001), esp. Chapter 3 "A Scottish Empire." In Pittock's view, two moments in the twentieth century are significant: the immediate postwar period of colonial devolution, and the 1980s and 1990s, from the failed referendum on Scottish devolution in 1979 to the restoration of the Scottish Parliament in 1998. These two moments might be marked in theater history terms by the Edinburgh Festival in the first instance and the resurgence of Scottish theater publishing and performance in the wake of the referendum, in the second.

26. The first quotation is from Michael Goldberg, Chairman of the Board, "Past, Present and Future," *A Conspectus to Mark the Citizens' 21st Anniversary as a Living Theatre in Gorbals Street Glasgow* (Glasgow: Citizens' Theatre, 1964), 3–4 (hereafter: *Conspectus*), who expresses the desire that Glasgow match theater in "any large Continental city." The second modifies Eileen Miller, *The Edinburgh International Festival, 1947–1996* (Edinburgh: Scolar Press, 1996), 21.

27. Shellard, Table of Significant Events, *British Theatre since the War*, x; the sole entry for 1944, "the Old Vic opens at the New Theatre," is misleading because it suggests that this company, which exemplified serious theater in *1930s* London, opened only in 1944. The Table includes the openings of regional theaters in Nottingham and Coventry, but no word of the Citizens', whose first season was in 1943.

28. Rebellato, "Something English: the Repatriation of European drama," *1956 and All That*, 127–55. Citizens' first two seasons included plays by Gogol, Ibsen and Molnar as well as Bridie, Corrie, Priestley and Shaw; *Conspectus*, 53.

29. Robert McLellan, *Jamie the Saxt*, and *The Flouers of Edinburgh*, Collected Plays Volume 1 (London: John Calder, 1981); the phrases in quotation marks are McLellan's subtitles for these plays.

30. James Bridie, *John Knox and Other Plays* (London: Constable, 1949); Sydney Goodsir Smith, *The Wallace: a Triumph in Five Acts* (London: John Calder, 1985); Terence Rattigan, *Adventure Story* (London: Samuel French, 1950). One could read Bridie's interest in *Adventure Story*'s Alexander the Macedonian as an oblique replay of Jamie the Saxt's acquisition of the supposedly greater power to the south, but that is a subject for another paper.

31. Relevant plays from the Restoration might include John Dryden's *Aureng-Zebe or the Great Mogul*, Nathaniel Lee's *The Rival Queens, or the Death of Alexander the Great*, or Aphra Behn's *The Moor's Revenge*. Tara Arts work that speaks back to the orientalism of the Restoration as well as the silent representation of the Indian servant S[h]iva in *The Flouers of Edinburgh* might include the company's adaptation of Molière's *Tartuffe* (1990) and the trilogy of plays on Asian migration to Britain, *Journey to the West* (1998–2000).

32. For the ground-breaking analysis of internal colonialism, see Michael Hechter, *Internal Colonialism: the Celtic Fringe in British National Development* (Berkeley: University of California Press, 1975); for recent critiques of binary oppositions between Anglo-Saxon core and Celtic fringes, using evidence of blurred linguistic,

religious and settlement patterns in the borderlands, which complicate any simple oppositions between English and Scots, Scots and Gaelic, Protestant and Catholic, Lowlands and Highlands, see Pittock, *Scottish Nationality* and Keith Robbins, *Great Britain: Identities, Institutions, and the Idea of Britishness* (London: Longman, 1997).

33. Colley writes of "runaway Scottophobia in England after 1760" (and the final defeat of the Jacobite rebellion led by the Young Pretender Charles Stuart) encapsulated in the cartoon figure of "Sawney Scot" (*Britons*, 117–18), clad in a crude version of the tartan which McLellan's Sidney finds "splendid." Pittock takes a longer view, arguing that, on the one hand, Scottish national feeling and the tartans representing it appear as early as the Battle of Bannockburn (1314) and, on the other, that the status of Scots as a national language, in print in the sixteenth century, was at the same time under threat; by 1580, 18 percent of books printed in Scotland use English forms; by 1625, the figure was 93 percent (*Scottish Nationality*, 42), long before Union (1707) and subsequent depredations of Scottish savagery expressed by English luminaries such as Samuel Johnson. Analogous descriptions of Boers as savage natives or "white kaffirs" abound in colonial British accounts of Afrikaners. For *Love and the Hyphen*, see Stephen Black, *Three Plays*, ed. Stephen Gray (Johannesburg: Ad Donker, 1984).

34. For the notion of "national modesty" and Guthrie's intervention, see Ivor Brown, "Birth and Growth," in *The Edinburgh Festival: a Review of the First Ten Years of the Edinburgh Festival, its Aims and its Origins, its Achievements and its Hopes for the Future* (Edinburgh: Edinburgh Festival Society, 1956), 14; for the apparent necessity of international, read *British* legitimation of national theater aspirations in the Commonwealth c. 1910, see Alan Filewod, "National Theatre, National Obsession," *Canadian Theatre Review*, 62 (1990), 5–10. "Cultural cringe" registers tension in post-war Australia between national cultural aspirations and the sense of British superiority; see A. A. Phillips, "The Cultural Cringe" (1950) in C. B. Christensen, ed., *On Native Grounds* (Sydney: Angus and Robertson, 1968), 451. Although Canadian and Australian nationalists match themselves against "British" models, their cultural references tend to be *English* and metropolitan. Born and educated in England of Irish and Scottish parentage, Guthrie worked in theaters from Canada to Australia, and major metropolitan centers in between. Although he found the *Satire* a "chore" to read, he far preferred it to the alternatives including *Douglas*, by John Home, a "much admired" patriotic "tragedy in verse" from 1756; see Guthrie, *A Life in the Theatre* (New York: McGraw-Hill, 1959), 306–11; here 306.

35. Although hosted by the Catholic Queen Regent, the *Satire* was ordered burnt by Scottish bishops in 1555, when Protestants were still officially heretics. Although not finally established as the Church of Scotland until 1690, the Presbyterians led by John Knox were ratified by the Scottish Parliament in 1560. For English/Scottish relations in Lindsay's time, see Pittock, *Scottish Nationality*, 41–5, and Robbins, *Great Britain*, 54–60; for comment on Lindsay's pageant, see Robert Kemp's Preface to Sir David Lindsay, *The Satire of the Three Estates*, Edinburgh Festival Version by Robert Kemp (London: Heinemann, 1951), xiii–xviii, and Matthew MacDiarmid's introduction to *A Satire of the Three Estates, a play adapted by Matthew MacDiarmid from the acting text made by Robert Kemp for Tyrone Guthrie's production at the Edinburgh Festival* (New York: Theatre Arts Books, 1967), 7–15

36. For the affirmative position, see MacDiarmid's introduction, 14–15; for the critique of Lindsay as a subtle equivocator, see John Arden's "General Notes" to *Armstrong's Last Goodnight* in Arden, *Plays: One* (London: Methuen, 1977), 238–9. Mentioning Lindsay's play prior to discussing Arden's, Peacock treats Arden's characters as

historical fact, describing James V in 1540 as a "boy king" (following Arden's description of the 17-year-old in 1530 (242)), in negotiation with Henry the Seventh of England; see Peacock, *Radical Stages*, 50.

37. The relevant versions are Sir David Lindsay, *Ane Satire of the Thrie Estaites*, adapted by Robert Kemp, published in *The Scots Review* in 1949, and *The Satire of the Three Estates*, Edinburgh Festival version by Robert Kemp, introduced by Tyrone Guthrie (London: Heinemann, 1951). Kemp describes the Edinburgh Festival version as "Scots of the present day" but the text is closer to London stage English than either the scholarly version of the *Satire* edited by MacDiarmid or the modernized version of seventeenth-century Scots used by MacLellan in *Jamie the Saxt*.

38. Miller, *Edinburgh Festival*, 14.

39. Guthrie, *A Life in the Theatre*, 311. Guthrie's pun rests on the homophony between the French *assister à* (to participate in, be present at) and the English *assist*.

40. For comments about the success of the production and the comparison with *Jedermann* see Miller, *Edinburgh Festival*, 15. MacDiarmid reiterates the comparison with *Everyman* in the introduction to his adaptation (15).

41. John Arden, "General Notes," *Plays: One* (London: Methuen, 1972), 238.

42. Ibid. Arden does not identify his citation (from either the Bannatyne ms. [1568] or the Charteris Quarto [1602], both reprinted by the Scottish Text Society) but it is noteworthy that he quotes a more thoroughly Scottish original than the Anglicized Festival text, which reads: "Here is a cord both great and long/Which hangèd Johnny Armstrong/ [. . .]/Good holy people, I stand for'ard/ Whoever is hangèd with this cord/ Needs never to be drowned! (*The Satire of the Three Estates*, 41).

43. Christopher Small, "English Reiver in Triumphant Border Foray," *Glasgow Herald*, 6 May 1964, 7. Arden's exposure to modern Scots dated from his architectural training in Edinburgh and the production there of his first play, "All Fall Down, a Victorian period piece," by the College of Art Drama Society in 1955.

44. Taylor wrote in *Anger and After* that "it was widely received with mystification and resentment even by those critics who had previously liked Arden's work. I suppose the first reason for this was the language" (102); and Edwin Morgan lamented, in full-blown cultural cringe, that "[t]he fairly thick Scots language . . . will prove a severe challenge to the goodwill of English audiences" and, claiming to speak for "we in Scotland," asserted that Scottish audiences preferred "plays in English"; Morgan, "Armstrong's Last Goodnight," *Encore*, 11,4 (1964), 51. The retrospective view of *Armstrong* as the "best 'Scottish play' ever written" and of the *second* twenty-one years at the Citizens as a "forbidden garden of . . . riot" is Michael Coveney's, in *The Citz: 21 Years of the Glasgow Citizens' Theatre* (London: Nick Hern Books, 1990), 57, 10.

45. Christopher Small, "The Playwright in a Hurry," *Glasgow Herald*, 2 May 1964, 8.

46. John Gross claims that "the play offers an image of violence and statecraft rather than analysis" in "Rebels and Renegades," *Encounter* (October 1965), 41, quoted in *Arden on File*, ed. Malcolm Page (London: Methuen, 1985), 37; Gross goes on to praise Arden for "respecting the sheer *otherness* of the past," expressing his own sense of the spatial and temporal remoteness of Scotland. Penelope Gilliatt exoticizes the characters further by describing their movements as "Japanese-looking," in "Adjusting the Focus of History," *The Observer*, 11 July 1965, *Arden on File*, 38. Irving Wardle is a notable exception to this "othering" of *Armstrong*; in an interview with Arden in 1963, he paid special attention to the importance of language as a means of communication and analysis as well as local color, a point reiterated by the director of the English production, William Gaskill; see Irving Wardle, "Arden Talking

about his Way of Writing Plays," *The Observer*, 30 June 1965, in *Arden on File*, 36, and William Gaskill, "Producing Arden," *Encore*, 57 (September/ October 1965), 23, *Arden on File*, 37.

47. Susan Bennett, "Brecht – Britain – Bakhtin: The Bridge of *Armstrong's Last Goodnight*," in *John Arden and Margaretta D'Arcy: a Casebook*, ed. Jonathan Wike (New York: Garland, 1995), 67–79; here: 69, 74. Bennett's essay highlights Arden's nuanced retrieval of local traditions of the ballad and the chronicle as forms of *history* and theater writing, as well as his thorough understanding and localization of the inter-national emblem of an avant garde theater, Brecht, as against the superficially "Brechtian" trappings affected by contemporaries such as Osborne or Robert Bolt, but her telling equation of the "English stage"(75) and "British theatre"(74) and her reliance on Brecht as *the* marker of innovation runs the risk of reducing the Scottish reception of the play to a minor role in the revival of the London scene while emphasizing Brecht's prestige as an international avant-gardist at the expense of his and others' engagements with local popular cultures.

48. The locus classicus for the still-influential argument that Brecht was an artist trapped by politics is Martin Esslin, *Bertolt Brecht: a Choice of Evils* (London: Methuen, 1962). Tynan noted famously in 1963 that Brecht's impact in Britain was greater on direc-tors than writers (see "Talk with Tynan" rpt. in *New Theatre Voices of the Fifties and Sixties*, 283–4). In "Brecht and the British," his review of John Willett's useful but in parts misleading translation of a fraction of Brecht's essays in *Brecht on Theater* (1964; rpt. in Arden, *To Present the Pretence: Essays on the Theatre and its Audience* [London: Methuen, 1977], 37–41), Arden suggests that awkward translation made Brecht more remote in English than he ought to be. Nonetheless, the publication of *Brecht on Theater*, as well as the turn to political theater in the late 1960s and 1970s, prompted a deeper investigation of Brecht's theory and practice by writers as well as directors; see Itzin, *Stages of the Revolution*; Janelle Reinelt, *After Brecht: Britain's Epic Theater* (Ann Arbor: University of Michigan Press, 1994), and, on Arden, David Graver, "John Arden," in *British Writers: Supplement II* (New York: Scribners, 1991).

49. Brecht's first usage of the term is in "Verfremdungseffekte in der chinesischen Schauspielkunst" (1935). The first English translation was "The Fourth Wall of China: an Essay on the Effects of *Disillusion* in Chinese Acting" (emphasis added), trans. Eric Walter White, *Life and Letters Today* (1936; rpt. Brecht, *Werke: Grosse kommentierte Berliner und Frankfurter Ausgabe* [Frankfurt: Suhrkamp, 1998], 22: 960–8); "disillusion" better captures the original sense of *Verfremdung*: undoing theatrical illusion so as to encourage the audience to understand and thus critique the world off- as well as on-stage (22:401), while "alienation" translates the Hegelian/Marxian *Entfremdung*, which characterizes the dispossessed subject of slavery or proletarianization.

50. Arden, "Telling a True Tale" (1960), in *New Theatre Voices of the Fifties and Sixties*, 125.

51. Ewan McColl, who had founded the Theatre of Action, later Theatre Workshop, with Joan Littlewood in the 1930s, left when the company moved to London in 1953 to work instead with folk and industrial song clubs. Charles Parker worked in Adult Education and folk clubs as well as for the BBC as Documentary Features producer. In collaboration with Peggy Seeger, Parker and McColl produced "experimental radio documentaries" combining received melodies with new lyrics, themes, and actuality recording or found sound; titles included *The Ballad of John Axon* (1958), about a railway accident, *Singing the Fishing* (1960), on the fishing industry, *The Big Hewer* (1961), on coal-mining, and *The Travelling People* (1964), on Roma in Britain. Alan Filewod and David Watt, in *Workers' Playtime: Theatre and the Labour Movement*

since 1970 (Sydney: Currency, 2001), 83–9, note that the music in these documentaries combined old melodies from regions around Britain with MacColl's interest in the international socialist legacy, including music in the style of Hanns Eisler, Brecht's collaborator and a major influence on socialist music clubs. I have no direct evidence that Arden knew these documentaries but, given his strong interest in ballads and his intermittent work with BBC Radio (from *The Life of Man*, which won the BBC Radio Drama Prize in 1956), the link is certainly plausible.

52. For the phrase "ballad history" and the critique of same, see Christopher Harvie, *Scotland and Nationalism*, 3rd edn (London: Routledge, 1998).

53. On Cyprus: two men in Famaguste, probably members of the Greek Cypriot movement EOKA, shot two women, wives of British military personnel, killing one and seriously wounding the other. In response, the British occupying forces arrested 640 Cypriot men. In the process over 200 people were injured, shops looted, and three people died: two men and a twelve-year-old girl. The "Famaguste incident" was in the news for about four months. Arden may also have been aware of the Morant Bay incident in Jamaica, October 1865, discussed by John Saville and E. P. Thompson, "John Stuart Mill and EOKA," *New Reasoner* (Winter 1958–9), 1–11. At Morant Bay, discontented locals killed twenty-one men, including local colonial officials; the British Army responded by putting to death 500 people and burning 1000 homes and buildings.

54. Arden maintains that he was "somewhat influenced" by Conor Cruise O'Brien's book, *To Katanga and Back: a UN Case History* (London: Hutchinson, 1962) and what he saw as a "similarity of moral problems", particularly in the ambiguous figure of the Western diplomat (*Plays: One*, 239) who contributes, willingly or not, to the destruction of indigenous leaders. O'Brien himself tackled the dramatic representation of this figure in his rendering of Dag Hammarskjöld in the play (or political history in dramatic form) on the UN intervention in the Congo, *Murderous Angels* (Boston: Little Brown, 1968), but resigned from the United Nations because, in his view, UN "officials played an important part in Lumumba's downfall, and in bringing about the situation in which Western influence became predominant in Leopoldville [Kinshasa]"; Conor Cruise O'Brien, "The UN, the Congo, the Tshombe Government," *Writers and Politics* (New York: Pantheon, 1965), 215–16.

55. Bertolt Brecht, "Nachträge zum 'Kleinen Organon,'" *Werke*, 23: 290; trans. John Willett, "Appendices to the Short Organum," *Brecht on Theater* (1964; rpt: New York: Hill and Wang, 1992), 276.

56. Guthrie's commitment to critical disillusion on stage is pre-Brechtian not in the sense that it happened before Brecht, since the two men were practically contemporaries, but rather in that his experiments with non-naturalistic staging and the use of non-theatrical spaces in the 1930s predate serious English-language interest in Brecht. Further, Guthrie's engagement with the revival of Elizabethan staging pioneered by William Poel and Harley Granville-Barker, alongside his un-British interest in Expressionism, reminds us that British experiments with dis-illusion took place before the imprimatur of Brecht; see Guthrie, "The Picture Frame," *A Life in the Theatre*, 195–214. The "fourth estate" in McGrath's play were professional journalists and other scribblers but his title also alludes to Guthrie's passing reference to another fourth estate: "the disenfranchised Poor" at the "end of the stage" near the "stocks" and the "gallows"; see Guthrie, Introduction, *The Satire of the Three Estates*, x. On Scots translation of, for example, Michel Tremblay's *Les Belles-soeurs* as *The Guid Sisters*, see Bill Findlay, "Translating Tremblay into Scots," *Theatre Research International*, 17,2 (Summer 1992): 138–47, or Sophocles's *Antigone*, Ian Brown et al.,

"Scots and Welsh: Theatrical Translation and Theatrical Languages," *International Journal of Scottish Theatre*, 1,2 (December 2000); <http://arts.qmuc.ac.uk/ijost/Volume1_no2/1_Brown.htm> (retrieved: 1 May 2002).

57. Simon Gikandi, *Maps of Englishness: Writing Identity in the Culture of Colonialism* (New York: Columbia University Press, 1996). "Postcolony," the post-colonial state in arrested development, is Achille Mbembe's term; see "The Banality of Power and the Aesthetics of Vulgarity in the Postcolony," trans. Janet Roitman, *Public Culture*, 4, 2 (1992): 1–30.

58. In 1960, Nigeria was still a Crown colony and South Africa still part of the British Commonwealth. For the Royal Court program, see Appendix 1, *At the Royal Court*, 206–9. Sóyínká makes a few comments on his early work in the interview with Nigerian theater scholar Biodun Jeyifo that prefaces his *Six Plays* (London: Methuen, 1984), but these plays remain unpublished and are not included in the Lord Chamberlain Collection of Plays in the British Library. Fugard received attention in London only with the London production of *The Blood Knot* at the New Arts Theatre in Hampstead in 1963; his first play at the Royal Court was *Boesman and Lena*, in the Theatre Upstairs in 1971. *Die Verminktes* was not performed in South Africa until the 1970s; it was directed at the Royal Court by Keith Johnstone after its première performance in Flemish at the Festival of Avant-garde Theatre in Brussels, which also hosted "A Kakamas Greek" written and acted by Fugard. For a comprehensive but not quite complete list of Fugard productions, see *Athol Fugard: a Bibliography*, comp. John Read (Grahamstown: National English Literary Museum, 1991) and, for comment on the early plays in production, Russell Vandenbrouke, *Truths the Hands Can Touch: the Theatre of Athol Fugard* (Johannesburg: Ad Donker, 1986).

59. Lewis Nkosi, author of one play *The Rhythms of Violence* (1964; rpt. New York: Thomas Crowell, 1973), was also an actor with Fugard in the 1950s, but he has had more impact as a critic and essayist. After leaving South Africa on an exit visa, he went first to Harvard University and to New York, and was only briefly in London, before working in Zambia and, since the 1980s, back in the United States; he appears nonetheless in *Contemporary British Dramatists*, ed. Berney. For a contextual account of the work of Fugard, Smit, Nkosi and other South African playwrights, see Loren Kruger, *The Drama of South Africa: Plays, Pageants, and Publics since 1910* (London: Routledge, 1999).

9

Deus ex machina in the Modern Theater: Theater, History, and Theater History

Freddie Rokem

"God is dead; but given the way of men, there may still be caves for thousands of years in which his shadow will be shown. – And we – we still have to vanquish his shadow, too."

Friedrich Nietzsche, *The Gay Science*

"We'll hang ourselves tomorrow. Unless Godot comes."

Samuel Beckett, *Waiting for Godot*

"What, has this thing appeared again tonight?"

W. Shakespeare, *Hamlet*[1]

The *deus ex machina* consists of the sudden and unexpected appearance of a god or a divine figure on the stage, usually at the end of the performance, in order to unravel the otherwise insoluble predicaments of the humans. This kind of supernatural intervention was prominent on the Greek and classical stages and continued to be an important theatrical device in the medieval as well as in the baroque theaters. But such god-like figures have also, as I want to show here, made their appearance on the modern, twentieth-century stages. The issue I want to examine here, in order to problematize the notion of history in general and of theater history in particular, is whether the *deus ex machina* became an anachronistic theatrical atavism after Nietzsche had declared that God is dead, or whether the gods, or the god-like figures, as they appear – and in some cases emphatically fail to appear – on our contemporary stages, still carry some form of metaphysical meaning. What is the significance of the *deus ex machina* on the modern and contemporary stages?

I want to argue here, trying to confront these issues, that the use of the traditional device of the *deus ex machina* and its transformations in the modern and contemporary theater is related to the notion of utopia as well as to

177

narrative closure. By using the basic iconographic features of the *deus ex machina* the modern and contemporary theater has confronted issues of how the individual, as well as the more general historical forces or developments, strive to reach some form of fulfillment. In employing the iconographic features of the *deus ex machina* the modern theater has also critiqued and in some cases even subverted the possibilities of such a utopian ending. In what follows I want to show that also after the death of God the *deus ex machina* has continued to serve as a powerful metaphor for such an open-ended futurity where different notions of Utopia – the ultimate ending of history – are critically reflected and refigured on the stage. Even in the cases where such a utopian fulfillment is radically questioned (and modernity as well as postmodernity has frequently adopted such a stance), the theater has quite openly employed certain features of the classical *deus ex machina* device. Alluding to the issues of representation raised by Plato through the well-known cave simile in *The Republic*, Nietzsche claimed in *The Gay Science* that even if "God is dead," there "may still be caves" where the shadow of God will be "shown for thousands of years."[2] The modern and contemporary theater is obviously one of these caves in which we are not only struggling with the issues of representation *per se*, but also how to historicize them, attempting to write the history of theatrical representations.

In order to confront these complex issues within this limited framework I will first discuss the general conditions for the use of the *deus ex machina* in the modern theater, examining the historical, the metaphysical, and the iconographic dimensions of this device. In the second part of my article I will analyze some specific examples where the device of the *deus ex machina* has been used in the modern and contemporary theater. The purpose of this second section of my paper is to provide a preliminary historiographical sketch, a kind of initial "genealogy" that I hope can point out some possible directions towards a much more comprehensive historiographic examination of the use of the *deus ex machina* in the modern theater.

The meeting of two worlds

"I'm not a historian," says Gogo, who together with Didi is waiting for the appearance of something that we must admit very much resembles a supernatural figure, and who as we all know too well by now, does not appear, again, alluding to the enigmatic question in the first scene of *Hamlet*, whether "this thing" has appeared "again tonight."[3] But that's exactly Beckett's point: the machinery of the *deus ex machina*, enabling the appearance of such a supernatural being, is out of joint. It does not function anymore. And this frustration of our expectations, that some form of supernatural power will finally appear, serves as a comment not only on the times in which we live (if we see

Beckett's play as an expression of the post-World War Two Zeitgeist), but will probably also influence our narratives about theatrical conventions at different times in history. Looking at *Waiting for Godot* as an aborted *deus ex machina* also establishes some kind of continuity with the "traditional" *deus ex machina* as a phenomenon with its own distinct history. In what sense, then, is the *deus ex machina*, as a theatrical narrative unit based on certain theological and metaphysical assumptions with more or less fixed constellations of verbal and visual elements conventionally employed to end the performance, still relevant for the modern and contemporary theater? And how can a discussion of this device with its distinct and fixed iconographic regime, which the modern theater has both preserved and transformed, illuminate our discussions concerning the historiography of the theater?

It is of course impossible to address all of these complex questions here. But they need to be introduced as the general framework for this presentation. To begin with, it is important to note that the *deus ex machina* has been marginalized or even overlooked by most critics. A fairly recent example is a handbook by Karl Beckson and Artur Ganz, written a few years after Beckett had published Godot; Beckson and Ganz sweepingly brush away the *deus ex machina* as a more or less non-existent phenomenon in the modern theater. They claimed that, "Serious modern writers avoid the *deus ex machina*, though it has sometimes been used in comedy."[4] But since they do not provide any concrete examples we are left with the question as to whether *Waiting for Godot* is a comedy by at least then a not very serious writer, or if Ibsen's social plays, August Strindberg's *A Dream Play* (1901–5), Luigi Pirandello's *Six Characters in Search of an Author* (1921), Bertolt Brecht's *The Threepenny Opera* (first performed in 1928 and published in 1929) and *The Good Person of Szechwan* (1938–9), as well as the visual, iconographic apparatus of most of Robert Wilson's performances, just to give a few examples of major modern plays and performances where the *deus ex machina* has been integrated as a dramatic and scenic element, will be given the same critical verdict. In the second part of this article I will analyze these examples in more detail.

But I will begin with some more general reflections. Aristotle, historian and theorist of poetics, surveying both the origins and the development of tragedy, argued that, "the unraveling of the plot should arise from the circumstances of the plot itself, and not be brought about *ex machina*."[5] The suspicious attitude towards the *deus ex machina* is clearly not a new phenomenon and can perhaps best be ascribed to the improbability inherent in the use of this device itself within the theoretical framework presented by Aristotle, where events have to be both probable and possible. For Plato such matters even led to the ban of the theater. In spite of Aristotle's critique of the *deus ex machina*, however, it was frequently used in the plays he examines, and not only "for matters outside the play proper," something that Aristotle clearly approved of, as opposed to the actual appearance of the gods on the stage itself, from which he distanced himself.[6] The appearance of the gods was apparently for Aristotle, as for Plato, basically a religious concern, not something for the theater where stage machineries like the tracks above the stage holding the ropes, the spring coils and the iron rods attached to the actors or the chariots on which they were suspended or transported in the air in view of the audience were used to make the gods appear. This was not an acceptable representation of the Greek pantheon.

What could be termed "theatrical immanence," the incarnation of supernatural forces, like "ghosts, apparitions, dibbuks, souls, demons, angels, and devils" on the stage (to quote the list of other-worldly beings cited by the character Aron in Ingmar Bergman's film *Fanny and Alexander*),[7] has given rise to a complex historical dialectics in which the theater, metaphysics and theology constantly interact. Aron is preparing a huge *deus ex machina* doll in the cellar while his brother Ismael, who is also kept imprisoned there, brings about the punishment of Alexander's vicious stepfather, the bishop, through some form of supernatural intervention. Nietzsche, in *The Birth of Tragedy*, commented that, "The *deus ex machina* took the place of metaphysical comfort,"[8] preserving life in the cave where the shadows flicker on the inner wall. Examples like these show how theater and performance occupy an ambiguous and sometimes even transformative middle ground, what Turner termed a "liminal" position, mediating between different worlds, while at the same time also commenting and reflecting on the medium of theater and performance itself.[9] The *deus ex machina* can even be seen as a basis for the theater to scrutinize its own means of expression, developing a heightened awareness of its own potential metatheatrical dimensions. The *deus ex machina*, perhaps because of its improbability, is inherently theatrical.

The concept of allegory developed by Walter Benjamin in his *Ursprung des deutschen Trauerspiels* was partly intended to meet the transformation of the ancient deities within the context of the religiously charged baroque period. According to Benjamin this transformation, even if it served as a basis for redemption, was at the same time also expressed through different forms of debasement. Benjamin argued that

> [t]here is a threefold material affinity between baroque and medieval Christianity. The struggle against the pagan gods, the triumph of allegory, the torment of the flesh, are equally essential to both . . . As can be seen, allegorical exegesis tended above all in two directions: it was designed to establish, from a Christian point of view, the true, demonic nature of the ancient gods, and it also served the pious mortification of the flesh. (220)

These tendencies of physical torment and demonization, which were complemented by some form of declaration of the holiness of the theater, can also be found in the examples that will be examined here, and they culminate in the theoretical thinking of Antonin Artaud, which was further developed by for example Peter Brook and Jerzy Grotowski after World War Two (which will, however, not be discussed here). According to Benjamin, allegory preserved "an appreciation of the transience of things," but only, he claims, after the ancient gods had actually died out.[10]

Erika Fischer-Lichte has pointed out, that Benjamin's extensive discussions of allegory,

> as a process of meaning-constitution, follows the guide-line of exposing and intensifying the principles of subjectivity and historicity, it becomes in itself an allegory in which the "mode of signifying" turns into the signified: as "fixed movement" the allegory signifies the "messianic standstill of history," which Benjamin describes as the messianic redemption at the end of history.[11]

Thus allegory, according to Benjamin, can even be seen as an aesthetic, self-reflexive category pointing at historical processes that are constituted in the world as forms of meaning as well as through the messianic longings for the end of history. This reflects the dialectics of the *deus ex machina* in the theater, simultaneously performing the contradictory processes of narrative and history from a temporal/social as well as a semiotic-aesthetic perspective, both of which, alluding to Frank Kermode's illuminating study, have the "sense of an ending" in view.[12]

The modern theater, I wish to argue here, has continued to develop these allegorical features on the level of theme, plot, as well as with regard to the uses of the stage and its theatrical machineries in their relationship to the meta-physical, divine immanence and the messianic utopias. The strategies through which the modern theater has so distinctly preserved both the position/location on the stage for the appearance of the *deus ex machina*, descending vertically from above in the focal point accompanied by heightened lighting on the back-stage, clearly show that the stage possesses a "language" on the basis of which it can both locate and isolate the interaction, the integration and the oppositions between the physical and the metaphysical as an integrative feature of performance, enabling these different worlds both to meet and to interact.[13]

The fact, however, that the theater during different periods, as Jonas Barish has convincingly shown, aroused such passionate opposition, in particular from religious circles, when they themselves, like the medieval church or the Jesuits, did not hesitate to use the theatrical spectacles for pedagogical purposes or even for indoctrination, is no doubt partially the result of the seemingly blasphemous aspects of the *deus ex machina* as a theatrical machinery.[14]

As long as the theater was intimately connected with the church or with clearly structured official, ritual activities, reinforcing the social and religious norms, it did not raise any resistance. But as soon as the theater and perform-ance, so to speak, tried to stand on their own, primarily on the basis of what I believe can be formulated in terms of their gradually expanding spheres of fictionality – what they are about and what they show – they were perceived as subversive by the hegemonic religious or in some cases even by the secular authorities.[15]

The theatrical concerns of how to enable a no-longer-extant metaphysical dimension to make some kind of physical appearance on the stage are no doubt also intimately connected with the attempts during the first decades of the twentieth century to formulate a complex relationship between aesthetic experience and the vision of utopia. The thinking of Ernst Bloch is perhaps even more relevant here than that of Benjamin. According to Richard Wolin, to Bloch:

> works of art remain merely aesthetic, symbolic totalities that fulfill an essen-tial *anticipatory* function in the re-creation of totality, but which can never embody the latter in and of themselves. They are for Bloch Messianic prom-ises which explode in the dark and meaningless continuum of contempo-rary life to light the way toward the long sought after homeland (*"Heimat"*). However, he is careful to point out that as aesthetic symbols they remain only fictive, imaginary incarnations of this ideal, and thus are merely one aspect of a larger process of coming to self-consciousness on the part of the species, a process whose traces are equally discernible in the mystical and esoteric aspects of the great world religious systems, the tradition of Western metaphysics, daydreams, fantasy, etc.[16]

The paradoxes of the aesthetic field as formulated in the thinking of Bloch no doubt touch the very core of the modern theater with respect to its use of the *deus ex machina* as well as the possibilities of the theater (and art in general) to create representations of this utopian state, a state (or a no-place) where history itself will both reach its end and its fulfillment. For Bloch the fulfillment of his-tory is seen both in temporal and spatial terms. The no-place of *utopia* is an open-ended futurity for which the appearance of the *deus ex machina* on the stage serves as a powerful metaphor.

In his commentary on Bloch, Jürgen Habermas emphasized the spatial metaphor for understanding this utopian spirit in a world where God is no longer present. Habermas's formulations are also relevant for the modern the-ater where the stage for a short but powerful fictional moment is transformed into the space where the void previously occupied by God is filled. According to Habermas:

God is dead, but his locus has survived him. The place into which mankind has imagined God and the gods, after the decay of these hypotheses, remains a hollow space. The measurements in-depth of this vacuum, indeed atheism finally understood, sketch out a blueprint of a future kingdom of freedom.[17]

How free the blueprint of the modern theater as a performance reality can make the spectators, and if, indeed, we are really able fully to appreciate and interpret it, remains an open question. The modern theater, and our contemporary performance traditions in particular, are constantly attempting to fill the voids in our systems of thinking, mainly by making us painfully aware of them. The modern theater can perhaps even be perceived as the very "locus" attempting to find the thread leading to this "kingdom of freedom," even if the awareness that the kingdom itself can probably never be reached, no doubt prevails, as it does in the work of Beckett. But the *deus ex machina* is one of the ways to confront this void, filling it with spectacle, at least as long as the performance itself lasts.

This implies (and perhaps I am jumping too quickly to conclusions) that besides developing a sense of what the theater is and can do, we also have to confront this sense with an understanding of what history is, and in particular how the theater itself performs history. In my book *Performing History* I wanted to examine how the theater has been representing the past in post-World War Two contexts.[18] What I am exploring here is how the theater imagines this open-ended futurity, the "future kingdom of freedom," which at least in fictional terms also represents the end of history itself. *Deus ex machina* figures this history, pointing out ways in which we can hopefully also re-figure the history of theater and performance.

Before looking more closely at some of the twentieth-century examples where the *deus ex machina* has been employed I want to add something on a more personal note in parenthesis. While working on this topic – and it has been on my mind for more than a decade now – I have frequently asked myself what my own reasons for this engagement are. Partly it stems from my interest in the relations between theater and history as well as what I believe is one of the most central issues concerning the dynamics of *mise-en-scène* in the theater, the appearance of a character or "being" on the stage who comes from another world. The question presented in the first scene of *Hamlet*, "What, has this thing appeared again tonight?" of course refers to the ghost, but also to the performance itself as something which inevitably appears again tonight, connecting the performance with the supernatural, while at the same time exposing a self-reflexive metatheatrical mode of expression through which theater and metaphysics become inevitably linked.

Thinking about these issues I also remember the first concert of the Beatles in Stockholm, in October 1963, before they had become universally famous.

I was one of a few thousand fans attending this concert, which began with the young group slowly descending on a crane to the stage singing "She loves you, yeah, yeah, yeah." The power and energy emanating from these initial moments, while the singers and their instruments were illuminated with spotlights remain with me as a liberating force which only later became connected to the traditional *deus ex machina* and the appearance of the otherworldly on the stage.

The *deus ex machina* as dream

After trying to set up the metaphysical and historical framework within which the issues of the *deus ex machina* in the modern theater can be examined, I now want to turn to an analysis of concrete examples. I will start with the work of August Strindberg.

The fictional universe of Strindberg's *A Dream Play* (1901–6) is divided between the heavenly sphere and the material, everyday world. It presents the journey and the investigations of a divine figure, Indra's daughter, in the world of human suffering. Even though she had hoped to find at least a spark of hope in the earthly form of existence she quickly realizes that the suffering of the humans is unbearable and she returns to the heavenly extra-terrestrial spheres from which she originated. The play, which opened with a descent from the heavens through the clouds, ends with an ascent to those same spheres, thus completing the cyclic movement of the birth and death of Indra's daughter.[19] The prologue, the actual *deus ex machina*, with which the play in its present form begins, was added during the Fall of 1906 for its first production at Svenska Teatern in Stockholm in April 1907. In this prologue, on the background of clouds and stars Indra's daughter is seen gradually descending, thus making the play begin with a *deus ex machina*, instead of as it was traditionally used, for ending a performance. In this prologue the voice of Indra himself, who never becomes visible though, can be heard warning his daughter:

> Thou hast strayed, my child.
> Take heed, thou sinkest.
> How cam'st thou here? (197)[20]

To which she answers:

> Borne on a cloud, I followed the lightning's
> blazing trail from the ethereal heights.
> But the cloud sank, and still is falling.
> Tell me, great father Indra, to what region
> am I come? The air's so dense, so hard to breathe. (197)

The descent is slow and painful and what she sees below is the earth, which according to Indra "is the darkest and the heaviest / of all the spheres that swing in space" (197).

However, when the clouds disperse the Daughter can hear their joy and their songs of "praise and thanks to heaven" (198) and her father asks her to

Descend and see, and hear, and then, come again
and tell me if their lamentations
and complaint are justified. (198)

Even at this initial point the whole movement of the play is presented. The descent of the goddess into this world is also the birth of an individual – who will later also be called Agnes in some of the scenes – to the pains and sufferings of this world. The pangs of birth, the *deus ex machina*, are depicted from the perspective of the newborn baby:

Now the cloud sinks. It's growing dense. I suffocate!
This is not air, but smoke and water that I breathe,
so heavy that it drags me down and down.
And now I clearly feel its reeling! (198)

This mixture of smoke and water, we learn, is the dust that the humans breathe on earth, and, as Indra explains, it makes them dizzy. The "birth" of Indra's daughter/Agnes and her descent into this world is in *A Dream Play* also compared with the notion of falling asleep and, according to Strindberg's "logic," life in this world is actually a dream. To wake up from this nightmare for Strindberg also means to die and to become liberated from this world.

The longing back of Indra's daughter/Agnes to the heavenly spheres is placed in constant opposition to the imprisonment in this world. This opposition between freedom and imprisonment can also be seen as an implicit discussion on Strindberg's part of the limitations of theatrical realism. The closed box stage of the realistic theater has no possibility to reach out beyond the limited material forms of earthly existence and one of the things Strindberg shows in this play is how this limitation, on the aesthetic level, can at least partially be overcome by giving the *deus ex machina* such a central position in the play.

Once the descent of Indra's daughter into this world has been carried out she is locked into the confined limits of the box-stage bourgeois existence. The strongest expression in *A Dream Play* of this confinement is the scene where Agnes marries the lawyer, representing justice and truth, albeit in its limited earthly version. In this scene, which takes place in their home, Kristin is blocking all the exits of the room by glueing newspapers around the windows, supposedly to keep the cold out. But what actually happens at the same time, on the metatheatrical level, is that Kristin is cutting off all the daughter's channels of communication with the "outside" world, including the metaphysical dimensions of her origins as well as the machinery which has made it possible for her to move between the different levels of existence, and which, temporarily at least, does not function anymore, just as in *Waiting for Godot*.

But *A Dream Play*, as opposed to Beckett's play, contains a mechanism of redemption for Indra's daughter as well as, on the aesthetic level, for the realistic theater, which enables them both to transcend the closed confines of the living-room existence. Seen from this perspective Strindberg's play is a metatheatrical allegory about overcoming the theatrical conventions of realism. The realistic scenes, which traditionally had to adhere to the unities of time, place and action, have instead become fragmented both in time and space through the intricate *Stationen*-drama form of the play.

The *deus ex machina* in the realistic theater

However, the realistic theater with its closed rooms also frequently employed the device of the *deus ex machina*, though in a modified form. In the plays of Ibsen the supernatural creature has been transformed into a dead father figure, who instead of saving the life of the protagonist at the end of the play carries a destructive force that usually leads to his or her death. The kind of benevolent otherworldly "God" or Fate, bringing some form of salvation, which was the traditional function of the *deus ex machina*, has in Ibsen been transformed into a psychological mechanism producing a destructive revenge both from within, resulting from some kind of inner character-flaw frequently caused by the hereditary influences from the father, as well as from without, through the social and symbolic influences of this destructive father figure.

Ibsen has carefully located this vengeful paternal power in the centrally located focal point at the back of the symmetrical box stage, exactly where the *deus ex machina* traditionally appeared, transposing the theatrical machinery into a psychological dynamics. The tragic fall leading to the death of the protagonist is caused by the intervention of this "supernatural" father figure in the central focal point of the stage. This form of vengeance has been realized in plays like *Ghosts*, *The Wild Duck*, *Hedda Gabler*, *Rosmersholm* and *John Gabriel Borkman*, to mention some of the more obvious examples.[21] In these plays the father figures directly interfere with and even destroy the lives of their descendants. This also takes place in a strong flow of light – because the focal point traditionally contains the light of divine illumination – as at the end of *Ghosts*, where the illness Oswald has inherited from his father overpowers him, while at the very same time the sun finally appears through the clouds that throughout have obstructed the view of the fjord.

The pistols in *The Wild Duck* and *Hedda Gabler* are the tools of divine vengeance connected to the respective fathers of Hedvig and Hedda. Hedvig intends to use the pistol to kill the duck, a present from her biological father, Old Mr Werle, but kills herself instead. Hedda takes her life under the portrait of her father, General Gabler, and the portraits of the ancestors in *Rosmersholm* also take their vengeance. In *John Gabriel Borkman* the protagonist himself descends from his high abode in order to bring vengeance, but here this descent leads to his own death. The *deus ex machina* represented by Borkman destroys itself. And in all of these cases the iconographic features of the *deus ex machina*, as it was inherited from the baroque tradition, a tradition Ibsen knew very well from his own work in the theater, have in different ways been preserved, relying heavily on the focal point of the scenic one-point perspective of the box stage, where the traditional *deus ex machina* had appeared.

After the turn of the twentieth century these psychologically oriented issues were radically reformulated. In the plays of Ibsen, and in the more general psychoanalytic contexts developed by Freud, we find a transformation of the mythic role of father figure into psychological energies carrying a destructive influence on the individual, within the limited framework of the bourgeois family in its final stages of disintegration. With the advent of the new century the issues dealt with by the theater were at the same time both existential and social in ways that strove to transcend the confines of the limited family. The social and psychological developments of the new century could not to the same extent be dealt with in terms of the more intimate family structures, and this also led to significant transformations of the *deus ex machina*. This development can be discerned in the work of Strindberg for whom the turn of the century as we can see in *A Dream Play* led to a radical reformulation of his stage language in relation to the device of the *deus ex machina*, now affirming its metaphysical dimensions.

Ibsen's use of the sudden appearance of the sun in the last act of *Ghosts* served as a challenge for Strindberg when writing *Miss Julie*. Strindberg even claimed that for this naturalistic tragedy he only needed one act for the sun to rise, while Ibsen had needed three in *Ghosts*. The sunrise in *Miss Julie* comes towards the end of the play, when the games of this short midsummer night are over and Julie has to face her situation while for Jean this night will probably only remain an incident. Julie's final confrontation is taking place in a state of sleep and hypnosis, and she asks Jean to bring her to this state. She orders him to be her hypnotist and in turn to order her to take the broom. For that, he claims, she has to be asleep, and she answers, "as if in a trance" (113), that

> I am asleep already . . . the whole room has turned to smoke – and you look like a stove – a stove like a man in black with a tall hat – your eyes are

glowing like coals when the fire is low – and your face is a white patch like ashes. (113)

At this point Strindberg's stage direction informs us that the sunlight has reached the floor and is illuminating Jean.

Jean's figure is apparently illuminated from behind and from the point of view of Julie he is transformed into glowing messenger of death who has come to bring her to the next world. This whole scene is no doubt inspired by the iconography of the *deus ex machina*, but here it is seen from the subjective perspective of her trance, while at the same time the action continues. "How nice and warm it is!" (113), she says, and warms her hands on what she believes to be the fire, and then, before Jean gives her the razor blade, which she thinks is the broom with which she will sweep away all pain, she adds: "And so light – and so peaceful" (113). She has only one question for Jean before she makes her final exit and that is whether he can promise her redemption. And, as the divine incarnation he represents for her at this moment, this too can be realized, at least from her subjective perspective.

But Strindberg's play presents a struggle between the divine figure of redemption represented by Jean, on the one hand, and the Count, the vengeful father figure, on the other. The stage presence of the Count, Julie's biological father, is only realized through the telephone-pipe from his apartment to the kitchen, obviously a modern transformation of the theatrical machinery through which the gods had previously intervened in the actions of the humans. Just before Jean gets enough power to command Julie to go, he imagines seeing how the bell, which will call him to the telephone, moved:

To be so frightened of a bell! Yes, but it's not just a bell. There's somebody behind it – a hand moving it – and something else moving the hand. (114)

Here the Count has become a divine figure diminishing Jean's power. But she relies on Jean in order to release her from the bonds of the material world, and it is he, with the threat of the ringing bell hanging over his head, who finally orders her to go.

The Ghost Sonata presents a similar split between the supernatural forces struggling over a young woman, Adele. They are materialized through the young student and the character of Hummel in his wheelchair, an ironic reversal of the chariot used by the gods. Here too, the light of the sun figures prominently. At the moment of Adele's death the student says:

The Liberator is coming. Welcome, pale and gentle one. Sleep, you lovely, innocent doomed creature, suffering for no fault of your own. Sleep without dreaming, and when you wake again . . . may you be greeted by a sun that does not burn, in a home without dust, by friends without stain, by a love without flaw. You wise and gentle Buddha, sitting there waiting for a Heaven to sprout from the earth, grant us patience in our ordeal and purity of will, so that this hope may not be confounded. (303–4)

The strings of the harp can be heard while the room is filled by a white light through which the pains of this world gradually dissolve and the student recites the poem to the sun through which the *deus ex machina* is actually carried out.

> I saw the sun. To me it seemed
> that I beheld the Hidden.
> Men must reap what they have sown,
> blest is he whose deeds are good.
> Deeds which you have wrought in fury,
> cannot in evil find redress. (304)

While these lines are recited we can hear Adele's final moans and the stage directions inform us that as the room disappears Boecklin's painting *The Island of the Dead* "is seen in the distance, and from the island comes music, soft sweet and melancholy."

In the three plays by Strindberg briefly examined here the final release of a young woman from the bonds of this world and her unification with some form of metaphysical principle are at the same time both thematically and iconographically conceived of as an ascent to or through a heavenly light. This ascent is administered by a young man – the poet (in *A Dream Play*), the student (in *The Ghost Sonata*) or the servant, Jean – all of whom are potential partners for these young women, while an older man, a father-figure, who in *Miss Julie* and *The Ghost Sonata* represents different forms of the avenger, and in *A Dream Play* the God Indra himself, but also the Lawyer, the husband of Agnes, are more or less passively or helplessly observing the final departure of this young woman. In *A Dream Play* and *Miss Julie* the godlike father figure does not appear on the stage, while in *The Ghost Sonata* he is very much present in the figure of Hummel.

The *deus ex machina* as aesthetic device

Luigi Pirandello's *Six Characters in Search of an Author* approaches the device of the *deus ex machina* from a completely different perspective, almost completely voiding it of its religious, mystical or theological substrata. Instead, this play presents a metatheatrical, self-contained aesthetic universe where the six so-called Characters as well as Madame Pace enter the "real", i.e. the fictional, world of the theater from their otherworldly sphere of the extra-theatrical reality where, according to the premises of the play, their lives have already been lived.

In his stage directions describing the first entrance of the Characters Pirandello has taken great care to emphasize their otherworldliness, pointing out that they wear masks in order "to bring out the deep significance of the play" and that they should be "designed to give the impression of figures constructed by art." Even if these Characters are supposedly more "real" than the fictional reality of the play into which they want to have their lives transformed by the actors, Pirandello, in his stage directions emphasized, that they

> should not appear as ghosts, but as created realities, timeless creations of the imagination, and so more real and consistent than the changeable realities of the Actors.[22]

Such "timeless creations of the imagination" are closely related to divine figures, but the paradox is that these Characters have through their own lives already enacted the banal family melodrama, which they now, through the help of the Director and the Actors, wish to see transformed into a work of art.

The appearance of Madame Pace, who is actually called an "apparition" in the stage directions, is even more clearly conceived of as a *deus ex machina* figure than the Characters. Since it is necessary for her to be present in order for the Characters to retell some of the crucial events of their melodramatic story, the Father places different clothes on the stage in order, as he says, to attract her "by the articles of her trade" (104), and since she is apparently a true fetishist, the incantation works. The Father then invites everybody to watch the door in the back and, exactly like the traditional *deus ex machina*, Madame Pace makes her magical entry. Some of the Actors think this is a cheap trick, but the Father retorts:

> Why do you want to spoil a miracle by being factual. Can't you see this is a miracle of reality, that is born, brought to life, lured here, reproduced, just for the sake of this scene, with more right to be alive here than you have? Perhaps it has more truth than you have yourselves. (105)

There is no solution to the aesthetic paradox Pirandello presents. It is clear though, that on a theatrical stage where reality can become a miracle it is necessary to activate the machineries of the *deus ex machina* in order to make the fragmented reality on which it is based appear.

In one of the first productions of *Six Characters in Search of an Author*, which was directed by the Russian-born director Georges Pitoëff in Paris at the Comédie des Champs-Elysées in 1923, he used the existing scene-lift in the back-stage area for the first entry of the Characters. I have not been able to establish if it was used for the entrance of Madame Pace as well. There is no doubt, though, that from the iconographic point of view, the entrance of the Characters as a group in the lift clearly emphasized the fact that they descend to the stage from another level of existence, from another world. The use of the stage-lift was very well suited the notion of their *deus ex machina* entrance as the consciously employed aesthetic device presented in the play itself. It is said that when Pirandello heard about Pitoëff's plans for this important scene he became so horrified that he personally made the trip from Rome to Paris in order to protest it. But after viewing the rehearsals and meeting with the director he became convinced that it worked.[23]

A short and preliminary ending (without a *deus ex machina*)

I have argued that the *deus ex machina* and its iconographic figurations are ubiquitously present in modern drama as well as on the contemporary theater stages. It exists in numerous variations, and an interesting feature of the modern theater with regard to this device is the fact that it frequently begins the theatrical narrative, as in *A Dream Play* and *Six Characters*. This, as well as other issues, however, still needs our careful attention. So does the work of Bertolt Brecht – and not only his plays like *The Threepenny Opera* where the last scene, written during the rehearsals for its first production at Theater am Schiffbauerdamm in Berlin in 1928, was explicitly called a *deus ex machina* by Brecht himself; or *The Good Person of Szechwan*, where the gods appear with a specific mission – because Brecht's epic theater is a scientific theater about the structure of the universe, a Planetarium where the spectator is ultimately bestowed with a divine point of view.

Robert Wilson's scenic images, which feature an illuminated backstage area in nearly every production, should also be investigated in this regard; so, too, Tony Kushner's *Angels in America*. Some recent Israeli performances like *The Boy Dreams* (analyzed in my book *Performing History*) and *Adam Resurrected*, featuring figures of Messiah, hopefully bringing some form of redemption to this world, also have to be examined in order to understand this form of divine intervention. In both of these performances, relying heavily on the classic Habima production of *The Dybbuk* from 1922, the Messianic hopes become thwarted through a subversive theatrical gesture. This is, however, only a partial list of plays and performances where the *deus ex machina* and what I have termed its iconographic regime, recalling the rule of death in *Hamlet* personified by a sergeant who "is strict in his arrest," appear on the twentieth-century stages. Such an extended version of this preliminary study also has to examine contemporary productions of classical plays like *Medea* where the *deus ex machina* plays an important role.

In view of the somewhat preliminary nature of this sketch, I hope that I have suggested that the *deus ex machina* seems to be an indispensable element of our theatrical machinery, one that we retain, despite the significant changes it has undergone with the radical challenge to its theological basis. In the pre-modern forms of the theater the boundaries between human characters and other kinds of creatures, regardless whether they were divine or monstrous, were relatively clear. The modern theater dismantled these boundaries. In Ibsen's plays the *deus ex machina* became an expression of psychological conflicts, while during the twentieth century its metatheatrical and even nihilistic dimensions have been much more strongly emphasized. With Hamm's total blindness in *Endgame* nothing remains of the divine machinery but the wheelchair inherited from Strindberg's Hummel in *The Ghost Sonata*, a pair of sunglasses, a broken toy dog and a few old jokes.

The traditional Jewish joke about the tailor, which Hamm likes to tell his so-called "progenitors," could perhaps be interpreted as a parable of the development of the contemporary theater. A man brings a piece of cloth to the tailor and after several attempts to make these trousers fit, the customer (or perhaps the spectator) gets angry at the tailor and screams:

> God damn you to hell, Sir, no, it's indecent, there are limits. In six days, do you hear me, six days, God made the world! Yes Sir, no less Sir, the WORLD! And you are not bloody well capable of making me a pair of trousers in three months![24]

The tailor retorts:

> But my dear Sir, my dear Sir, look – (disdainful gesture, disgustedly) – at the world – (pause) – and – (loving gesture, proudly) – at my TROUSERS! (103)

The theater is striving to reproduce this act of creation. In the meantime the tailor has become a post-modern director collecting his materials from the garbage piles of history. The first seven days passed a long time ago, which means, to develop the argument of the tailor, that the result will perhaps eventually become much more perfect than the world, as we know it, is. And while what could be a child is perhaps approaching, Hamm chants: "You cried for night; it falls: now cry in darkness . . . Moments for nothing, now as always, time was never and time is over, reckoning closed and story ended" (133). Theater history has not yet reached this condition, and hopefully will not. But we have to bear in mind that this is certainly one of the ways to end the story, with Hamm saying to himself: "You . . . remain" (134).

Notes

1. Friedrich Nietzsche, *The Gay Science*, trans. Walter Kaufmann (New York: Viking Books, 1974), 167. Samuel Beckett, *Waiting for Godot* in *The Complete Dramatic Works of Samuel Beckett* (London: Faber & Faber, 1986), 88. William Shakespeare, *Hamlet* 1. 1. 21.
2. Nietzsche, *The Gay Science*, 167.
3. Beckett, *Waiting for Godot*, 61.
4. Karl Beckson and Artur Ganz, *A Reader's Guide to Literary Terms* (London: Thames and Hudson, 1961), 48.
5. Aristotle, *On the Art of Poetry*, in *Classical Literary Criticism*, trans. and introd. T. S. Dorssch (Harmondsworth: Penguin Books 1965), chapter 15, 52.
6. Ibid. Aristotle's "blindness" to the basic conditions of the phenomena he discusses is a subject in itself worth detailed attention. Why does he fail to acknowledge signs on the body as an important aspect of the *anagnorisis*, while Oedipus, whose name is marked by his bodily scars, serves as his prime example of tragedy? For a discussion on this issue see my article "One Voice and Many Legs: Oedipus and the Riddle of the Sphinx," in *Untying the Knot: On Riddles and Other Enigmatic Modes*, ed. G. Hasan-Rokem and D. Shulman (New York: Oxford University Press, 1996), 255–70.
7. Ingmar Bergman, *Fanny och Alexander* (Stockholm: Månpocket, 1984), 201 (my translation).
8. Friedrch Nietzsche, *The Birth of Tragedy*, trans. Walter Kauffmann (New York: Vintage Books, 1967), 109.
9. See, for instance, Victor Turner, *From Ritual to Theater: the Human Seriousness of Play* (New York: Performing Arts Journal Publications, 1982).
10. Walter Benjamin, *The Origin of German Tragic Drama*, trans. John Osborne (London: Verso, 1985), 220, 223.
11. Erika Fischer-Lichte, *The Show and the Gaze of Theatre: a European Perspective* (Iowa City: University of Iowa Press, 1997), 283.
12. Frank Kermode, *The Sense of an Ending: Studies in the Theory of Fiction* (London: Oxford University Press, 1967).
13. See Gösta M. Bergman, *Lighting in the Theatre* (Stockholm: Almqvist & Wiksell International, 1977).
14. Jonas Barish, *The Antitheatrical Prejudice* (Berkeley: University of California Press, 1981).
15. These issues (though I will not be able to discuss them in detail here) can also be formulated in terms of a related historical dialectics: between the fictional forms of *mimesis* as opposed to the religious/Christian expressions of *imitatio*.

    The expressions of the theater that are independent in this sense contain several points of conflict with different forms of religious orthodoxy that are relevant in this context. The most basic point of conflict and, one could even argue, the competition between theater and religion focuses on the different forms and interpretations of the fundamental concept of *mimesis*, what is usually translated as imitation or representation. The complex tradition of the *mimesis* concept is in different ways also intimately connected to the *deus ex machina*, the representation of divine creatures in the theater, especially after the emergence of Christianity. The major reason for this complex connection between *mimesis* and *deus ex machina* seems to be that, in addition to the different classical interpretations of *mimesis*, either as a gradual distanciation from the true forms of reality, as argued by Plato, or as an independent aesthetic reality with its own internal laws, a view basically held by Aristotle, Christian theology developed its own understanding of imitation and representation, *imitatio*, as a spiritual relation to the Christian God and in particular to the life of Jesus and his role as the Savior.

It was through the incarnation of Jesus in this world in the form of a human being, a very special form of divine descent, that the salvation of the individual was made possible. The salvation of each individual was dependent on his ability to create a spiritual relationship of *imitatio* to Christ. Since the historical incarnation of Christ in this world is, at least metaphorically speaking, also a form of *deus ex machina*, there arose, one could argue, an extremely strong cultural conflict with regard to the different competing forms of representation. *Imitatio* was perceived as the source for religious elevation and personal salvation, while *mimesis* was basically understood as a fundamental aesthetic principle, a more objective and depersonalized mechanism on which playwriting and scenic presentation were based. The distinctions between *imitatio* and *mimesis* are extremely complex and deserve to be discussed and analyzed independently. But they are clearly connected to the discussion of the *deus ex machina*, insofar as both *imitatio* and *mimesis* are concerned with different and even competing perceptions and interpretations of the notion of divine immanence or embodiment.

16. Richard Wolin, *Walter Benjamin: an Aesthetic of Redemption* (New York: Columbia University Press, 1982), 25.
17. Jürgen Habermas, "Ernst Bloch – A Marxist Romantic," *Salmagundi*, 10–11 (Fall 1969–Winter 1970): 313.
18. Freddie Rokem, *Performing History: Theatrical Representations of the Past in Contemporary Theatre* (Iowa City: University of Iowa Press, 2000).
19. For extensive discussions of this play see Harry Carlsson, *Strindberg and the Poetry of Myth* (Berkeley: University of California Press, 1982); Evert Sprinchorn, *Strindberg as Dramatist* (New Haven: Yale University Press, 1982); and Egil Tornqvist, *Strindbergian Drama: Themes and Structure* (Stockholm: Almqvist & Wiksell International, 982). See also Gunnar Ollen's notes to the new Swedish edition of Strindberg's collected works, *August Strindbergs Samlade Verk*, vol. 46 (Stockholm: Norstedts, 1988), where the process of composition of *A Dream Play* and its early reception in Sweden are discussed.
20. The translations from all the Strindberg plays used for this version of my paper are from *Six Plays of Strindberg*, trans. Elizabeth Sprigge (New York: Doubleday Anchor Books, 1955). Page references are included in the text.
21. It could even be argued that the mailbox in *A Doll's House* contains features of the *deus ex machina*, both on the basis of its position on the stage and because of its threat to Nora. However, according to Ibsen's stage directions between the two doors on the back wall, the entrance door with the mailbox and the door to Helmer's room, there is a piano which serves as the central focal point. In the first production of the play, in Copenhagen in 1879, there was a painting of Mary holding the Child above the piano. This arrangement pointed in two directions for spiritual redemption: through music and dancing, on the one hand, and through religious belief on the other. Nora, however, is not able to reach fulfillment through any of these options, and flees through the door with the mailbox, instead of chosing the door of her husband, which is the acceptable social solution to her dilemma. The iconography of this play points towards a spiritual and a social solution to Nora's dilemmas.

22. Luigi Pirandello, *Six Characters in Search of an Author*, trans. John Linstrum, *Three Plays* (London: Methuen, 1985), 75.
23. Jean Hort, *La vie héroique des Pitoeff* (Geneva: Pierre Callier, 1966), 177 ff.
24. Samuel Beckett, *Endgame, The Complete Dramatic Works*, 102–3. Page references are to this edition.

10
Improvising/History

Susan Leigh Foster

How might the historian research and write about improvised performance? Because of its allusiveness and resistance to documentation, improvisation has most frequently eluded the historian's focus. The improvised event, even the fact that improvisation occured as part of a performance, is frequently omitted from the historical record or glossed over as insubstantial or indescribable. Rather than lament this absence or ineffability, I want here to celebrate improvisation as an object of study that foregrounds theoretical dimensions of history writing. I will use improvisation as a catalyst for a new consideration of how history is researched and written.

In improvisation, the fact that performers don't know what they are going to do next draws viewers' attention to their decision-making process. It encourages viewers as well as performers to reflect on, at the same time that they attend to, what they are doing. Performers open their physicalized imaginations to entertain the possibility of many different next actions. They also track the results of acting upon or rejecting those impulses. Viewers likewise open to the flow of events and also critically engage with that going. Like the performers, they ask themselves, what is going to happen next and what difference will it make to the performance's significance? The fact that performers are improvising draws viewers into what Roland Barthes has called a "writerly" relationship to the performance text.[1] No longer the passive consumers of what is presented as performance, they become engaged, along with performers, in developing the form of the event.

In what follows I will attempt to reconstruct three specific improvised performances that took place in the 1960s, using each to formulate a distinctive approach to historical research. I offer this enquiry into history writing alongside those of Lena Hammergren, Randy Martin and Peggy Phelan, each of whom constructs a theoretical device that problematizes the way that dance can be reconstructed and deciphered. Hammergren's *flaneuse*, a purposeful regendering of Walter Benjamin's casually observant meanderer, strolls through the archival remains registering the remnants of a physicality once experienced. Siting herself at the 1930 Stockholm World Exposition, the *flaneuse* foils attempts to erect distinctions between high art and popular forms, savoring equally leisure, art, and innovation so as to elucidate the socialist utopian vision of the 1930s.[2] In contrast, Randy Martin's maniacal critic stuffs a single dance with more meaning than it could ever be thought to bear. Arts administration policies, economic theory, labor history, global flows of bodies and capital, are all summoned up through the process of overreading Bill T. Jones's *Last Supper at Uncle Tom's Cabin/The Promised Land*.[3] Phelan's computer-loving psychoanalytically inclined Balanchine ballerina mines the act of dancing for clues to Freud's choreography.[4] Performing an anatomy on both ballet and psychoanalysis, she shows how the symptoms of each reveal crucial lineaments of one another and of the sign of the feminine that they share. Each of these interpretive paradigms signals the means through which the analysis takes place by fabricating a characterological and textual embodiment of reflexivity.

The conjectured performances discussed below join hands with Hammergren's, Martin's, and Phelan's choreographic devices in order further to proliferate these kinds of approaches to history writing. These reconstructed performances do not set the record straight, but instead attract attention to the relation between subject and method of study. They also demonstrate the way improvisation occurs as a mediation between known and unknown parameters that shape the performance's argument and significance.

Improvising choreography

Dominant paradigms of improvisation in the 1950s and 1960s saw it as an abandoning of all structure in order to be free in the moment. Performers utilized improvisation as a way to unsettle routinized responses to the world and thereby contest normative patterns of behavior. Artists espousing this approach to improvisation had come of age in the wake of World War Two and the corporatized bureaucracies that had formed to respond to it, and many concluded that social renewal could only come about through a renewal of critical and perceptual faculties. Improvisation was seen as one vehicle for this sensory renewal. By clearing the mind of all preconceived structures and habituated responses, artists might summon up new ways of perceiving and orienting towards the world. In his book *The Culture of Spontaneity* Daniel Belgrad argues that this aesthetic agenda, rather than lacking in political commitment, especially when compared with the socialist and communist initiatives of the 1930s, contained a new notion of the political, one dedicated to the overthrow of bureaucratized regimens that defined both work and leisure activities. The best way to challenge this corporatized ordering of the world was through the introduction of entirely unanticipated, and hence chaotic events and stimuli.[5]

Body, in this view of improvisation, was endowed with a specialized access to the spontaneous which was cultivated through an amalgam of physical practices such as yoga, encounter-group exercises, chanting, Candomblé and massage – all seen as ways to develop sensory awareness and to construct a porous and sensitive corporeality. Training programs instituted by the Living Theater, the Open Theater, Jerzy Grotowski, the Judson Church dance group, and influential acting teacher Viola Spolin all devised open-ended encounters among performers that emphasized experiencing the scene with the entire body – seeing, smelling, hearing the environment and moving responsively through it.

Avant-garde theater experiments such as those conducted by Grotowski and the Living Theater developed text out of these kinds of physical exploration and encounters among bodies. Rather than begin with a play text, their dialogue often derived from spontaneous encounters among actors in rehearsal. Groans, shouts and whining sighs all signaled the performers' investment in the moment and authenticated their access to the deepest states of feeling. In performance the periods of silence that featured bodily movement reinforced this claim to a more raw and unmediated realm of human experience, a potential source of inspiration for social change.

Dance experiments such as those conducted by Judson choreographers focused on the physical facts of actions such as falling, running and pedestrian tasks rather than on body as an indicator of an interiority prior to or deeper than words out of which the action developed. Yet the playful messiness celebrated in these concerts privileged body as a special locale for accessing perceptual possibilities that might yield genuinely new discoveries. Arguing in favor of the serious fun that the Judson choreographers' concerts provided, critic Jill Johnston analyzed them this way:

> The demonstration of play as a mode of action central to dance is a significant regression. Central to play is improvisation. To improvise is to compose on the spur of the moment, as the dictionary says. Children compose things offhand in this manner and don't worry about alternative ways of behaving. When children like something they've done, they repeat it, thus achieving a set form, such as hopscotch or red-light. Adults who regress to childhood do the same.[6]

Here Johnston sets up childhood as a space in which random, non-habituated exploration can lead to marvelous new frameworks of behavior. Engaging in these indeterminate explorations of physical capacities, Judson artists conceptualized the body's diverse potentialities as a democratic range of possibilities. They dehierarchized parts of the body – treating head, torso, pelvis, fingers, legs or elbows with equal interest. Space and place were equally disencumbered from the traditional associations to them: high, low, in and out enjoyed reversals, juxtapositions, and scatterings, the result of improvisations dedicated to unsettling regimented responses.

Dance historian and critic Sally Banes characterizes this prevailing notion of improvisation succinctly when she comments: "In a way improvisation in its purest form would call for no choreography . . . it stands in direct opposition to choreography. So in a way improvisation is very subversive . . . And in that subversive role that improvisation has – in its purest sense, improvisation really does away with all the conventions that we know, that we recognize a dance work by."[7] Banes places the spontaneity of improvisation in opposition to the structural concerns of choreography. Choreography, she implies, consists in the judicious selection and utilization of the conventions of representation through which a danced message is crafted. Improvisation, in contrast, abandons all awareness of such conventions in favor of the performance of anti-form. Where choreography entails a reckoning with structure and craft, improvisation offers an escape from these formal concerns, and in this escape it functions subversively, if not to overthrow at least to deviate from established protocols.

In contrast to this oppositionality between structure and discovery, musicians working in the tradition of jazz envision improvisation as synthesizing the pre-established with the unknown. They utilize their mutual understanding of rhythmic, harmonic and melodic principles as a map to new musical territories. Often based on a popular song form or blues tune, jazz improvisations engage in a continuous reshaping of known material, moving it out into unknown varieties of musical utterance. Jazz not only moves unhaltingly between structure and immediacy, form and originality, craft and spontaneity, but it also provides for an exceptional opportunity to negotiate between individual and collective needs and desires. Solos, for example, take place within the shared structure of passing them around among band members. Experimentation with jazz forms as elaborated in bebop and eventually in the free jazz ensembles of the 1960s distribute responsibility collectively among all members of the group. Free jazz players, no longer implementing a shared tune or even standard harmonies, nonetheless work to develop a coherence within each performance based on an ongoing awareness of the material set forth from the opening moments of the performance.

Jazz, a tradition that has evidenced perpetual renewal in the face of calcifying demands of commercialism, served as an inspiration for white and African-American artists alike, and it was especially influential for theater and dance practices during the 1960s. Many artists went to jazz clubs regularly and listened to jazz as an edifying synthesis of unpremeditated innovation and social critique. The militant propulsiveness of bebop, its speed and harsh harmonies, the agility of its montage-like sequencings, all crafted a defiant opposition to racial oppression. Its adeptness at the unpremeditated dazzled listeners with the possibilities for maneuvering outside and against the system.

Applying these insights of jazz performance to dance improvisation, it is possible to reconceptualize improvisation as a continual negotiation between known and unknown physical experience, between previously mastered skills and impromptu discoveries, between learned patterns for choreographic thought and fresh insight, between established protocols for artistic performance and spontaneous deviations from those protocols. No matter how hard the improvising dancer works to jettison the habitual, its effects endure. Whether theorized as Marcel Mauss's "techniques of the body" or as Pierre Bourdieu's *habitus*, the systems of patternings that constitute the dancer's articulateness provide the armature through which exploration and discovery occur.[8] Similarly, expertise at making dances and knowledge of prior and contemporaneous dance productions deeply affect the performer's choreographic judgement. By exercising these influences and concerns, however impulsively and spontaneously, dancers engage with the conventions of representation through which danced meaning is constructed. That is to say, rather than exemplifying Banes's oppositional formulation between improvisation and choreography, the dancers are improvising the choreography.

Taking this view of the improvisatory process, I turn now to performances by pianist Cecil Taylor and choreographer Fred Herko, visual artist Carolee Schneeman, and performance artist Shigeko Kubota. Together these performances highlight the importance of assessing sexual orientation, gender, race, and disciplinary affiliation, as part of constructing the historical significance of the work. Together they also argue for the partial and culturally specific nature of historical investigation. In presenting this analysis, I want to summon up in the descriptions themselves part of the process through which I, as a historian, work at reconstructing the past.

Camping out in history

Ta-dah, ta-dah-ta-dah, ta-dah.

6 July 1962; the first "Concert of Dance" at Judson Memorial Church: Fred Herko and Cecil Taylor perform an improvised duet entitled *Like Most People – for Soren*. According to Banes, the "movement style ran the gamut from everyday gestures to Cunninghamesque movement to quotations of ballet."[9]

A year earlier, 31 July 1961 Herko presented *Possibilities for a Pleasant Outing*, his choreographic debut, at a concert organized by James Waring. According to drama critic Michael Smith: "Mr. Herko seems, more than the others, to derive direct delight from moving, which I'd think would be the basis of all dances . . .

he is dancing about infantile pleasure in a world dominated by inhibiting adult rationality."[10]

Hmmm. Already, Herko is located at odds with the mainstream of the avant garde, singled out among other proto-Judson performers, Yvonne Rainer and Aileen Passloff, as the one who likes to move. He is also isolated from adult aesthetics because of his infantile, not even childlike, pleasure-oriented motion. And these preliminary assessments are later amplified with descriptions that disagree in intriguing ways: Steve Paxton remembers that Herko

> seemed very campy and self-conscious . . . he was a collagist with an arch performance manner. You would get ballet movement, none of it very high energy. Maybe a few jetés every now and then. As a dancer his real forte was some very, very elegant lines. But in terms of actual movement, transitions from one well-defined place to another, he did it rather nervously. Holding a position was more what he did than moving from place to place.[11]

And critic Allen Hughes describes his work this way:

> His dances were architecturally organized. He didn't just go willy-nilly from here to there. He always had a sense of theatrical structure. Herko was a performer with charisma. He had a performer's instinct . . . He vitalized . . . movement . . . gave it a vividness that many of the others did not. Herko was the brightest performing star of all. he was a happy exhibitionist, which makes theater. Therefore he really wouldn't allow himself to go too far off into inner-somethings, because he never wanted to lose his public.[12]

But choreographer and critic Maxine Munt sums it all up when she writes: "Fred Herko is indeed the enfant terrible, and his *Little Gym Dance* . . . shouted 'look at me, look at me'; he has yet to prove he belongs with this group."[13]

Here I am; don't I look great?

Herko started dancing by taking ballet lessons beginning at the age of nineteen. He first performed professionally with Yvonne Rainer and David Gordon in (gay) choreographer James Waring's company. During the early period of his work with Judson, he lived with lighting designer Billie Linich who moved shortly thereafter to the Warhol factory. Andy Warhol writes: "[Herko] was one of those sweet guys that everybody loved to do things for simply because he never remembered to do anything for himself."[14]

On the same concert as his duet with Taylor, Herko presented a solo *Once or Twice a Week I Put on Sneakers to Go Uptown* to music of Erik Satie, with a costume by Remy Charlip. Jill Johnston describes it this way:

> Herko did a barefoot Suzie-Q in a tassel-veil head-dress, moving around the big open performing area . . . in a semi-circle, doing only the barefoot Suzie-Q with sometimes a lazy arm sneaking up and collapsing down, [and] with no alteration of pace or accent.[15]

Allen Hughes describes it this way:

> Fred Herko came out dressed in multi-colored bath or beach robe with a veil of light-weight metal chains covering his head and face . . . One's attention was riveted to his dance, which was no more than a kind of unvaried shuffling movement around the floor to the accompaniment of a piano piece by Erik Satie (Satie, incidentally, would have loved it) . . . This was the *Sneakers* dance, but Mr. Herko was barefoot all the while.[16]

E.M.B.L.A.Z.O.N.E.D.

For his collaboration with Fluxus member Joe Jones, *Binghamton Birdie* (May 1963),[17] Hughes writes that:

> Herko flashed in looking beatific. He wore black tights, a yellow-and-blue jersey with "JUDSON" emblazoned across the front, and, on one foot, a black shoe and his means of locomotion – a roller skate. His other foot was bare. Continuing to look beatific, he skated around the floor for a time, moving his arms and the unencumbered foot through various balletic positions. Before vanishing behind the white curtain, he did a bit of toe-dancing – roller skate and bare foot notwithstanding.[18]

And for *Elephant Footprints in the Cheesecake-Walk: For Shirley* (1964), co-choreographed with Deborah Hay, Herko began the piece, according to John Herbert McDowell, "on a swing with the curtain closed, so that suddenly the whole curtain went PUNCCCHHHHH and blew out at the audience, because he swang in the swing against the curtain and knocked the curtain way out into the audience."[19]

Deborah Hay remembers "Freddie" as someone who

> Would arrive late and très flamboyantly always. His movement mannerisms, as I remember them, made him look like he was flying. No surprise about the nature of his death, although it was a shock . . . I don't remember much about the duet we did. I think there was a swing or a sling of some sort,

maybe a hammock. I did some tap dancing. I believe the whole thing was pieced in little campy parts.[20]

I adore ballet; [I want to torture ballet]

"Continuing to look beatific, he skated around the floor for a time, moving his arms and the unencumbered foot through various balletic positions. Before vanishing behind the white curtain, he did a bit of toe-dancing – roller skate and bare foot notwithstanding."[21]

"It seemed very campy and self-conscious . . . he was a collagist with an arch performance manner. You would get ballet movement, none of it very high energy. Maybe a few jetés every now and then. As a dancer his real forte was some very, very elegant lines."[22]

In "Notes on Camp" Susan Sontag calls *Swan Lake*, in particular, and all ballet, in general, Camp.[23]

I am a homosexual

According to George Chauncey, camp has been utilized since the 1920s to refer to "a style of interaction and display that uses irony, incongruity, theatricality, and humor to highlight the artifice of social convention."[24] Alan Berubé observes that camp gave homosexuals an opportunity to distance themselves from the humiliation of their marginalized status, and also to build an alternative aesthetic and social sensibility.[25] Susan Sontag asserts that camp is the "victory of 'style,' over 'content,' 'aesthetics,' over 'morality,' irony over tragedy."[26] Camp sensibility alert us to a double sense in which "the thing means something, anything, and the thing is pure artifice."[27] Herko's style of presentation, alternately understated and emblazoned, accomplished just this placing of quotation marks around his movement.[28] His non-sequitur eclecticism, dead-panning ballet and then punching up the spectacle, all with unabashed "beatific"-ness, highlighted the artificial.

Al Carmines, Associate Minister at Judson Church and grantor of permission to perform there, remembers Herko as the most "out" (no, he didn't mean it *that* way) of step with the general aesthetic of the Judson concerts:

> Fred Herko seemed to me the most "out" of the general tempo and style of the Dance Theatre as a whole. His work was often piquant and ironically flamboyant, with cadenzas of pure lyrical movement. His work tended to be more directly commentary-like than most of the other dancers.[29]

How did it go? What did you think?

Camp explains Herko to a "T," but it does not account for what must have happened in the duet with Taylor. For one thing, as Sontag observes, "Camp taste is by its nature possible only in affluent societies, in societies or circles capable of experiencing the psychopathology of affluence."[30] And Taylor did not come from an affluent society. Nor did his role as improviser constitute a rebellion against his society as Herko's did.[31]

Did they ever rehearse?[32] Did Taylor create the kind of sonic propulsiveness evident in his first recordings from 1955? Did he ever look up from the keyboard? Did he feel the energy and intelligence in Herko's motion? Yes, if the liner notes to his 1966 album *Unit Structures* are any indication.[33] In these notes, Taylor advances a theory of improvisation that places the body at the center of the creative process. He writes: "Physiognomy, inherent matter-calling-stretched into sound (layers) in rhythms regular and irregular measuring co-existing bodies of sound." Here Taylor conceptualizes body as the organization of matter and energy out of which music issues. He also envisions the body as the locus of knowledge, sensation and memory that determines musical composition as a social response.[34] Intriguingly, for Taylor, ballet is a *techne* that can cultivate the richness of articulation; it is "the studied manipulation of extremities, a callisthenic procedure away from body center," assisting a "physical conversation between all body's limbs: Rhythm is life the space of time danced thru."

But how did Taylor's black body signify in the white world of Cage-influenced modern dance? Did he take a look around at the mostly white Judson audience looking at the all-white dancers rolling on the floor, running or gallivanting around, shouting and colliding, and determine he needn't return?[35] However deeply incommensurate their histories and artistic approaches were, Herko and Taylor shared their love of ballet and their homosexuality, and this tacit bond must have trumped other differences that night.

Slipping into History

Shhhhhhh. Listen to your body. Feel its impulses. Shhhhhhh. Feel what it senses. Go with what it says . . .
We'll show those mother-fuckers.
I'm an organism . . . with parts. My parts rub up against each other, bump into one another, intervene in one another's projects, build actions together.

Trained as a visual artist, Carolee Schneeman began to work in the area of live performance in the early 1960s. *Stop being so linear.* Works such as *Newspaper Event* (1962), *Lateral Splay* (1963), and *Meat Joy* (1964) developed the tactility and sensateness of corporeality as a communal labor. Taking collage into live time and space, they asked bodies to engage in disparate yet intersecting activities, whose frictive encounters yielded up an unordainable sensuality.[36] *Shhhhhh. You're never going to understand if if you keep talking like this. Just give them the score*. For *Newspaper Event* Schneeman assigned to each of seven dancers focus on a different body part, type of action, and possibility for speech. As prelude to these discrete yet overlapping improvised actions, dancers flung stacks of newspaper into the space, thereby creating the malleable, slippery, responsive milieu in which they moved. For ten minutes they folded into, romped through, tore, tossed, and tumbled among the sheets of paper. *Just try it for a few minutes, even without the newspaper, even in your imagination.*

Driving these experiments was Schneeman's belief in the power of art as excess. She writes:

> I have the sense that in learning, our best developments grow from works which initially strike us as "too much"; those which are intriguing, demanding, that lead us to experiences which we feel we cannot encompass, but which simultaneously provoke and encourage our efforts. Such works have the effect of containing more than we can assimilate; they maintain attraction and stimulation for our continuing attention. We persevere with that strange joy and agitation by which we sense unpredictable rewards from our relationship to them. These "rewards" put to question – as they enlarge and enrich – correspondences we have already discovered between what we deeply feel and how our expressive life finds structure.[37]

Here, Schneeman imagines art's mission as one of expanding, but also integrating and balancing, what we feel and how we structure that feeling.

In order to pursue this "and-and" rather than "either or" *Yes, and-and*, approach to art-making, Schneeman left the visual art world for the world of performance, developing what she called kinetic paintings, or concretions, performances through which "the fundamental life of any material used is concretized."[38] For Schneeman the privileging of the body as a site of sensual eventing – *Each part of the body is a special event – spine, legs/face, shoulders/arms, neck/feet, hands, head, fingers* – worked to expose the masculinist assumptions underlying "abstract" expressionism, while at the same time offering a palpable vision of what "action painting" might look like.[39] She observes:

> In 1963 to use my body as an extension of my painting-consciousness was to challenge and threaten the psychic territorial power lines by which women were admitted to the ArtStudClub.[40]

Where the male artist worked to secure a self, distant from and in control of the work of art, Schneeman's performances catapulted both performer and viewer into a newly energized sensorium.

As dance historian Karen Schaffman has observed, Schneeman's efforts fell between the cracks of two artistic disciplines, neither of which wished to claim her. Excommunicated from the visual art world for her messy, in-your-face, eroticized subjectivity, she was equally shunned by choreographers, whose efforts were being directed towards masculinizing the gynocentric world of modern dance.[41] Thus critic Jill Johnston, who is quoted above extolling the virtues of childish play exhibited at the Judson concerts, dismisses Schneeman's *Chromelodeon* as a "messy, brainless 'happening' with lots of clothes, paper, rags, burlap, and paint."[42] And she described *Newspaper Event* as "a wild orgy."[43]

In their championing of a non-expressionistic approach to choreographic inquiry, Judson artists largely adopted an aesthetics of randomness, using a variety of aleatory procedures or simply the look they produced to organize their dances. Like their mentor composer John Cage, they borrowed extensively from Zen and Taoist philosophies of chance, using those abstract formulations of the order of things to deconstruct interiority-driven methods of composition. Although some Judson participants remarked on the similarity of their investigations to jazz music, African-American approaches to improvisation went largely uncredited while Asian influences were celebrated repeatedly.

Schneeman characterized this use of chance methods as "Fro-Zen," arguing instead for an alternative implementation of chance as a "depth run on intent," a means of accessing the necessity of desire that lay tentacled beneath the surface of things.[44] Although she appeared on the Judson concerts, her rhetoric of surface-depth and intuitive excess ran counter to Judson's principle focus on task-like neutrality with which they approached any and all movement possibilities.[45]

Did you feel anything different? Could you get beyond the embarrassment? Could you, just for once, let go of all those worries about your appearance and tune in to physicality?

Like Herko, Schneeman was at odds with the main "thrust" of Judson experimentation. Her jumbling of sensations failed to seep into the world of their masculinizing project, just as his swishy choreography swirled around its margins. At the beginning of the century, the founding gestures of modern dance had sacrificed African-American dance styles so that a new femininity could gain credibility. The Judson movement similarly shunned the "in poor taste"-ness of Herko's camp and the earthy revelry in Schneeman's feminism so as to intensify its overhaul of modern dance. Both performances expose the whiteness of the Judson project and also its masculinist inclinations.

Scarring the face of history

Its title is Vagina Painting, and in order to perform it, I, Shigeko Kubota, am fastening a paint brush to my underpants. No one can see it under my Coco Chanel style dress. No one will know it is there until I walk over to the container of red paint and squat so as to dip the brush in the red paint. Then I must walk carefully across the paper-covered floor, yes, leaving a little trail of blood-like paint.

Where shall I begin? Ahhh, I can feel the brush make contact with the floor. Now, back and forth, a little on the diagonal. The brush goes along and then it flops when I change the motion of my pelvis. I can't control it with any precision. There, that's better, if I hover over it, I can direct the line, although it's somewhat faint. And then I can lower a little and make a splotch. Ummmm, out of paint already.

OK, which spot next? Where shall I go now? It's so precarious. I feel rather pathetic, only being able to maneuver the brush this much. If it wasn't such a great comment on the art world, I wouldn't do it. Hmmm. It's dripping more than I thought. Keep the body crouched so that the paint doesn't get on my legs. It needs to get to the floor. It needs to fill the floor with its peculiar designs. You see? We, too, have ways of making our mark.

Time for more paint. Ummm, I think I'll go over here. I'm not getting much better at manipulating this brush. Is this how they see us? Incapable of technical mastery?

I'm dipping, walking and then stroking. It's preposterous, but why not? Jackson Pollock placed his canvases on the floor, and sloshed the paint onto them. Now I want them to see a woman do it. But they think we're different, don't they? So, I will show them the version that represents that difference. I will show them menstruation and fecundity, women's assigned actions in the natural rather than cultural realm.

More paint. Where now? Maybe I'll continue to develop this area over here. Jackson Pollock claimed influence from Asian and Native American forms.[46] Sand paintings? I wonder. The Gutai painters in Japan have been doing action painting for years.[47] Somehow, I don't think that's the influence Pollock had in mind.

This is a Fluxus performance, an "event," it is called.[48] And George Maciunas has invited me to join the group.[49] I like how diverse the artists are: African-Americans, Asians, Asian-Americans, whites. But I'm not getting a good feeling from them tonight. What did Carolee Schneeman write: "You have to be tidy to be a member of Fluxus"? It's the underpants. No, it's the closeness of the paintbrush to my crotch. I'm feeling like they want me to stop. It's boring them now; they got the point. But women's work is never done, right?[50] Why not continue?

Where shall I go next? Maybe they think my vagina is somehow different. British and Dutch colonists often imagined that we Asian women had slanted or sideways vaginas.[51] Do they think our vaginas paint differently?[52] Whoops, don't laugh. It makes the paintbrush jiggle against my legs.

Look them right in the eyes and don't stop yet. Walk to one more place, at least. Not your painted white-faced geisha; not your ethereal source of perfect manners; not your fleshless concrescence of the exotic East; not your essence of femininity. NO. I bleed.[53]

My thighs are killing me from all this squatting. If I'm not careful I'll topple over. Maybe it's enough.

Improvising history

Where Schneeman privileges a superabundance of sensation, Kubota manufactures multiple layers of ironic commentary. Both use performance as a counterforce to the dominant masculine politics of the visual art world, and both rely on improvisation as a tool for opening up new forms of embodied knowledge. Like Herko, they operate on the outskirts of an avant garde, revealing its focus and values through their sagacious and mischievous attempts to jolt its nervous system.

In describing their improvisations, I have tried to show how a historian might undertake to write about performances such as these, first, by reconstructing them in the imagination, and then by contemplating how the written translation could summon up both the form and the content of the event. Such writing can make more evident the historian's efforts to interrogate and reproduce the premises on which the performances were based. These premises – evident in the residue of assessments, calculations, inspirations that determined what happened – are part of the conceptual paraphernalia that choreographers move with and against when they make dances. At the same time, I have kept the reflecting, doubting, questioning voice of the historian (not dissimilar to that of the performer during and after the event) present. History writing occurs in the matrix constituted by these voices. Watching and/or practicing improvisation highlights just this intercalation of spontaneous and reflective impulses, because in improvisation the choreography is being made and evaluated as the performance progresses.

I have also tried to show how improvisation might provoke a reconsideration of history writing by affirming multiple tactical moves that dismantle the monolithic in history, or what Hayden White has called the "proper history."[54] To "camp out in history" entails an indulgence in the contradictory evidence, a savoring of the telling detail, a cultivation of the artifice of documentation – all undergirded by the pressure that margins exert to tell their stories in a distinctive way. In contrast, "slipping into history" centralizes the sensorium in all its frictiveness as an antidotal epistemology from which history could be generated. And finally, "scarring the face of history" inscribes upon the historical text layers of ironic commentary that defile its wholesome complexion. Responding to the improvised status of their objects of study, all three approaches share a capacity to generate both a text and a critical positioning of that text.

Often perceived as incommensurate, the simultaneous doing and reflecting on that doing could provide a new perspective on the activity of writing history. Conceptualizing history writing as a kind of improvisation could move us past objective/subjective binaries and also provide new models for how to situate the historian as part of the research project. Improvisation's reflexive stance towards one's actions preserves agency as contingent yet palpable – the result of an ongoing process of making as well as reflecting on choices, and assessing their consequences as part of a continual negotiation between past and present.

Notes

1. Barthes develops the distinction between the "readerly" and "writerly" in *S/Z: an Essay*, trans. Richard Miller (New York: Hill and Wang, 1970). See especially 3–4.
2. See "The Re-turn of the Flaneuse" in *Corporealities: Dancing, Knowledge, Culture and Power*, ed. Susan Leigh Foster (London and New York: Routledge, 1996), 53–69.
3. See "Overreading the Promised Land: Towards a Narrative of Context in Dance" in *Corporealities: Dancing, Knowledge, Culture and Power*, 177–98.
4. See "Immobile legs, stalled words: psychoanalysis and moving deaths," in *Mourning Sex: Performing Public Memories* (London and New York: Routledge), 44–72.
5. Daniel Belgrad, *The Culture of Spontaneity: Improvisation and the Arts in Postwar America* (Chicago: University of Chicago Press, 1998).
6. Jill Johnston, "Dance Journal: Play," *Village Voice*, 18 November 1965: 15.
7. Panel Discussion on Improvisation. Sponsored by the University-wide Committee on the Arts, SUNY Purchase, Spring 1980. Panelists: Margaret Beals, Richard Bull, Remy Charlip, Peentz Dubble, Diane Frank, Cynthia Novack, Deborah Riley, Sarah Voegler, David Woodbury. Moderator: Sally Banes. Richard Bull Archives, New York Public Library for the Performing Arts at Lincoln Center.
8. Mauss develops the notion of cultural training of basic bodily patterns and habits in "Techniques of the Body," *Economy and Society*, 2,1: 70–87. Bourdieu develops his concept of the *habitus* in *The Logic of Practice*, trans. Richard Nice (Cambridge: Polity, 1990).
9. Sally Banes, *Greenwich Village, 1963. Avant-Garde Performance and the Effervescent Body* (Durham: Duke University Press, 1993), 67.
10. Sally Banes, *Democracy's Body: Judson Dance Theater, 1962–1964* (Durham: Duke University Press, 1983), 19.
11. Steve Paxton, quoted in Banes, *Democracy's Body*, 44.
12. Allen Hughes, quoted in Banes, *Democracy's Body*, 44.
13. Maxine Munt, quoted in Banes, *Democracy's Body*, 92. See also Jill Johnston's review of the piece in "Judson 1964: End of an Era," *Ballet Review*, 1,6 (1967): 7–14.
14. Banes, *Democracy's Body*, 45.
15. Johnston, quoted in Banes, *Democracy's Body*, 43.
16. Hughes, quoted in Banes, *Democracy's Body*, 43–4.
17. Sally Banes astutely notes that Binghamton Birdie was also the nickname of one of the A-men from the San Remo coffee shop who visited Linich at Warhol's Factory; *Democracy's Body*, 136.
18. Hughes, quoted in Banes, *Democracy's Body*, 136–7.
19. Waring thought the dance "really rather awful"; quoted in Banes, *Democracy's Body*, 163.
20. Email interview by the author with Deborah Hay, conducted 8 March 2002.
21. Hughes, quoted in Banes, *Democracy's Body*, 136–7.
22. Steve Paxton, quoted in Banes, *Democracy's Body*, 19.
23. Susan Sontag, *Against Interpretation, and Other Essays* (New York: Farrar, Straus, & Giroux, 1966), 277–8.

24. George Chauncey, *Gay New York: Gender, Urban Culture, and the Making of the Gay Male World, 1890–1940* (New York: Basic Books, 1994), 290.
25. Quoted in Richard Meyer, *Outlaw Representation: Censorship and Homosexuality in Twentieth-Century American Art* (Oxford and New York: Oxford University Press, 2002), 109.
26. Sontag, *Against Interpretation*, 287.
27. Ibid., 281.
28. Sontag observes that "Camp sees everything in quotation marks," Ibid., 280.
29. Al Carmines, "In the Congregation of Art," *Dance Scope* 33, 1–2 (Fall/Winter 1967–8): 29.
30. Sontag, *Against Interpretation*, 289.
31. White artists, alienated by society's repudiation of their vocation, identified with the position of African-American artists, whose art was shaped by the racial discrimination that had exercised oppression for generations. This affiliation by whites with African-Americans created new alliances that fueled the Civil Rights movement and its important advances in the rights of African-American citizens, but it also spawned misunderstandings, especially if whites, impervious to the differences in class and racial histories, presumed that improvisation served a common rebellion.

    Amiri Baraka elucidates the distinctive roles played by improvisation in white and African-American cultures in this comparison between Bix Beiderbecke and Louis Armstrong: "The white middle-class boy from Iowa was the product of a culture which could place Louis Armstrong, but could never understand him . . . [Beiderbecke] had an emotional life that . . . was based on his conscious or unconscious disapproval of most of the sacraments of his culture. On the other hand, Armstrong was, in terms of emotional archetypes, an honored priest of his culture – one of the most impressive products of his society. Armstrong was not rebelling against anything with his music. In fact, his music was one of the most beautiful refinements of African-American musical tradition, and it was immediately recognized as such by those Negroes who were not busy trying to pretend that they had issued from Beiderbecke's culture. The incredible irony of the situation was that both stood in similar places in the superstructure of American society: Beiderbecke, because of the isolation any deviation from mass culture imposed upon its bearer; and Armstrong, because of the socio-historical estrangement of the Negro from the rest of America." See Amiri Baraka, *Blues People: Negro Music in White America* (New York: W. Morrow, 1963), 153–4.

    The aesthetics of spontaneity elaborated in Armstrong's music issued from a cultural matrix that valued highly improvised action, whereas the white, middle-class culture that produced Beiderbecke condemned improvisation. Hence Beiderbecke was moving against normative values in his culture whereas Armstrong was implementing a respected tradition of improvisation to fortify African-American culture as well as to critique its history of racial oppression. The legacy of that oppression endowed the two artists with very different privilege. Thus, even while jazz offered an aesthetic-political practice that provided a refuge from and critique of mainstream white society, it did not constitute the same kind of resistance in both cultures. See Amiri Baraka, *Blues People*.
32. Or did they simply hang out together at Diane DiPrima's loft as part of the Greenwich Village alternative art scene and then somehow determine to perform together on that first Judson concert? Herko lived above Diane DiPrima and was a close friend of hers. Along with Taylor, he assisted her in publishing *The Floating Bear*. Banes speculates that this is where they might have met. DiPrima references

Herko as a choreographer who was "pushing at its so-called boundaries" and she particularly notes "Freddie's costumes and that jazz." Quoted in Banes, *Democracy's Body*, 132.

33. For a fuller analysis of Taylor's philosophy as evidenced in the liner notes, see Andrew W. Bartlett, "Cecil Taylor, Identity, Energy, and the Avant-Garde African American Body," *Perspectives of New Music*, 33, 1–2 (Winter–Summer 1995): 272–94.

34. He writes: "At the controlled body center, motors become knowledge at once felt, memory which has identified sensory images resulting social response." Liner notes for *Unit Structures* (1966). Blue Note Records number 84237.

35. Whatever his response that night, we know that Taylor's attraction to dance continued, for in 1972 he begins an extensive collaboration with choreographer Dianne McIntyre, one that profoundly influences the vocabulary and syntax of her choreographic approach. See Susan Leigh Foster, *Dances That Describe Themselves* (Middletown, Conn: Wesleyan University Press, 2002) for a fuller explication of their collaboration and its impact on McIntyre's work. We also know that Herko involved African-American dancer Gus Solomons Jr. along with white dancers Trisha Brown, Ruth Emerson, Valda Setterfield and himself in his choreography for *Edge* (1962).

36. Choreographer Deborah Hay, who performed in many of Schneeman's pieces, observes that sensuality was a distinguishing feature, especially in comparison with the chasteness of most other Judson choreographers. Personal communication with author, November 2000.

37. Carolee Schneeman, *More than Meat Joy: Complete Performance Works and Selected Writings*, ed. Bruce McPherson (New Paltz, NY.: Documentext, 1979), 9.

38. Schneeman, *More than Meat Joy*, 9.

39. Schneeman identified seven areas of the body in her score for *Newspaper Event*. The full score is printed in *More Than Meat Joy*, 32–5.

40. Schneeman quoted in Amelia Jones, *Body Art/Performing the Subject* (Minneapolis: University of Minnesota Press, 1998), 3.

41. Karen Schaffman, "Excavating the Dinosaurs: Carolee Schneeman and Prehistoric Contact Improvisation," paper presented at the 32nd International Congress on Research in Dance, Pomona College, Claremont, California, December 1999.

42. Johnston, quoted in Banes, *Democracy's Body*, 149.

43. Ibid., 96.

44. Ibid., 94.

45. As evidence of this incompatibility, Schaffman points out the extraordinary similarities between Schneeman's investigations for Lateral Splay and the development of contact improvisation by Steve Paxton a decade later. See Schaffman, "Excavating the Dinosaurs."

46. Pollock described his method of action painting as follows: "On the floor I am more at ease. I feel nearer, more a part of the painting, since this way I can walk around it, work from the four sides and literally be in the painting. This is akin to the method of the Indian sand painters of the West." Quoted in Brenda Dixon Gottschild, *Digging the Africanist Presence in American Performance: Dance and Other Contexts* (Westport, Conn: Greenwood Press, 1996), 40. Pollock also cited "Oriental" influences on his work, yet never mentioned jazz, despite his avid interest in it. Dixon Gottschild, providing ample documentation of Pollock's involvement with jazz, argues persuasively for the significance of the omission. Dixon Gottschild, *Digging*, 39–40.

47. Michael Kirby notes that the Gutai group may well have influenced the creation of the Happenings. See Kirby, *Happenings* (New York: E. P. Dutton, 1965), 28–9.

48. The term "event," introduced by Fluxus performance collective member George Brecht in 1959, aptly titled the open-ended encounters among audience, performers and score that improvisation enabled. George Brecht along with LaMonte Young produced numerous scored events that called for audience interaction with a set of open-ended instructions. For example, LaMonte Young's 1960 scores for performances called for the performer to build a fire or to let loose one or more butterflies for the audience to watch. See La Monte Young, ed., *An Anthology of Chance Operations . . . by George Brecht [and Others]* (New York: La Monte Young and Jackson Mac Low, 1963). Before coming to New York in 1960, La Monte Young had collaborated with Anna Halprin, a San Francisco-based choreographer, on several events that similarly worked the divide between art and life. See Anna Halprin, *Moving Toward Life: Five Decades of Transformational Dance*, ed. Rachel Kaplan (Middletown, Conn: Wesleyan University Press, 1995). For a lucid analysis of the encounter among audience, score and performers that Fluxus artists constructed, see Kristine Stiles, "Between Water and Stone," in *In the Spirit of Fluxus*, ed. Elizabeth Armstrong and Joan Rothfuss (Minneapolis: Walker Art Center, 1993). In addition, see Armstrong and Rothfuss, *In the Spirit of Fluxus*, for an excellent overview of Fluxus and their various activities.
49. Kubota emigrated to the US from Japan in 1964. In 1962, she had seen a performance by John Cage and was impressed with his interest in Asian philosophies. She married Korean-American video artist Nam June Paik and went on to make video the focus of her artistic work.
50. For a good overview of Kubota's subsequent work and also her brief but significant participation in the mixed-race feminist art collective known as Red, White, Yellow, and Black, see Melinda Barlow, "Red, White, Yellow, and Black: Women, Multiculturalism, and Video History," *Quarterly Review of Film and Video*, 17, 4 (2000): 297–316.
51. Karen Shimakawa, personal communication with author, May 2001.
52. My speculation that this level of commentary existed in Kubota's piece is supported by her subsequent participation in an all-woman performance and video group entitled "Red, White, Yellow, and Black." For descriptions of their performances, see Barlow, "Red, White, Yellow, and Black."
53. I thank Shimakawa who pointed out to me how Kubota's performance debunks the stereotype of the Asian woman/geisha as ethereal and "detached" – to the point of bloodlessness – by making her "bleed" in such a spectacular and (to conventional Asiaphiles) grotesque way. Karen Shimakawa, personal communication with author, May 2001.
54. Hayden White, "The Value of Narrativity in the Representation of Reality," *Critical Inquiry* 7,2 (1980): 5–27.

11

The Imprint of Performance

W. B. Worthen

What is the work of "literature," or, to use a less contested term, "writing" in the theater? What is the status or being or force of dramatic writing relative to the drama's existence as performance? Is it possible to understand performance through the scripted form of dramatic texts? Is there a theoretical relationship between dramatic writing and stage performance that is worth pursuing? Is the form of the printed book an adequate delivery system for plays? Is it a delivery system at all?

To ask such questions means bracketing a number of crucial issues. An understanding of theatrical performance has everything to do with everything that is beyond the text, the practices and ideologies of directing and design, of acting and dance, of architecture and economics that are the material modes of stage production. This may sound, for the moment, as though I am bracketing *all* of theater, and in one respect I am: to the extent that we consider bodies, spaces, and the practices that use them the stuff of drama in performance, then writing (in those forms of theater that use writing at all) is merely one among many such materials, not the abstract cause or governing logos, but a substance entirely refashioned in the densely pragmatic working out of the creative business of the stage.

We often take the idiom of drama – Chekhov's approach to action and character, or Beckett's – to bear directly on performance; isn't it the function of the stage to embody, fill out, even fulfill that design? And yet, as the changing forms of stage Chekhov in the past century or of stage Beckett in half that time imply, the rhetoric of embodiment and the panoply of practices deployed with, around, and beyond the text to create a significant theatrical event are remarkably unstable. Here, I would like to try to gain a different purchase on this problem by contracting our vision from the outlines of the whole play to the marks of its materialization on the page. Does the material form of modern drama in print have any bearing either on performance practice, or on a wider understanding of dramatic performance? Texts cannot determine performance; they

213

do not even determine the performance of reading. Nonetheless, the material properties of a given dramatic text – typography, layout, page and cover design – matter to the ways specific groups of readers (actors, directors, audiences, reviewers) understand its potentialities for performance, insert them into the conventional behaviors – the "performative regimes," so to speak – of theater practice. The material form of the text is a similarly contingent performance, a materialization of the play that might both record and prompt an understanding of the momentary implication of print and performance culture. Can we consider the materiality of writing not in opposition to performance (or, much the same thing, as governing or determining performance), but in a more dynamic, even cybernetic relation to the practices of the stage?[1] If we take the printform of a work to be like a performance, materializing a historically contingent, socially inscribed instance of the work (and not, as both the New Bibliography and the New Criticism might have said, as the work itself), we may be able to seize a more dynamic sense of the changing interplay between these two enduring, and volatile, modes of production.[2]

To frame this question is to raise some larger theoretical concerns about the identity of both kinds of artwork, in ways that trouble the attributes usually ascribed to print – fixity, durability, repeatability – and to performance. On the larger scale, a specific performance cannot be extrapolated from text alone, much as a table cannot be extrapolated from a tree (though if you have ever made or used a table, you know that oak is more durable than pine, and much harder to work with). To make a table, you need to know a hawk from a handsaw, and how to use them. It makes some difference whether a production of *Hamlet* takes Richard Burbage or Ethan Hawke as its physical prince; does it also matter whether it uses a hand-copied playhouse side or an edited modern text, the embodiment of four centuries of the developing ideology of print culture? The text of a play cannot imply a specific performance: its theatrical signification is subdued, like the dyer's hand, to the theatrical work that shapes it into a performance, practices which are themselves articulated by the tensile resistance of the writing. Some of those practices were familiar to the playwright (the thrust stage and boy actors for Shakespeare; the box set for Ibsen), but if the history of performance tells us anything it is that playtexts are susceptible to reuse in ways that generate performances unanticipated by the playwright, impossible in the originating theater, and so uncoded in the text of the play. The kind of theater that uses scripted texts is only one kind of theater; yet even in this theater, texts are subjected to the labor of performance in a disarming variety of ways, as they are transformed into something else, something that takes place, an action, an event, *performance*.

The form of the text records the work's historical materialization, but it cannot alone tell us about its use, the strategies deployed for its performance; these, too, are historically bound. Reading is one of these practices, though the act of reading usually disappears behind its theatrical consequences.[3] As students of literacy have shown, reading is not the absorption of the dynamics of the text, but the application of trained interpretive strategies. Reading a text, in other words, means applying a practice of performance to it: you have to know *how* to read a modern poem as opposed to a Shakespeare sonnet, a Victorian novel, a phone book, a cook book, a play (the first dictionaries in English, after all, had to explain the principle of alphabetical ordering to their users). More to the point, differential literacies reflect different kinds of production. Victorian novels often had a variety of print identities, published in serial form in periodicals and later bound as triple-decker books, forms of publication that imply different audiences and locate different sociologies of reading. Although literary culture's fetishization of "the text" has seemed to narrow this range of identities (*Middlemarch* is always itself, the same thing, regardless of its material form), republication can only multiply the work's materiality, and so ramify and complicate its performance in history. Reading the Norton *Middlemarch* is different from reading a cheap, unannotated paperback; so, too, to read *Middlemarch* from the perspective of social history – what does it tell us about labor history, or gender, or indoor plumbing – is to produce a different *thing* than, say, reading the same novel as a beach book. As Jerome McGann suggests in his brilliant dialogue "The Alice Fallacy," students (like actors in this respect) are trained to apply interpretive schemata that define and legitimate appropriate performance, all the while insisting on the "freedom" of interpretation; at the same time, both the materiality of the text and the "appropriate" contexts of reading undergo constant change, change sometimes visible as the process by which outrageous, illicit performances, and the reading strategies that generated them, are normalized as legitimate, even ordinary.[4] Needless to say, reading a playtext if you have been cast in the play is itself a specific kind of reading, as is reading it as a director or designer; it involves the trained, disciplined ability to apply a range of reading and interpretive strategies, some of which are not unique to the theater ("what is Hamlet really thinking?") and some of which are ("what do I *do* here and how do I do it?").

The practices of reading, of any kind of production, are not constrained by or even visible in the text (different kinds of texts relate to their embodiment in different ways, cookbooks, car repair manuals, poems). Yet the materiality of the text is the thing that gets read. How much does it matter – matter as matter – what we read? This question has come to be a crucial question in textual studies, where the material appearance of writing is seen as a crucial record (and instigation) of a work's historical and social identity: much as the theatrical identity of a given production of *Hamlet* depends on whether it took place in London or the provinces, with a professional or an amateur cast, on the opening or on a benefit night, whether it included Rosencrantz and Guildenstern, and so on, in the sphere of textual criticism, the question of whether one is reading Yeats's "September 1913" in the Dublin newspaper in which it initially appeared, in a volume published by a nationalist press, or in the more impersonal – and internationalized – context of a British-published collected edition, makes a difference in what the words on the page might mean, how they have been materialized in time and space, and so what practices of reading they might have engaged.[5] Like performances, texts are surprisingly volatile in the ways they materialize writing in history.

Reading the traces of performance in the materiality of the text has a long history in certain corners of literary studies: in the work of playhouse practice that may be inscribed in stage directions, speech prefixes, and other elements of early modern printed plays; in various efforts to develop notation systems for performance, as well as in the partly discredited idealism of some versions of modern "performance criticism" of various playwrights. Yet the rise of print and its dominion over modern literary studies has tended to preempt such enquiry of the modern and postmodern theater. It might be said that the pervasive ideology of print is also partly responsible for the chasm that has opened historically between the "literary" and the "theatrical" conceptions of drama in the modern era, institutionalized in university departments, forms of pedagogy, the practices of scholarly enquiry and production. Even those of us interested in a more reciprocal, historically inflected sense of this relationship would have to admit that the theoretical account and interpretive practice of drama studies – how we account for the multiform meanings, slippages, and identities of dramatic texts and dramatic performances – remains seriously underdeveloped.

Here, I want to take a narrow, extremely narrow, view of this question, as a way to locate some of the issues before returning to the larger question of dramatic texts and performance in the modern era. I want to begin by troubling a common distinction between the printform of modern poetry and that of modern plays: that the typographic "surface" of modern poetry is designed to slow reading, to force attention to the process and materials of the poem, while the typography of modern plays is designed to speed reading, to render the text in a purely instrumental form so that it can be readily digested by performance. This alimentary sense of the materiality of dramatic texts naturalizes the practices of theatrical reading, and has other implications, too. It implies that modern dramatic writing is unlike other artforms of the modern era, which characteristically, insistently call attention to the materiality of their materials: paint, stone, metal, sound, words, silence. When drama does participate in this modernist tradition, it does so by rendering its *theatrical* (rather than its *textual*) material opaque: think of plays like *Six Characters in Search of an Author* or *The Measures Taken* or *Play*, to say nothing of the immaculate challenge to textuality characteristic of dada, of Artaud, or – in a significantly more compromised way – of performance art. At the same time, I think we should also be skeptical of the apparent transparency of dramatic writing, for preventing the natural assimilation of words on the page to speech may enable us to take a different, alienated perspective on them, and on the naturalized practices of their articulation.[6] Is it possible to begin to rethink the relation between print and performance by refusing the abstract and universalizing "logic" of print, and instead putting print and performance into dialogue as materializing practices? Does the material form of dramatic writing matter, matter as matter, in the late age of print culture?

So much depends

The poetic revolution of the first decades of the twentieth century was undertaken by a generation of writers who conceived their work within the forms of mechanical reproducibility. As the imagists, vorticists, futurists, dadaists, and others recognized, the page itself could render the text as a visual icon, a different materialization of the text that might prompt materially different acts of reading, might even prompt kinds of reading – as Susan Howe's poems do – that do not always feel like reading if what we mean by reading is the ability to see distinct, legible words on the page, and confidently to assemble them in a speakable series.[7] The various use of capital letters and foreign scripts typical in Ezra Pound's poems is one measure of this tendency; composing on the typewriter is also relevant (reading T. S. Eliot's manuscript of the poem that became *The Waste Land*, Pound responded to some sections written in longhand, but generally preferred to edit from typescript: "Bad – but cant attack until I get typescript" he wrote over the first draft of "Death by Water").[8] James Joyce's *Ulysses* is unimaginable without typographic play – the headlines in "Aeolus," the centered speech-prefixes of "Circe" (where the dramatic status of the episode is emphasized by the intrusive, centered speech prefixes, as opposed to the more novelistic blocks of type used in Bernard Shaw's plays), the famous blot at the end of the "Ithaca" chapter.

XXI

The Red Wheelbarrow

> so much depends
> upon
>
> a red wheel
> barrow
>
> glazed with rain
> water
>
> beside the white
> chickens.

William Carlos Williams's work is particularly suggestive in this context.[9] In poems like "The Red Wheelbarrow," "so much depends" on how we move from line to line, hanging on the poet's mastery of rhythm and image to give us, finally, something to rest "upon" . . . a mild irony in the poem, in that the word "upon" provides only a momentary rest before we slip into space again towards that part-object, the "red wheel," landing finally on "barrow." So like Williams, so pedestrian, an everyday thing in the workaday world. It seems so solid, that we hardly notice how little realized it is (what color red? wood or metal? large or small? dirty or clean?) until, after a pause (here, the syntax does not force us to move on, we have to choose to take action), it is changed (though not in a way that answers any of those questions) by the most unexpected, modestly metaphorical, "poetic" word in the poem, *glazed*, a word which, alongside the whiteness of the chickens (still to come), seems, somehow, without actually putting it into words, to evoke the indelible redness of the red wheelbarrow, upon which so much finally depends. e. e. cummings's "Grasshopper" emblematizes this drive towards iconicity, but Williams is less interested in mimicry than in the poetics of *printed* language. Later in life, surviving strokes that broke his speech and paralyzed his right arm, Williams composed on the typewriter, guiding his right hand with his left, indenting new lines three spaces, more easily to find them. Williams's famous "three-ply line" is integral to the movement of his later poems, embodying and memorializing the act of writing, white space signaling, and perhaps enacting, forcing us to enact, a kind of duration, suspension, translating Williams's struggle to compose into the force of poetic motion itself.[10] Yet this is nothing new in Williams: the earlier poems dramatize the deft use of print to materialize the movement of language, and to render the space between the words significant, part of poetic *composition*, so to speak. It has become conventional, following Fredric Jameson, to describe the postmodern's relation to the modern in spatial terms, as "today dominated by categories of space rather than by categories of time, as in the preceding period of high modernism."[11] Yet what may at first seem a rupture or transformation may also seem a continuity: modernist poetics drives the temporality of poetic discourse with the spatializing engine of type, and its beguiling absence from the printed page.

Learning to read – at least learning to read in what Michael Joyce calls the "late age of print" – involves learning to read spatially, to account for the rhetoric of typographic space; this strategy is visible in modernist print, and sustains the rhetoricity of the computer screen and of print-emulating hypertextual writing.[12] It involves learning specific kinds of reading strategies, as our ancestors once had to account for the physical or affective (rhetorical) and signifying or conceptual (syntactic) effects of punctuation.[13] There are important distinctions to observe here, though: the typographical play of modernist poetry is often designed to slow reading, to isolate and materialize "language" as an object, to trouble the transparency of the page, even to prevent the direct assimilation of written language to performance, to speech. To this extent, the materiality of modern poetry poses problems for the poetics of performance, at least to the extent that we believe that a play in print should be designed for easy assimilation to the conventional practices of theater. As Michael Goldman suggests, "Memorizing a part is actually a means of freeing oneself from its mere textuality."[14]

And yet the practices of reading that now seem obligatory for modern poems could not be created by poems alone; the dialectical interplay between the structure of the text and the changing practices of its use is readily seen in the evolution of interpretive practices now seen as not merely legitimate, but as essential to the reading of the work of, say, Pound, or Eliot, or Joyce. It is striking to note a parallel in the history of modern performance – the bafflement not of audiences (they were baffled) but of actors and directors over what to *do* with plays like *The Master Builder* or *The Seagull* or *Waiting for Godot*. We do not often take this to be a reading problem, but it is: how can *we* read this text as theatrically *producible*? What is it telling us to *do*? How can we apply what we know how to do to it, in order to make it into a recognizably, effectively theatrical event? Jerome McGann draws an analogy between the "alienation" implied by poetry's foregrounding of typography and Brecht's similar efforts to alienate theatrical conventions. Attending to the material form of plays in print may also provide a means to "alienate," and so to observe, other aspects of our understanding of dramatic performance, the interplay between the text and the naturalized strategies of its production onstage.[15] Modernist poetry is one of the things that stands between us and the novelistic, even bookish plays of Ibsen and Shaw: it is one of the things that makes Shaw's elegant volumes – to say nothing of the plays they contain – look old-fashioned, positively Victorian in their earnest effort to conquer the page, to expand the imperious, rational eloquence of (Irish?) English to the very margins of discursive space. The printed page may, in this sense, point to a shifting relation between writing and enactment in the conception of modernist writing's unwanted orphan: "modern drama."

(Pause.)

I want now to look at the opening pages of Harold Pinter's *The Homecoming*.[16] Pinter's description of the set is notable for its combination of literary/descriptive and theatrical/practical stage directions, locating the "old house" at once in the geography of "North London" and in the geography of the stage, mapped for us in practical terms ("a staircase, ascending U.L., well in view. The front door U.R."). More to the point, the opening page of dialogue reflects many of the conventions of dramatic publishing today: stage directions are noticeably spaced out, the two lines *"He wears an old cardigan and a cap, and carries a*

stick" and *"He walks downstage, stands, looks about the room"* appearing on different lines (7).

> *Evening.*
> LENNY *is sitting on the sofa with a newspaper, a pencil in his hand. He wears a*
> *dark suit. He makes occasional marks on the back page.*
> MAX *comes in, from the direction of the kitchen. He goes to side-board, opens top*
> *drawer, rummages in it, closes it.*
> *He wears an old cardigan and a cap, and carries a stick.*
> *He walks downstage, stands, looks about the room.*
>
> MAX. What have you done with the scissors?
>
> > *Pause.*
>
> I said I'm looking for the scissors. What have you done with them?
>
> > *Pause.*
>
> Did you hear me? I want to cut something out of the paper.
> LENNY. I'm reading the paper. (7)

While Shaw wanted his plays "set solid," Pinter's page seems considerably less
dense, certainly less novelistic, even more iconic, poetic in its use of white
space.[17] And, of course, there are the famous *Pauses*, here each occupying a separate line, and surrounded by extra spacing above and below. As your students
have surely complained, the publishers of contemporary plays tend to be prof-
ligate with paper and penurious with ink: Pinter's later plays are even more
exemplary of the expense of ink in a waste of shame.

In terms of play publishing, if not much else, the 1950s resembled the 1890s,
as first Penguin and then Methuen and Grove began to publish dramatic texts
for a general audience, once again dispensing with the technical apparatus of
acting editions, as Shaw, Pinero and others had done a half-century before.[18] Is
it possible for us, now, as readers of Pinter – and of course I include actors in
that number – to read Pinter as anything other than Pinteresque? This may
seem a purely intentional question, but it is not, or not entirely: it has to do
instead with the sociology of print, how printed texts materialize writing in
human history, as specific objects in that history. Shaw's plays were originally
published as the inverse of the Victorian triple-decker novel (three – or four –
plays in one densely printed volume), by a publisher adapting, under Shaw's
obsessive supervision, William Morris's modernist aesthetics for a broader reading public. Pinter's plays are published in a standard format, in paperback, by
publishers on both sides of the Atlantic striving – successfully – to establish a
niche for published modern plays. More to my point here, the printform of

Pinter's plays was apprehended at the interface between two reading practices: the poetics of modernist verse, which renders punctuation, white space, typography all as part of the text's legible signification, and the poetics of modernist acting, particularly acting in the realist tradition, which tends to ignore the material accidentals of the printed text (stage directions, the placement of speech prefixes, punctuation) but which, on the other hand, often regards silence – the absence of type, or the space between type – as an especially meaningful instigation of meaning, of subtextual "speech." Is it possible for us (*Pause.*) not to see the "*Pause*" (*Pause.*) as one of the features most characteristic of Pinter's dramatic writing, of his use of language? I don't think so; nor was it possible for the first generation of Pinter's directors, audiences, and reviewers: in the first decade of Pinter's real celebrity, the material idiosyncrasies of Pinter's printed texts drove the understanding of Pinter's dramatic writing, and the relation between print and performance they appear to claim.

Martin Esslin's landmark study *The Peopled Wound: the Plays of Harold Pinter* (1970) is a useful case in point, marking what we might call the normative reading practice for Pinter's plays in the period. Esslin works to evoke the poetic mystery of Pinter's prosaic prose, framing Pinter as "Basically a lyric poet." Although "He has been reproached with a mannerism of silence, an excessive use of long pauses," for Esslin, Pinter's "use of language is that of a poet" to the extent that "there are no redundant words in true poetry, no empty patches, no mere fill ins "[19] But to read Pinter *as* poetry, New-Critical fashion, to attribute "the density of texture of true poetry" to his page, means reading the "empty patches" as texture, the white spaces, and the *Pause*s they hold, as significant, signifying, not merely as irrelevancies intruding into the dramatic dialogue. How do we know, or why do we think, the *Pause*s are "long," unless it is the space on the page surrounding them that seems to amplify them, translating the space of the page into the imagined time of performance? Esslin takes what would become a familiar stance towards the Pinter text, seeing the *Pause*s as textual, part of *the* text, the Author's writing: "That is why – as in poetry the caesura, as in music the pause – silences play such a large and essential part in Pinter's dialogue" (219).

Bernard Shaw's plays provide a useful contrast to Pinter. Shaw is well known for the attention he gave to the design of his books, an obsession reflected by his obvious interest in spelling and punctuation reform, by the use of dialect, and by a desire for consistent conventions of dramatic printing (the use of italics for stage directions and spacing between letters for e m p h a s i s); more important to me here is Shaw's desire to blacken the page, his instructions to his early printers (notably Grant Richards, who published *Plays: Pleasant and Unpleasant*) to space tightly and evenly, to hyphenate words at the end of the line rather than using leading to justify (which would create more white space between words). Shaw's plays are nothing if not, to use a favorite undergraduate term, *wordy*: words are the stuff of drama for Shaw, so it is appropriate that the page has lots of words on it, words that so densely reify their status as words as nearly to eliminate all non-linguistic space. At the same time, we might just think that the layout of Shaw's plays is part of what makes them now seem a bit antique, too rhetorical to enact in our idiom – what would we think of Shaw's plays had he decided to follow David Greig's example, starting a new sentence on a new line, writing *in*, so to speak, the rhythm of stage speech.[20] Alternatively, I wonder whether Pinter's *Pause*s and *Silence*s would have seemed so freighted with complexity had the plays been laid out differently on the page, which uses the design – at least, now that we are all prepared to read the space of the page as significant – to assign considerable weight to what are, in the theater, normally considered as moments in which the author is stepping on the performers' prerogatives, their trained ability to *decide* the pace, rhythm, emphasis, and significance of speech, in part through the syncopation of silence.

The portentously "literary" character of the *Pause* emerges in a very different light if we compare "reading" and "acting" editions of a slightly earlier play, *The Collection*. There are many differences between the two texts – the specificity of description is notably less extensive or prescriptive, more Pinteresque in other words, in the trade/"literary" than in the practical/"theatrical" text – but the most suggestive difference between the two versions is the handling of *Pause*. Although both texts put *Pause*s in the dialogue on separate lines, spacing them out on the page, the acting edition does so less frequently, and tends to use an arresting phrase: *"There is a pause."* The Methuen trade edition (like the American Grove Press edition in this matter), lays out the page in the manner to which we have all become accustomed, appearing (to us) to mark the density and significance of different kinds of silence by signifying it textually on the page, here as *Pause* and ellipsis:

STELLA: I'm going.

>   *Pause.*

Aren't you coming in today?

>   *Pause.*

JAMES: No.
STELLA: You had to meet those people from . . .

>   *Pause. She slowly walks to an armchair, picks up her jacket, and puts it on.*

You had to meet those people about that order. Shall I phone them when I get to the shop?[21]

The Samuel French acting edition tends to place the *Pause*s on the line, sometimes accompanied by a personal pronoun, as in *She pauses*, or a demonstrative pronoun, *There is a pause*; the final stage direction, like others in this text, is considerably more ample than those in the trade editions used by non-theatrical readers.

> STELLA. I'm going. (*She pauses*) Aren't you coming in today?
> JAMES (*after a pause*) No. (*He puts down his cup*)
> STELLA. You had to meet those people from . . .
>
> (*There is a pause.* JAMES *sits still*)
>
> (*She moves slowly to the sofa, picks up her coat, puts it on, then turns to James*) You had to meet those people about that order. Shall I phone them when I get to the shop?[22]

The acting edition, with its weird locution ("*There is a pause*") tends to equate the *Pause* with other stage directions, "*She pauses.*" Esslin's sense of the *Pause* as intrinsic to Pinter's poetic writing is muted here, where the *Pause* is pulled towards the practicalities of recording and prompting performance, a text outside the dialogue commanding the actor to *stop talking*, *put down the cup*, and *sit still*. These material differences do not signify on their own, of course, but gain significance in the ways they are apprehended within different – but, arguably, related – reading formations. In the practice of modernist reading, the isolated *Pause* on the page tends to be absorbed into the functions of action and character, particularly if we are trained to think of that white space as a form of poetic signification, a significance it has gained for actors and directors as well as for general readers. Running the *Pause* into the line of stage directions tends to move it out of the focal discourse of acting and characterization and into the dispensable discourse of the *didascalia*, a discourse whose authorizing necessity is differently weighted in literary and in theatrical practice.

In their material mise-en-page, Pinter's plays appear to inscribe the meaning of performance with a certain temporality, a temporality – and perhaps a psychological complexity – that emerges more palpably from the trade text than from the acting edition, and that emerges finally from the habits of certain kinds of reading, the interpretive practices that legitimate appropriate reading among different interpretive communities.[23] It is a very different page from the page of *Plays: Pleasant and Unpleasant*, yet there is a paradoxical sense here in which the white space, not the density of type, locates Pinter's texts in what might otherwise have been a doomed, Shavian project: to arrogate the actor's freedom to the designs of the printed page.

Niggling about typography and layout in this way smacks of the purely, even comically literary, but in contemporary theater practice Pinter's *Pause*s are

emphatically observed as an essential part of the theatrical texture of the dialogue. Rehearsing *The Homecoming* in 1965, Peter Hall once had "a dot and
pause rehearsal," forcing his actors to run their lines beginning to end, reciting
where the ellipses, pauses and silences occurred in the text, and distinguishing
between them.[24] Writing in 1988, having just directed *The Birthday Party* at
CSC Repertory Theater in New York, Carey Perloff remarked:

> I was not aware in rehearsal that we were "tightening the pauses," but I
> wanted to make sure that there was a clear distinction between a *pause* and
> a *silence*. And I wanted to be sure that if a pause was not marked, we didn't
> take one, no matter how "emotionally true" it might seem.[25]

It seems unimaginable that *pausing* would be regarded as an illegitimate,
actorly intrusion in the plays of, say, Shakespeare, or Ibsen, or Shaw, or even
Chekhov; granted *Pause*s are frequently marked in Pinter, but it strikes me that
it is their isolation and emphasis on the page that transforms their status for
modern readers, rendering them not only definitively Authorial, but as part of
that part of the text that, in theater practice, tends to be regarded as the legitimate sphere of the playwright's work – the dialogue – rather than as part of
that part of the text contested between playwright and director – the stage
directions. The fact that stage directions mark contested cultural territory –
contested by the divergent ideologies of theatrical and print production – is
confirmed, of course, by the various efforts of the Beckett estate to police the
performance of *all* of "Beckett's text," the dialogue *and* the stage directions. But
just to point the question, we might ask of the opening stage direction of
Endgame – "*Bare interior. Grey light*" – how grey is grey? ("Light black. From pole
to pole" does not help much.)[26]

Pinter has often denied the significance of the *Pause*s in ways that confirm
the absorption (and irrelevance) of his intentions to the signifying armature of
print. Interviewed by Mel Gussow, Pinter confessed:

> I made a terrible mistake when I was young, I think, from which I've never
> really recovered. I wrote the word "pause" into my first play. [Laughter] I
> really do believe that was a fatal error because people have been reading my
> plays and acting my plays most of the time concerned, really obsessed with
> this pause. I meant it merely as a natural break in the proceedings, or even
> a breath. [Pause.] But it's become something metaphysical.[27]

Pinter evokes the *Pause* as a rhetorical marker, recalling one of the original purposes of punctuation that persists to the present day: to mark the manner of
speaking the written text. Yet Pinter has also come to describe his composition
of *Pause*s and *Silence*s as meticulously conceptual, and so to imply that they –

again like punctuation – perform important work in the syntax of action and characterization. Revising *Old Times*, Pinter seems to recall Flaubert, said to have spent a full day's writing adding a comma and a second workday taking it out: "I did change a silence to a pause. It was a rewrite. This silence was a pretty long silence. Now it's a short pause." Pinter describes his revisions of *Betrayal* as similarly exacting.

> HP: In rehearsal in London, I did three things. I cut one word, "please". I also took out a pause and I inserted a pause.
> MG: And that made all the difference?
> HP: That made all the *damn* difference.[28]

Confirming Gussow's sense that "they stand in for the dialogue," Pinter sees the *pauses* and *silences* as inscribed in and directed by the text.[29]

My point here is not that Pinter's writing somehow governs theatrical practice. Rather, it seems to me that the printform of plays like *The Homecoming* (and, even more appropriately, *Old Times*) materializes the play in ways that appeal to certain practices of reading, practices that legitimate which features of the text appear to signify. The *Pause* seems to us to participate in the design of modern poetry (we read the space around it as important); it also shares the tension between rhetorical and syntactic features of punctuation, seeming to mark both a temporal and affective rupture and possibly a conceptual shift as well. Although stage performance and dramatic performativity have been decisively altered by print, the theater remains a space where "print logic" is regularly turned to other purposes, deploying "concrete practices and . . . procedures of interpretation" that sometimes seem – from the partial perspective of textually oriented literary studies – to depart from the (only) apparently determining order of the text.[30] Here, though, the material form of Pinter's printed texts participates in the historical forms of modernist print, and so in the historical formation of a recognizable set of reading strategies, strategies – to judge by the accounts of Esslin (a literary critic of considerable theatrical experience) and Hall and Perloff (practicing directors with literary pedigrees) – that have clearly affected the productive practices of page and stage. Writing in any form cannot itself govern or determine performance; at the same time, in the modern era printed drama does not exist in an impermeable discursive realm, a cultural space distinct from the world of theater practice. To the extent that the materiality of texts marks their historical formation, they participate in other forms of meaning-making with which they are contemporary (let alone other forms of meaning-making that use them). To say that both Esslin and Hall apply a kind of New Critical poetics to Pinter would be one way of linking the materiality of print in the 1960s to emerging ways of transforming these plays into theatrically legible objects (as the history of Pinter criticism suggests, what is *in* the *Pause* – if anything – remains a key interpretive controversy both for literary critics and for performers).

So much depends here on so little. Yet if we want to trace the relationship between writing and performance as forms of signification at a given moment in history, it is important not to overlook the details, the material traces that may connect writing and performance in a common cultural tissue. The sense that the placement of the *Pause* marks a tension not only in the use of printed drama but in its cultural identity at a given moment may suggest that the material form of printed drama can tell us something else, perhaps point to different kinds of questions about the status of writing and performance in the cultural understanding of the work of drama (what are the limits of Authority as they are understood by readers, actors, directors, for instance). Although the *Pause* now dwells in the portmanteau of the Pinteresque, Pinter's plays are not unique in galvanizing the interface between print and performance. For the past twenty years or so, printed plays have been making much ado about nothing, well about nearly nothing – punctuation. I am thinking of the famous slash-mark [/] that punctuates the dialogue of many of Caryl Churchill's plays, and which has become more or less conventional in plays developed for the Joint Stock Theater Co. and its successor, Out of Joint. Patrick Marber's *Closer* regularly uses italics, underlining and under-lined italics to signify – well, I think they are supposed to signify – different kinds of emphasis, though what actors are meant to do with these marks is not really clear (describing what "men want" from women, Alice remarks: "she must come . . . like a *train* . . . but with *elegance*").[31] In the collected edition of her plays published after her death, Sarah Kane's *Blasted* begins with the note:

Author's note

Punctuation is used to indicate delivery, not to conform to the rules of grammar.

A stroke (/) marks the point of interruption in overlapping dialogue.

Words in square brackets [ ] are not spoken, but have been included in the text to clarify meaning.

Stage directions in brackets ( ) function as lines.

Cleansed, on the other hand, surprisingly notes that "Where punctuation is missing, it is to indicate delivery."[32] David Greig's *Victoria* comes with a similar caution about how the text must be read spatially, using both punctuation and layout to prompt elements of performance:

A note on punctuation

. . .

This tends to mean that the character has intended to complete the sentence but is either unwilling or unable to do so.

–

This tends to mean the character has jumped to a new thought, or suddenly jumped to silence.

dialogue continues on a new line
This asks the performer to take note of the rhythm of the speech. It can, but does not necessarily, imply a short beat.[33]

Here, writers attempt to use punctuation at once to record and to instigate a certain kind of performance, a sense of the rhetorical use of print that conventional histories of theater, and conventional critics of print, typically confine to the past. It is possible to see this as a continuation of print culture's effort to imprint the stage, to restrict the rebarbative freedom of theatrical practice – in what is often seen as a director's or a designer's theater – by appearing to locate the signs and signals of "appropriate" performance within the text itself. This is a doomed enterprise, perhaps, but it develops from the implicit logic of Pinter's *Pauses*. Greig and Kane recall the many efforts throughout the history of print to use the text as a kind of score, noting movement, posture, delivery, as a way to fix the relation between print and performance.

The desire to mark the oral, rhetorical force of performance in print is surprisingly widespread in recent published drama, though I think we have to read that persistence less as nostalgia for the waning power of print to determine performance (it may signify that fiction, too) than as a sign of the contested ground in which dramatic writing finds itself today. At the same time, there are a number of examples, writerly examples it should probably be said, of texts that appear to extend modern poetry's effort to make the material form of the page opaque, resistant, to deploy the kind of verbal and typographic friction that slows reading and so attempts to enforce innovative ways of negotiating the page, perhaps to stimulate innovative ways of negotiating the stage. In the modern era, we do not often pay much attention to what we typically accept as the "accidentals" of a play's layout on the page: the structure and location of stage-directions, the use of roman and italic font, the form, appearance and placement of speech-prefixes. These events are considerably more consistent than they were, for instance, in Shakespeare's era, where a printed play might refer to the same "character" with a number of different prefixes (Lady Capulet is, variously, Lady Capulet, Wife, Capulet Wife, Old Woman), might occasionally refer to the "character" by inscribing the actor's name in the text, and sometimes plainly puts the wrong character name in place (Edmund for Edgar in the Dover Cliff scene). Most readers have never seen those "errors," which have been erased from modern editions, as print has been used to regularize and standardize the text, and so has apparently simplified – and arguably falsified – what may well have been a much more interesting, complex and abrasive relation between print and performance. These early-modern errors point to an important fact: while modern readers – actors and otherwise – tend to take the dialogue as the work of the poet, these "accidentals" often lie on the interface between writing and its enactment, and might be seen to represent an ongoing effort to work out the relationship between the forms of writing and performance (in print and otherwise, to say nothing of the range of printed forms of plays, which are much less consistent or standard than, say printed fiction) that persists to the present day.

Much as various forms of concrete poetry and some of the poems of the L=A=N=G=U=A=G=E school prevent the ready assimilation of writing to conventions of speech, we might think that some of Suzan-Lori Parks's plays challenge actors and directors – to say nothing of mere readers – to figure out what, precisely, depends on the material organization of the text. Here is Scene 19 of her play *Venus*, in its entirety:

Scene 19: A Scene of Love (?)

The Venus
The Baron Docteur
The Venus
The Baron Docteur
The Venus
The Baron Docteur
The Venus
The Baron Docteur
The Venus[34]

Parks has numbered the scenes of her play in reverse, and uses a character in the play, The Negro Resurrectionist, to announce each scene as it occurs. In her attention to the ways that documents of the past make their way into the contemporary performance of history – a persistent theme of her plays – Parks tends to find ways to mark the textual process of the play in its performance. So, a director inclined to eliminate this scene will have some serious rewriting to do, and renumbering as well: Parks structures the play as a whole to bring this challenging print object into play. In her notes to *Venus*, Parks reminds her readers that such textual moments should be understood as *spells*:

An elongated and heightened (*Rest*). Denoted by repetition of figures' names with no dialogue. Has sort of an architectural look:

The Venus
The Baron Docteur
The Venus
The Baron Docteur

This is a place where the figures experience their pure true simple state. While no action or stage business is necessary, directors should fill this moment as they best see fit. (n.p.)

Kane uses punctuation (or the lack of it) in basically rhetorical ways, to articulate delivery; Greig emphasizes the syntactic value of his marks, how they contribute to the formation of "character." While Parks's marks here seem both rhetorical and syntactic, they also strike me as standing outside or beyond an obvious, conventional practice: directors and actors have to develop a practice to articulate this text onstage – what does experiencing your "pure true simple state" call on you to experience and what are you supposed to *do* about it? They will have to begin by reading the page, which suddenly transforms those nearly invisible speech prefixes into something else, objects to be engaged differently, though precisely how we might or should engage them remains, I think, an open question. This materialization strikes me as something more like the challenge first offered to readers of *Waiting for Godot*, or perhaps to readers of "The Love Song of J. Alfred Prufrock," a material text that appears less to direct our performance than to claim a space outside contemporary conventions of reading, theatrical or otherwise.[35]

In this sense, now, in the "late age of print," the printform of drama may provide a kind of evidence for what we might have suspected in other ways, a tension, perhaps even an anxiety not only about the persistence of print, but about its cultural meaning, its power relative to embodied regimes of performance. For Pinter's *Pauses* – unlike Parks's rests and spells – were immediately assimilated to theatrical production, arguably because the reading habits trained on other kinds of modernist texts enabled them to be read in theatrically useful ways. The material form of Pinter's printed texts enabled – though it could not alone create – what we take to be one of the most salient dimensions of the performance of his plays. In this regard, Greig and Kane seem rather nostalgic, pointing to a standard relation of print to performance that has passed, or is passing, out of view: the notion that print can or should determine performance. It is fair to say that the landscape, ideological as well as practical, in which theatrical performance takes place has changed dramatically since the première of *The Homecoming* in 1965. Western theater practice has both expanded and diversified in the past forty years (Grotowski, Schechner, Barba, Boal, Suzuki, Bogart, Brook, intercultural performance, deconstructive performance, performance art); directors, designers and performers have come to exert a kind of authorial presence in the work of theater (Robert Lepage, Julie Taymor, Anna Deavere Smith); the hegemony of dramatic theater as the index of performance has been rightly and successfully challenged by the contestatory instigation of performance studies; in the refined precincts of literary studies, reading strategies have multiplied and diversified; the death of the author and his/her intentions has been accompanied, surprisingly enough, by the announcement of the death of print and print culture itself, as digital forms have provided new ways to represent – and possibly supplant – writing. (In this sense, the long-foretold death of that magnificent, residual invalid – the dramatic theater – is hardly news.) This is the context in which plays today are published, in which their materiality takes shape. Whether we see a given text as evoking a desire to govern ready-made conventions of performance, or to summon new forms of production, printed drama today lies in the suspension of a defining relation between print and the stage, a suspension that takes place, of course, at the moment that the authority of print and printforms is being contested on other "performative" fronts.

Pauses, ellipses, the appearance and disappearance of commas, the placement of speech prefixes (to say nothing of cover design, trim size, and so on, the material properties of books): surely this isn't the stuff of drama, particularly since many of these marks do not even originate with the writer, but are assigned (as stage directions sometimes are) as an after-effect of a given production, or as the design protocol developed by the play's publisher. And, *really*, since actors and directors – increasingly, perhaps, given the autonomy of performance from print as a space for the realization of drama – are perhaps personally inclined and institutionally trained to ignore such trivialities, what difference can these make to our understanding of modern and postmodern performance? Does the printform of modern drama help to articulate its relation to performance? To modernism? I'm afraid that I cannot answer these questions here; yet I am struck by the extent to which such questions arise from a surprisingly contradictory impulse: to regard the practice of theater as the site of the play's materialization in history, while regarding the material form of the play's public identity as a text – print, in this case – as materially irrelevant, absorbed into the abstractions of the merely literary. This strikes me as a lost opportunity to seize on one of the ongoing dimensions of the drama's cultural identity in the West, its historical formation at the intersection between literary and performance culture. More to the point, it tends to preserve the unexamined ideology of print, and so to preserve the equally unexamined ways in which the normative values assigned to print – regularity, reiteration and so on – may be said to persist in spheres of activity (theater, performance studies) that sometimes see their work as repudiating the order of the book.

Finally, while I think it is critical to recognize that the book has been responsible for the persistence of dramatic writing, and for its partial incorporation within the canons of literature and literary study, we are only beginning to understand the consequences of print as a delivery system for works of art in general, and for dramatic writing in particular.[36] It has been fashionable to mark the incomplete realization of plays on the page, the ways in which plays have another form of existence, different kinds of meaning, when they are realized in the practice of theater. Yet the rise of digital culture has not only displaced print as the single dominant form of writing-production, and not only displaced theater and film/video as the dominant forms of live and recorded performance: it has also provided us with an analytic instrument for the analysis of both print and performance in a non-print medium. One consequence of digital culture (think of the many versions of any extended writing you have done that exist as files on your computer) has been not only the ability to transform and distribute texts online, but a sense of the differential quality of print itself, the ways in which print's many instances and versions of a work, the distinctive apparition of a given instance of the work, participate in its history (a kind of history that is in most cases obliterated by the present-tense of digital writing – do you save *all* your drafts, or simply revise them on the screen?). Both the ideological and the practical properties of print have become more visible in the past twenty years, in ways that enable us to open a different kind of perspective on the history of something that has always seemed poorly represented by print: drama. Print, that is, bears on the poetics of performance, not only because the material form of printed plays provide the raw material for many theatrical productions, but because – particularly in the modern/postmodern period – print has provided the model, and so the point of resistance, for our understanding of the identity of a certain sphere of cultural production, a sphere that shades off into performance in the production of dramatic theater. To the extent that contemporary conceptions of performance, theater, performance studies and drama have arisen in an era in which drama has itself been partly instantiated by print and in print, they remain partly captive to the ideology of print. Reading the signs of that ideological work, even in the accidentals of the printed page, may provide one way to reopen the narrative of modern drama's role in modernist culture, and to sharpen our understanding of the relation between writing and performance in the modern era.

Notes

1. On the sense that "theatrical instruments (staging, acting skills and so on) transform the 'raw materials' of the text into a specific product which cannot be mechanically

extrapolated from an inspection of the text itself," see Terry Eagleton, *Criticism and Ideology: a Study in Marxist Literary Theory* (London: Verso, 1978), 65. For one among many accounts of the implications of a cybernetic understanding of texts and textuality, see Espen J. Aarseth, *Cybertext: Perspectives on Ergodic Literature* (Baltimore: Johns Hopkins University Press, 1997).

2. For a summary of contemporary controversies in editorial theory, see Peter L. Shillingsburg, *Resisting Texts: Authority and Submission in Constructions of Meaning* (Ann Arbor: University of Michigan Press, 1997), 215–16.

3. It is not clear, for example, that all of the actors in early modern companies could read, or could read handwriting; for some of the possible consequences of this observation, see Leah S. Marcus, *Unediting the Renaissance: Shakespeare, Marlowe, Milton* (London: Routledge, 1996), 162–77. Tiffany Stern has investigated the possible rehearsal practices of Shakespeare's company, suggesting the possibility that some actors may have learned their parts extensively – or entirely – from working with more literate actors. See *Rehearsal from Shakespeqare to Sheridan* (Oxford: Clarendon, 2000).

4. Jerome McGann, *Radiant Textuality: Literature after the World Wide Web* (Basingstoke: Palgrave Macmillan, 2001), 38–9.

5. George Bornstein, "Yeats and Textual Reincarnation: 'When You are Old' and 'September 1913,' " *The Iconic Page in Manuscript, Print, and Digital Culture* (Ann Arbor: University of Michigan Press, 1998), 223–48.

6. Jerome McGann, *Black Riders: the Visible Language of Modernism* (Princeton: Princeton University Press, 1993), 168–70.

7. As Craig Dworkin points out in "Reading the Illegible," PhD dissertation (Department of English, University of California, Berkeley, 1998), Howe's poems foreground "the so-called 'accidentals' of written language: conventions of capitalization, abbreviation, spelling, and alphabet. With all of these elements, Howe calls attention to the illusion of the transparency of the printed page, and she thus emphasizes her own works' status as printed artefacts" (47). This kind of poetry "stands in marked contrast to the dominant Anglo-American traditions of twentieth-century typographic design, which maintains an unobtrusive clarity as its aim" (59).

8. T. S. Eliot, *The Waste Land: a Facsimile and Transcript of the Original Drafts Including the Annotations of Ezra Pound*, ed. Valerie Eliot (New York: Harcourt Brace Jovanovich, 1971), 55.

9. William Carlos Williams, *Collected Earlier Poems* (New York: New Directions, 1966), 277. I am grateful to New Directions for permission to reprint this page.

10. On "The Red Wheelbarrow," Williams's use of white space, and on the development of the "three-ply line," see Hugh Kenner, *The Pound Era* (Berkeley: University of California Press, 1971), 398–9, 541–2.

11. Fredric Jameson, *Postmodernism, or, The Cultural Logic of Late Capitalism* (Durham: Duke University Press, 1991), 16.

12. See Michael Joyce, *Othermindedness: the Emergence of Network Culture* (Ann Arbor: University of Michigan Press, 2001), 3.

13. As McGann suggests, "We want to recall that this highly evolved set of marks [punctuation] represent signs that were originally introduced as notations both for oral articulation and syntactic differentiation, and that they function in both registers to this day. As a set of oral cues – whether in silent or articulated reading – punctuation is a foundational element in the affective (as opposed to the conceptual) ordering of the poem. As a set of syntactic cues it is also a signifying system foregrounding dominant sets of conceptual relations in the text" (*Radiant Textuality*, 156).

14. Michael Goldman, *On Drama: Boundaries of Genre, Borders of Self* (Ann Arbor: University of Michigan Press, 2000), 52.

15. McGann, *Black Riders*, 168–70.

16. I refer here to *The Homecoming* (London: Methuen, 1965), 6. Page references to *The Homecoming* are to this edition, and are included in the text. In design and layout, this edition is very similar – though in smaller format – to the 1965 hardback edition published by Grove Press; it is slightly more similar to the 1967 Evergreen paperback edition, also published by Grove. I am grateful to Grove Press and to Faber and Faber for permission to reproduce this page of *The Homecoming*.

17. Shaw is quoted in Michael Holroyd, *Bernard Shaw. Volume I, 1856–1898: The Search for Love* (New York: Random House, 1988), 403.

18. Methuen's impact on play publishing in Britain in the 1950s is discussed by Dan Rebellato, *1956 And All That: The Making of Modern British Drama* (London: Routledge, 1999), 121–2; on the printing of plays in the 1890s and after, see John Russell Stephens, *The Profession of Playwright: British Theatre 1800–1900* (Cambridge: Cambridge University Press, 1992), 132–41. On Shaw's work with Grant Richards and their adaptation of William Morris's aesthetics, see Katherine E. Kelly, "Imprinting the Stage: Shaw and the Publishing Trade," *Cambridge Companion to George Bernard Shaw*, ed. Christopher Innes (Cambridge: Cambridge University Press, 1998), 25–54.

19. Martin Esslin, *The Peopled Wound: the Plays of Harold Pinter* (London: Methuen, 1970), 44, 46. Page references to *The Peopled Wound* are to this edition and are incorporated in the text.

20. See David Greig, *Victoria* (London: Methuen, 2000), 5.

21. Harold Pinter, *The Collection and The Lover* (London: Methuen, 1963), 10. I am grateful to Faber and Faber, and to Samuel French, for permission to reproduce this passage from *The Collection*.

22. Harold Pinter, *The Collection* (London: Samuel French, 1963), 3.

23. Writing in 1993, for instance, Alice N. Bentson distinguishes between the use of silence in Chekhov and Beckett, but finds as Esslin did that the point of these directions is in fact to indicate meaning, textually (they are lines after all): "Silences, then, are not the absence of speech but the true, raw, and frequently brutal or vulnerable self. Spoken (heard) dialogue is but a cue to the subtext, which itself is the pure unadulterated thing." Indeed, discussing Max's first long speech about MacGregor ("I used to knock about with a man called MacGregor . . ."), Bentson notes that Lenny neither confirms nor denies the veracity of Max's story. But she does so in a way that elides psychological and textual space with the temporality of performance – "The failure of the other, here Lenny, to move into the spaces and confirm the biographical statement casts doubt on their veracity at the same time as they fail to confirm or activate Max's power over Lenny." "Chekhov, Beckett, Pinter: The St(r)ain upon the Silence," in *Pinter at Sixty*, ed. Katherine H. Burkman and John L. Kundert-Gibbs (Bloomington: Indiana University Press, 1993), 117, 120.

24. John Lahr, ed., *A Casebook on Harold Pinter's The Homecoming* (New York: Grove, 1971), 16–17.

25. Carey Perloff, "Keeping Up the Mask: Some Observations on Directing Pinter," *Pinter Review*, 2, 1 (1988): 64.

26. Samuel Beckett, *Endgame: a Play in One Act. Followed by Act Without Words: a Mime for One Player* (1: New York: Grove, 1958), 1, 32.

27. Mel Gussow, *Conversations with Pinter* (New York: Limelight, 1994), 82–3.

28. Gussow, *Conversations*, 56–7.

29. Gussow, *Conversations*, 36. Pinter's plays themselves illustrate the typical mutability to be found in works that go through more than a single edition: Pinter has revised his plays on several occasions, sometimes without making this known in published editions; in other cases, several different editions of the same play exist, in complex relation to one another; see Scott Giantvalley, "Toying with *The Dwarfs*: the Textual Problems with Pinter's 'Corrections,'" in *Harold Pinter: Critical Approaches*, ed. Stephen H. Gale (Rutherford: Fairleigh Dickinson University Press; London: Associated University Press, 1986), 72–81. While I have compared Pinter's use of white space to Williams and to modernist poetry in general, it should be noted that Pinter's own poetry tends to be more formal, and to use verse forms which generally displace the force of white space. And yet even Pinter finds the force of emptiness on the page, for example in poems like "Before They Fall"; see Harold Pinter, *Collected Poems and Prose* (London: Methuen, 1986), 49.

30. Roger Chartier, *The Order of Books: Readers, Authors, and Libraries in Europe between the Fourteenth and Eighteenth Centuries*, trans. Lydia G. Cochrane (Stanford: Stanford University Press, 1994), 2.

31. Patrick Marber, *Closer* (New York: Grove, 1999), 11.

32. Sarah Kane, *Complete Plays* (London: Methuen, 2001), 2, 106. My thanks to Methuen Publishing Company, Ltd. for permission to reprint these pages.

33. Greig, *Victoria*, 5. My thanks to Methuen Publishing Company, Ltd. for permission to reprint this page.

34. Suzan-Lori Parks, *Venus* (New York: Theatre Communications Group, 1997), 80. My thanks to Theatre Communications Group for permission to reprint these pages. I would also like to thank Kathy Sova for her helpful insights into the production process of this volume, and of the printing of Parks's plays generally.

35. Elizabeth Dyrud Lyman presents a cogent overview of the dynamics of Parks's use of typography and typographic space, including a superb reading of the different materializations of Parks's texts – as typescript, printed trade editions and acting editions. See "The Page Refigured: the Verbal and Visual Language of Suzan-Lori Parks's *Venus*," *Performance Research*, 7, 1 (2002): 90–100. She discusses this scene at pp. 94–6.

36. The most inclusive study of drama in print is Julie Stone Peters, *Theatre of the Book, 1480–1880: Print, Text, and Performance in Europe* (Oxford: Oxford University Press, 2000).

Index